Mosul under ISIS

Mosul under ISIS

Eyewitness Accounts of Life in the Caliphate

Mathilde Becker Aarseth

I.B. TAURIS
LONDON • NEW YORK • OXFORD • NEW DELHI • SYDNEY

I.B. TAURIS
Bloomsbury Publishing Plc
50 Bedford Square, London, WC1B 3DP, UK
1385 Broadway, New York, NY 10018, USA
29 Earlsfort Terrace, Dublin 2, Ireland

BLOOMSBURY, I.B. TAURIS and the I.B. Tauris logo are trademarks of
Bloomsbury Publishing Plc

First published in Great Britain 2021

Copyright © Mathilde Becker Aarseth, 2021

Mathilde Becker Aarseth has asserted her right under the Copyright,
Designs and Patents Act, 1988, to be identified as Author of this work.

For legal purposes the Acknowledgments on p. viii constitute an
extension of this copyright page.

Cover design by Liron Gilenberg
Cover image: Rubble of the Old City of Mosul, Iraq, 2018.
(© Paul Jeffrey / Alamy Stock Photo)

All rights reserved. No part of this publication may be reproduced or
transmitted in any form or by any means, electronic or mechanical, including
photocopying, recording, or any information storage or retrieval system,
without prior permission in writing from the publishers.

Bloomsbury Publishing Plc does not have any control over, or responsibility for,
any third-party websites referred to or in this book. All internet addresses given
in this book were correct at the time of going to press. The author and publisher
regret any inconvenience caused if addresses have changed or sites have
ceased to exist, but can accept no responsibility for any such changes.

A catalogue record for this book is available from the British Library.

A catalog record for this book is available from the Library of Congress.

ISBN:	HB:	978-0-7556-0709-9
	PB:	978-0-7556-0708-2
	ePDF:	978-0-7556-0710-5
	eBook:	978-0-7556-0711-2

Typeset by Integra software solutions Ltd. Pvt.
Printed and bound in Great Britain

To find out more about our authors and books visit www.bloomsbury.com
and sign up for our newsletters.

Contents

List of Figures vi
Acknowledgments viii
Notes on Transliteration—Arabic x

1. Introduction 1
2. The Road to Power 15
3. Policing the Caliphate 45
4. Resistance in the Classrooms 71
5. A Reign of Terror in Mosul's Hospitals 95
6. Conclusion 121

Notes on Sources and Methodology 129

Notes 142
Bibliography 173
Index 186

List of Figures

1. Map of Mosul vii
2. Photo of Mosul's Old City 4
3. Sunni protesters 24
4. From Mosul General Hospital 46
5. Cigarettes sold by ISIS 61
6. ISIS school books 79
7. Destruction of Mosul University 88
8. ISIS-imposed dress for women 100
9. Jumhuri Hospital 107
10. Civilians escaping the Old City 122
11. Camp for displaced people 130

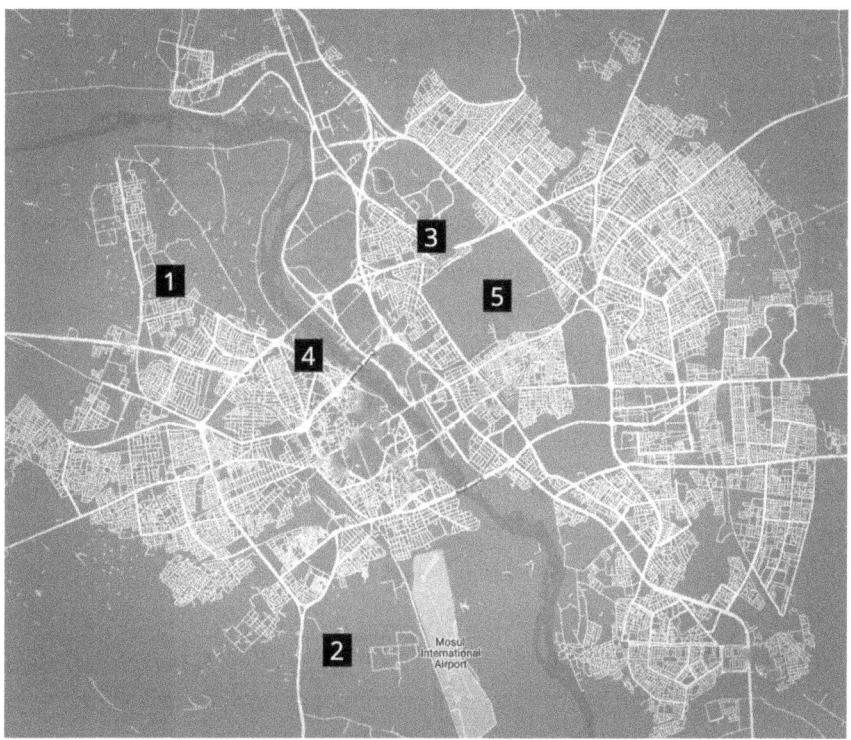

Figure 1 *Map of Mosul. 1. 17 Tammouz neighborhood. 2. Ghazlani Military Base. 3. University of Mosul. 4. Al-Jumhuri Hospital 5. Nineveh ancient ruins.*

Acknowledgments

The material in this book has been shaped by invaluable help and input from many dear colleagues and friends. First and foremost, I want to thank my PhD supervisor Brynjar Lia for his encouragement and wise comments on my work throughout and for inspiring me with his own open-minded and thought-provoking perspectives on the field. I have benefitted a lot from discussions and comments on early drafts of my research from my many great colleagues at the Department of Cultural Studies and Oriental Languages (IKOS), University of Oslo, and other research institutions. I want to especially thank my second supervisor Truls Tønnessen for valuable advice; my fellow PhD students, friends, and colleagues at IKOS for generously spending time to dig into the world of ISIS governance with me; Charles Tripp for lending his expert ear to an early draft of parts of my research; and anonymous reviewers for helping me sharpen my focus. A special thank you to Kjetil Selvik and Benedetta Berti for their thorough and insightful comments on my PhD thesis. Thank you also to Aymenn Jawad Al-Tamimi for your help and insight, and for sharing valuable material. I would also like to thank George Washington University for giving me access to unique ISIS files, and the Fritt Ord Foundation for financial support to develop this book.

Most importantly, however, I owe this research to the people of Mosul who courageously and with endless hospitality opened their homes, tents, fruit stands, hairdresser salons, and offices to me, sharing their stories and experiences despite personal risk and unimaginable trauma. Without this generosity, their pieces of history would remain in the dark. Although interviewees are anonymized in the text, I remember and appreciate every encounter.

The roads to knocking on the right doors can be windy, and some people have been extremely helpful in getting me there. I want to especially thank the excellent Halan Sheikha for making sure I had safe trips to Mosul, always staying patient and professional even in the strangest situations and making me laugh despite grim circumstances. I also want to thank Wael Roso and Basel Rasol for invaluable assistance and company in the IDF camps and Erbil. Thank you to Ahmed Al-Abadi, Thee Yazan Al-Obaide, Ali Ghaleb Al-Amry, Kamaran Palani, Tine Gade, Amir Grgies—you were all helpful in keeping the snowball rolling, in different ways but always with enthusiasm. Many Iraqis who remain anonymous did the same.

I want to thank my loving family and friends for always being so encouraging throughout the work on my PhD. Last, but not least, thank you my dearest Michiel for your patience, love, humor, and unrelenting support. I am lucky to have you.

Notes on Transliteration— Arabic

In the main part of this book, I have removed diacritical marks in Arabic words except ʿayn and Hamza. In the notes, I have followed the transliteration guidelines provided by the *International Journal of Middle East Studies* (IJMES). This means that some of the Arabic words are spelled without diacritical marks: names of persons, groups, organizations, and political parties. Arabic words that have a widely accepted spelling in the English language are usually written without transliteration.

1
Introduction

«Welcome to the Islamic State»

On the 4th of June 2014 Karim drove to work at the University of Mosul, crossing the bridge over to the East bank of the river Tigris, together with his wife Noor, who was eight months pregnant. Traffic was dense, and the June heat was sweltering. It was a normal day, as far as normalcy go in Mosul. It was true that the city had over time become an epicenter for violent insurgent groups—they were too many for Karim to remember most of their names. It was a well-known, but unofficial truth that the city was in the chokehold of armed militiamen. Chief among them was the entity known among most Maslawis as simply "Al-Qaida," who operated as a mafia organization and had grown as a tumor in the city since 2005. This group of militant, self-proclaimed Salafis now had tentacles in all parts of the economic and political life of Mosul, from the smallest corner shop and all the way up to the governor's office. If someone received a phone call from "Al-Qaida," he had to yield to its demands or face abduction, a bomb on his family`s doorstep, or being targeted in a drive-by shooting. "Iraqis must have a short memory in order to survive," some say in Mosul. And Karim, like other Maslawis, tried his best to maintain a regular life in the midst of smoldering violence. He and Noor were excited to receive their first-born child, mixed with worry because Noor's first pregnancy had ended in a miscarriage.

This workday, however, was cut short already at ten o'clock in the morning, when Karim´s colleagues told him that a big bomb had gone off in the center of Mosul.[1] Even this was nothing far away from the usual; it happened every two-three months that an armed group staged an attack against an Iraqi army checkpoint, a military installation, or a political representative. The last months the attacks had become more frequent. "Usually when there is a bomb in Mosul, they close all the bridges, and then it can take four or five hours to return home. So my employer let everyone go home before the bridges closed," Karim remembers. He jumped in his car and picked up Noor, heading back across the bridge. Usually, the way home would be scattered with checkpoints manned by Iraqi security forces, hampering the everyday movement of the inhabitants and causing a great deal of anger among the locals. If checkpoint guards had a bad day, it could mean that Karim and Noor would spend three hours each way. On this day, Karim remembers, they were home in just fifteen minutes. The soldiers usually manning the checkpoints had vanished into thin air.

A citywide curfew was announced in Mosul, and the couple stayed in their home, located right next to Ghazlani military base, one of two Iraqi army bases in Mosul. But unlike normal curfews, this was not lifted after a few hours—it lasted for three days. Unprepared, Karim and Noor quickly ran out of drinking water and food. On the third day, the 6th of June, they heard on the news that the group that called itself "the Islamic State" had seized control over the North-Western suburb Tamuz 17 and that armed militiamen were closing in on the city center from four additional suburbs. At this point, the name Islamic State was something most Maslawis knew only from TV news reports on Syria. Karim was unsure what to think of the news that the group might be coming for Mosul. If it was true, the army base next door would be a prime target. "You have to leave your area, now," a close friend of Karim living in East Mosul urged him on the phone. On that day, Noor started bleeding, and the couple worried for their unborn baby as they were cut off from medical help. After several hours of phone calls, Karim finally got the permission to leave the house from an acquaintance in the army. On the way out, it struck him that their closest neighbor was a Christian family with an elderly woman. If it was true that violent jihadis were approaching, he feared for their safety, so he knocked on their door and offered them to leave together. They accepted the offer and hurdled together in the car.

When Karim's car reached the bridge going over to the East side of the Tigris, they realized that the army had blocked the bridge with concrete blocks and it was only possible to pass by foot. All streets leading up to the bridge were jammed with cars desperately trying to cross. Karim turned back, but from a distance, he spotted three pick-up trucks at the entrance of Ghazlani military base, with armed men wearing something that looked like dark brown uniforms. The base had been captured by jihadi militants, and thousands of Iraqi army soldiers were escaping in full speed, without a fight. Shocked, Karim, Noor, and their neighbor hurried back to the bridge to cross by foot. "Then we saw that the Iraqi army had removed the concrete blocks, and they were driving fast across the bridge to escape from Daesh. They escaped before the citizens, leaving us in the middle of the bridge. Daesh was behind us, the army escaping in front of us. People were screaming around us and shots were fired," he recalls. Both Noor and the elderly neighbor had problems walking. Little by little, they managed to cross the bridge in the midst of the chaos, and Karim left the others in a relative's home, then returned to get his car in the early hours of June 7th.

Their whole area was deserted. When he reached his house, a sniper's bullet whizzed past his head, and he ran to the back entrance. The doors and windows of his house were open, and outside lied deserted military boots and uniforms. "All our clothes were strewn around the house, the soldiers had been looking for civilian clothes to escape among the civilians," Karim says. He heard a man shout from the outside: "Who are you? Welcome to the Islamic State." Karim peeked out and saw eight armed men dressed in black and brown. He shouted back and convinced the men that he was an unarmed civilian. "One of them had an Iraqi dialect, but he had hidden his face. They didn't have beards, they were young, 16–17 years old," Karim recalls. The new rulers of the neighborhood gave him five minutes to grab the belongings he wanted, "the rest is the *mulk* [war booty] of the Islamic State," he was told. He grabbed his and Noor's identification papers, some clothes, and his laptop, and drove off in his car. That was the last time he saw his home. The next day they drove to relatives in Mosul Dam, and then to Erbil in the autonomous Kurdish region, where Noor finally had a caesarian and gave birth to their daughter.

Figure 2 *View of Mosul's Old city across the Tigris before it was destroyed in 2017 (Photo: Ammar Galala).*

Each of the nearly two million inhabitants of Mosul has his or her own story of the confused first minutes, hours, and days of the ISIS occupation of Mosul, and the first encounters with their new rulers. Following the shock of having been left alone by their own government, in the weeks following June 6th, impossible choices had to be made. Leaving entire lives behind and going into exile in the Kurdish region or abroad, facing years of difficulties as outsiders? Or staying at home, protecting belongings and old relatives, under unknown rulers who had proclaimed an Islamic State? More than half a million people fled the city during the first days, as it became clear that the army was not going to return to protect the population.[2] For the ones who stayed behind, three years followed under the harsh rule of the Islamic State, one of modern history's most elaborate examples of rebels ruling a civilian population. After the unexpectedly easy capture of Mosul, Iraq's second largest city, and the entire Ninawa province, caravans of ISIS hummers continued their rampage South and West. To the South, they captured territory all the way to Tikrit, the provincial capital of Salah al-Din, and temporarily controlled Kirkuk, Ramadi, and Fallujah before they were pushed back. To the West, they took full control over the mountainous Sinjar province. At its peak in October 2014, it was one of the most powerful non-state armed forces in the world, controlling an area of more than 100,000 square kilometers[3]—the home of more than eight million people. With rhetoric familiar from other jihadi-Salafi groups,[4] ISIS portrayed itself as a revolutionary, anti-systemic movement that wants to alter the existing world order. In a July 2014 audio message, its leader Abu Bakr al-Baghdadi underlined that the Islamic State was indeed a state, and that it would return "dignity, might, rights, and leadership"[5] to the worldwide Muslim community. National borders, ethnicity, culture, and traditional hierarchies had all become irrelevant. In the new "caliphate," Al-Baghdadi professed, "the Arab and non-Arab, the white man and black man, the Easterner and Westerner are all brothers. It is a caliphate that has brought together the Caucasian, Indian, Chinese, *shami*, Iraqi, Yemeni, Egyptian, *maghribi*, American, French, German, and Australian."[6] The only categories that mattered in the world view of the Islamic State, the group claimed, were Muslim and non-Muslim. And it was up to the new rulers to decide who qualified as a true Muslim.

The message of ISIS shares many characteristics with those of other state-building revolutionary movements in history. Compromise with its enemies is impossible; its victory is inevitable, as long as supporters remain steadfast; and its model is universally applicable.[7] For ISIS, governing civilians was more than an unavoidable by-product of territorial control and economic dominance. Ruling the population in accordance with *shariʿa* was at the core of its project and central to its communication toward new recruits, the world's governments, and Iraqis and Syrians. Its slogan was *baqiyya wa tatamaddad*, "remaining and expanding," and its ambitions for territorial expansion were, in theory, never-ending. Overnight, Mosul's remaining inhabitants were left in a city with no Iraqi state presence, a city that they were told was the center of a new state encompassing a third of Iraq and large parts of Syria. After six months, the exit option was closed by ISIS. There would be no "caliphate" without civilians, and the group imposed death sentence on those trying to flee Mosul. After that point, the exiled Maslawis (residents of Mosul) could only communicate with their remaining friends and relatives via broken, self-censored phone conversations.

The view from the street

Four years after the liberation of Mosul from the clutch of ISIS, there is little systematic knowledge about how the group ruled the population that happened to become its citizens. Because of the sudden relevance the group had for Western security establishments, a large number of non-academic policy reports, research notes, and papers by think thanks and governmental bodies have been published on the group since 2014.[8] Naturally, the academic conversation on the complexities of the group and its rule is still evolving, and important work has been published that sheds light on various aspects of the group. Most publications have focused on the historical explanations for its rise[9] and the characteristics and ideology of the group.[10] Some have dealt with its finances,[11] its foreign fighters,[12] or the background of its members and leaders. Some publications are built on administrative documents,[13] available propaganda sources,[14] or interviews with militants. However, most existing accounts have relied heavily on journalism and secondary sources; partly because it has been challenging to gain access to primary sources. While excellent journalism has been produced on various aspects of ISIS, most often journalistic accounts fall short of providing generalizable information on ISIS governance. Because of security concerns, funding, and the nature of journalism, it has most often offered snapshots of its governance, specific to time and place. Over-reliance on journalistic sources is a limitation when it comes to accuracy, bias and underreporting.[15] This has been a weakness for studies of violent insurgent groups more broadly.[16] Furthermore, partly because of funding and government interests, many such reports analyze ISIS through a security or military lens.[17] While policy-oriented research reports can contribute important insight, they also have their limitations. Systematic empirical data are often lacking, and the group is often described in a language of "exceptionalism," focusing on the extreme violence that has become its trademark, sometimes ignoring the wider historical and academic framework necessary to further our understanding of the group. Documentation of the group's most violent sides is important, not least in trying to build legal cases against perpetrators. The group's violence has posed an existential threat to certain ethnic, religious, professional, or other groups in Iraq and Syria. The true extent of ISIS's atrocities is slowly being discovered in mass graves since the liberation of its strongholds in Syria and Iraq. At the same time, in the context of these countries' recent history, the extreme brutality shown in ISIS propaganda material and recounted by refugees is not as exceptional as is often portrayed in Western media and in some scholarship. Without minimizing the extreme suffering brought on by ISIS, it is necessary to move beyond the language of exceptional violence and situate the group in the context of existing literature on comparable conflicts. Furthermore, most of the existing material on this topic describes the group's activities in Syria,[18] even though the group's Iraqi roots and leadership have been more decisive for its development, and are crucial in order to understand its focus on territory and governance. Iraqis have occupied a disproportionate number of governor positions in the "caliphate." While ISIS's forerunners only became active in Syria after 2011, they have been in Iraq for more than fourteen years.

Many publications touch upon the issue of ISIS governance, but comprehensive studies of this important aspect of the organization are lacking.[19] The existing and expanding trove of ISIS-produced documents has been a source for many reports on its governance. Although they can give unique insight, such documents must be seen as a part of ISIS's constant propaganda machinery—produced to justify their "state." The best available corrective to the descriptions found in ISIS-produced sources is interviews with people who were on the receiving end of these "state" functions. Civilians who tried to go about their daily lives in Mosul are probably our best sources to describe what the "state" functions looked like in practice for the people they were, according to its propaganda, constructed to serve. The findings in the book are based on interviews conducted on three field trips to Northern Iraq in 2016, 2018, and 2019, and the method, challenges, and possible pitfalls are described in detail in the last chapter of this book. Most of the interviewees are civilians who experienced more than seven months of ISIS rule; users and providers of public services under ISIS. They had children in ISIS-run schools; they were treated in ISIS-run hospitals; they studied at the university, or worked as bureaucrats, teachers, nurses, doctors, priests, and other professions where they had face-to-face encounters with their new rulers. The interviews were conducted in camps for internally displaced persons in Northern Iraq, as well as in Mosul, Erbil, and Duhok. Additional interviews were done remotely. The interviewees also include Iraqi politicians, researchers, and NGOs, and the interview data is analyzed in the light of the information gathered from a wide range of ISIS-produced administrative documents and propaganda as well as secondary sources.

Interview data are indirect representations of people's experiences. Interviews are also interactions, and as an interviewer, I choose what to follow up on, when to open or close a topic. This is inevitable; what the informant says is always influenced by the interviewer and the interview situation. In qualitative research, it is not the goal to eliminate this influence of the researcher, but to understand it and use it productively. I strove to achieve as wide a scope of interviewees as possible. The fact that I am a female researcher from a Western country may have affected the interview situation in several ways. At the time of my first trip, Norway was directly involved in the coalition that had destroyed many of my interviewees' homes. This was never brought up during interviews, but it says something about a potential power imbalance. Being a woman in a conservative male-dominated society like Iraq can potentially limit both my own freedom to do interviews where and when I want, and the informants' answers. However, in my experience, being a woman created more possibilities than obstacles, because it granted easy access to female interviewees, and interaction with men was not a problem with a male assistant. Post-ISIS Mosul was a methodological and ethical minefield—as well as a literal one. At the time of my field trips, the social tissue of this proud and diverse city had been ripped apart after three years of mass trauma, on top of a decade of predatory rule by mafia-like extremist networks. The trust between ethnic and religious groups, between citizens and politicians, between rural and urban populations was already worn thin in 2014. In the aftermath of the battle against ISIS, many were scared to be interviewed out of fear from ISIS remnants, the government, or armed militias. There are possible methodological and ethical pitfalls in a situation with post-ISIS crackdowns on any sympathizers for the group's cause, as described in more detail in Chapter 7. Most interviewees are anonymized for their own safety. Despite the sensitivity of the subject, interviewees were not hesitant to describe positive aspects of ISIS governance or lamenting the corruption and inefficiency of the Iraqi government. This study is not an exhaustive study of ISIS's state-building functions, and many areas and aspects of their governance attempts deserve further scrutiny, including the ones studied here. Nevertheless, the fields of governance covered here each in its own way sheds light on the complexity of ISIS governance project and rebel governance in general. Because of the lack of comprehensive first-hand accounts of ISIS rule in Mosul, three years with momentous importance for

Iraq, I have chosen to give more room to the empirical data than to theory development. Giving much-needed space to the voices of civilians that were on the receiving end of ISIS governance adds a building block to our steadily growing knowledge on rebel governance.

This book is a contribution to filling the knowledge gap on ISIS governance by looking at Mosul, the heart of the "caliphate," through a magnifying glass. Cities are power centers for rebel groups because they are economic hubs—and anchor points for religious and cultural identities. Mosul is a prime example of the independent role taken on by cities throughout Middle Eastern history. In 2014, Mosul was the city where ISIS had the largest room of maneuver to implement its state-building plans, but also where it risked the most civilian resistance because of the size of the population. An estimated 300,000 people fled the city during the first year of its rule, nearly one fourth of its original population of up to two million.[20] An additional 200,000 people fled between mid-2015 and mid-2016. However, the restrictions on movement that the group imposed on the population meant that the majority of the population stayed in the city. This makes Mosul an interesting case for studying how the group's behavior vis-à-vis civilians evolved during its reign.

In this book, I understand rebel organizations as "consciously coordinated groups whose members engage in protracted violence with the intention of gaining undisputed political control over all or a portion of a pre-existing state's territory."[21] I here use the term *rebel group* for ISIS. This does not imply that I do not see the group as a terrorist organization, but analytically I find the term more fruitful than the more normatively charged terms *terrorist* or *extremist* group. I agree with Anthony Richard's assessment that "terrorism is best conceptualized as a particular method of political violence rather than defined as inherent to any particular ideology or perpetrator."[22] Rebel governance is the organization of civilians within this rebel-held area for a public purpose,[23] which takes many forms with various degrees of involvement in civilians' lives. Some rebels have no interest in creating a government, but see the population only as an opportunity for exploitation—or ethnic cleansing. Yet, a surprisingly large proportion of rebel groups across the globe do engage in some sort of governance.[24] Mao Zedong and Ernesto "Che"

Guevara, still influential among rebel groups of various kinds, stressed the importance of rebels' engagement with civilians when building an alternative order. Political mobilization of the peasants and provision of public goods were central for both of them. Rebel governments emerge in areas where state presence is weak.[25] In the contemporary Middle East and North Africa, rebel groups have engaged in various degrees of governance in Iraq, Syria, Yemen, Libya, Afghanistan, and other countries. Even so, despite the abundance of attempts by rebels to govern in the Muslim world, this important field is surprisingly understudied. The armed conflicts of our time most often include non-state actors within the borders of fragmented nation states. Areas ravaged by civil war have traditionally been seen as political black holes and ungoverned territories, especially in policy-oriented literature.[26] Rebel groups, sometimes called "warlords," have mostly been described as agents of destruction taking advantage of so-called "failed states," not as political actors seeking to create a new order. The Hobbesian view that only a state can provide political order still often prevails, despite the many examples of rebels that create institutions, form alliances with local actors, and provide public services, sometimes even better than the incumbent regime. This traditional state-centric approach is also problematic because the absence of a monopoly of force is often framed as a security risk in Western societies and used to justify military interventions.[27] In recent years, a more nuanced picture has started to emerge, and scholars have increasingly started to understand conflict as a form of order, and not the antithesis of the state.[28]

Rebel governance cases are as diverse as civil wars, but several scholars have tried to identify common patterns in the behavior of rebels and civilians across space and time. Rebels' violent behavior toward civilians has received more attention than its non-violent activities,[29] but a growing number of studies deal with questions such as civil administration and service provision by rebel groups.[30] Some theories of rebel governance focus on rational choice arguments and downplay social and ideological factors. A general line is often drawn between "opportunistic" or "predatory" rebel groups on the one hand and "activist" rebel groups guided by ideology on the other hand. Yet, as Zachariah Mampilly writes, "the distinction between 'opportunistic' and 'activist' rebellions, despite its intuitive appeal, does not hold when one looks closely at the actual evolution of different insurgent organizations' governance systems."[31] Few studies have attempted to explain variations *within* a given organization. In most groups, particularly ISIS, there is a variety of motivations within one group, as well as the combinations of various governance styles within a group. Many circumstances can lead a group to change its approach to governance; it is not locked on a predetermined path. Furthermore, it is a simplification to place agency only with the rebel leadership. What sort of rebel governance emerges is not just a reflection of the rebel leadership's preferences, but also the result of some sort of negotiations with civilians and other actors. Evidence from war zones suggests that the relationship between rebels and civilians is fluid and shifting, and the two influence each other in both subtle and overt ways.[32] Civilians are not just victims of rebel violence. They also engage with and affect how rebels rule, as is apparent in this book.

Apart from academic interest, rebel governance studies are important to understanding the power dynamics that develop under rebel rule and have a profound impact on civilians' lives. Knowledge of rebel institutions can have practical use for organizations working to save lives. It can give us an idea of the prospects for post-conflict peace, because state structures used during conflict may prove to be important for recovery and rebuilding when the conflict is over. After all, in most civil wars, the large majority of deaths happen because of the breakdown in social and political order, not because of direct combat. For instance, in the second Congo war from 1998 to 2003, battle deaths accounted for about 6 percent of the total 2.5 million deaths, which were mostly caused by disease.[33]

The book

The main aim of the book is to draw a clearer picture of what was going on inside ISIS institutions, weighing accounts from civilians against the image constructed in propaganda and bureaucratic documents. By doing so, the book sheds light on what it looks like in practice when a rebel group has to balance ideology and political expediency. In studies of rebel governance, the two have often been construed as separate and mutually excluding.

As mentioned above, rebel groups have often been categorized as either motivated by short-term "predation" or by long-term ideological goals, and the categories are used to predict the rebels' behavior vis-à-vis civilians'. ISIS was, and still is, often portrayed as an organization with unique ideological rigidity. This is in line with how the group wanted to be understood based on its propaganda. Jihadist rebel groups in general have been portrayed as more ideologically rigid than other rebels, and less likely to sacrifice ideology for pragmatism to advance their state building.[34] For example, in Nelly Lahoud's analysis, jihadist groups' religious strictness, their obsession with declaring others as infidels (*takfir*), their individualism and lacking respect for authorities and strategic alliances have so far locked them on an unavoidable "path to self-destruction."[35] The findings presented in this book offer a more nuanced view of jihadi groups. Seeing these groups as merely ideological hardliners is a simplification. The findings in the book demonstrate the malleability of the ideology once it met realities on the ground. Faced with governing a large population—in the midst of a war zone—the group's approach to governance was highly opportunistic and constantly shifting, often straying far away from its official ideological path. I found that ISIS channeled significant resources to run civilian institutions, at times filling them with new content. Many of its activities were geared toward building legitimacy for its ideology and its rule among the population. However, it simultaneously behaved as a so-called predatory group in many ways and made choices that deepened civilian suffering to serve the immediate interest of their military campaign or the interests of individual ISIS members.[36] The choices that ISIS made in governing Mosul did not only lead to immense suffering and death, but also contributed to the downfall of the group.

ISIS's takeover of Mosul did not become possible only because the central government forces fled. The following chapter sheds light on how it was possible that Mosul, this multi-ethnic city, wedged between the nationalist aspirations of Sunni Arabs and Kurds, to become a hotbed for militant jihadis from the mid-2000s. Furthermore, how was it possible for a few thousand ISIS fighters, many of them teenagers, to capture all public institutions in a few days and control several million citizens for three years? Building on interviews with Iraqi officials and civilians, a picture emerges of a city where sympathy and receptiveness for extremist groups had grown steadily over time—even if only a small minority of the population were convinced supporters of ISIS. This happened partly as a response to the growing feeling of being left out by the post-2003 nation-building project. The security of the Sunni-majority city, many Maslawis thought, was seen as less important by the government than Shia-majority areas. As violence grew, so did the government forces' intrusion into Maslawis' everyday life. Many felt collectively branded as terrorists. At the same time, some influential Muslim leaders in the city held extremist views that hinged on some of the principles of the Islamic State that would come: Intense hatred of Shia Muslims, contempt for secular politics, and a literal reading of Islamic scripture.

Chapters 3–5 investigate three of the central building blocks in the ISIS "state" in Mosul. Policing, education, and healthcare are all part of the new social contract presented by ISIS. The inhabitants were promised security, justice, and public services in exchange for taxes and subordination to laws and regulations. Chapter 3 nuances the question of legitimacy for rebel groups in the midst of a war zone, by taking a closer look at civilians' perceptions of the ISIS police that patrolled their streets, manned their checkpoints, and acted as ad hoc judges. Police forces were, along with courts, the first institutions established by ISIS in any area after they secured territorial control. Rooting out existing police and justice system, and policing the civilian population are crucial for choking potential organized opposition. The various branches of the ISIS police enabled the group to go about its looting, stealing, and extracting of resources. At the same time, the justice system was construed in the propaganda as a benevolent service to the population, providing long-needed stability, predictability, and accountable justice according to the *shariʿa*. And ISIS did spend extensive resources on small-scale conflict resolution between the inhabitants, seeking to replace the Iraqi government and local tribal courts. In some cases, it succeeded in winning the trust of locals, who were starved for predictability after many years of arbitrary militia rule. In the end, however, my study indicates that these positive feelings most often were replaced with anger and disillusionment, as corruption, arbitrariness, and discrimination made the new rulers resemble too much the previous regime.

ISIS launched an all-encompassing education reform throughout the territory it controlled. This reform was partly geared to serve ISIS's short-term military needs by militarizing the curriculum for children. But it also showcased the group's long-term ambitions to shape the ideal citizen of the new state—a long-term and costly project which only makes sense for an organization with a sincere ideological commitment. Chapter 4 shows how unexpected resistance from the local population blocked the realization of this important part of the ISIS governance project.

Chapter 5 highlights how a rebel group's conflicting policy aims can have direct and devastating results for the population. The health system, central in ISIS's projected image as a service provider, ultimately became a battleground between ISIS's conflicting interests. The chapter shows how the efficiency of vital institutions like hospitals was undermined by ideological micromanagement—to the detriment of not only civilians, but also ISIS members.

2

The Road to Power

If monsters are always about to jump out of the shadows, it is because the shadows in question are those we cast ourselves.
PETER CHAMBERS [1]

O Muslims, rush to your state. Yes, it is your state. Rush, because Syria is not for the Syrians, and Iraq is not for the Iraqis.
ABU BAKR AL-BAGHDADI, JULY 2014 [2]

On the 7th of June, as Karim, Noor, and their neighbors were escaping Western Mosul on foot across the bridge along with deserting military battalions, the urgency of the situation had sunk in for the city's political and military leadership. The governor of Ninawa Athil al-Nujaifi had gone to Erbil on that day to ensure military help from the Kurdish Peshmerga, which he was promised by the Kurdish president Masoud Barzani. But the Maliki government, wary of the Kurds, refused any help. Even as a handful of neighborhoods had fallen to the advancing jihadi forces, he insisted that the Iraqi military was equipped to fight back. Shock and disbelief was spreading among the leadership of the city's police, who was painfully aware of the state of the security forces. Athil's son Abdallah al-Nujaifi, who later became a leader of their Mutahidoun party in Ninawa, urged his father to return to Mosul—time was running out. The governor returned empty-handed from Erbil and went to the Ninawa operation command in Mosul. The prime minister had sent his military confidants to reclaim control, as the matter was now one of national security. What was their plan? The response Nujaifi got was not reassuring. Abdallah Nujaifi recounts the meeting: "They said that they had a plan, and that they would restore normalcy. That was their comment. And that was naïve. My father told them that they were basically handing over the city."

Without knowing any more details about the army's alleged plan, the political leaders of the city administration gathered in the Nujaifi family's home on the West bank, where they tried to follow the situation via their network and social media. ISIS convoys were now only a few kilometers away, and tens of thousands of civilians had fled in horror toward the North. The Ghazlani military base was deserted. It was risky for Athil al-Nujaifi to stay; if he was caught by jihadi militants he would be executed in a gruesome way to embolden the extremists. But what message would it send if the governor himself was driven out of his city? At 11 pm in the night, the governor, his family, and the remaining members of the political establishment finally were among the last officials to leave the West bank. They took shelter in the police department in the East bank, but on social media they read descriptions of Nujaifi's whereabouts, which was risky for security reasons. The group moved again, this time to the police academy. Athil made a televised address to Mosul's inhabitants, telling them to stand their ground and fight the intruders. But a few hours later, as the sun rose over the Tigris and gunshots could be heard in the distance, the Mosul police chief informed Nujaifi that they were within mortar range from the jihadis and that they could be hit any second. So they decided to exit the city on its eastern side, and drove to the village where the affluent Nujaifi family owns 10,000 acres of agriculture land and breeds world-class Arabian horses.[3] They tried to get some sleep, but were soon woken up by their security personnel who said that the jihadis were in the next village. The Kurdish president Masoud Barzani called Nujaifi and told him that if he did not get out of the area, he would personally send Peshmerga forces to bring him as a matter of courtesy. Athil al-Nujaifi escaped Ninawa, which he had governed for five years under increasingly harsh circumstances, and arrived in Erbil with his entourage at 3 p.m. on the 10th of June. He would not return for many years.

At the time when ISIS seized Mosul, it was unclear even to the political establishment exactly who they were dealing with, and the advancing jihadis were still called simply "al-Qaida." In the summer of 2013 in the countryside of Northern Syria, fighting had broken out between the Free Syrian Army (FSA) rebelling against the Syrian president Bashar al-Assad and a group calling itself the Islamic State of Iraq and Syria (ISIS). By the beginning of 2014, ISIS had wrestled the control of the Syrian city al-Raqqa from FSA and other competing groups, and installed a terrorizing rule in the city that brought headlines worldwide. According to the dominating media narrative, ISIS then swept across the porous border to Iraq and took control of "swaths" of territory in a shock-and-awe campaign, capturing Mosul within few days in June before its forces marched on toward Baghdad.

Although the rapid military advance of the group did take many experienced analysts by surprise, this account of a *blitzkrieg* obscures the deep roots ISIS already had in Iraq, reaching back a decade. The movement that grew out of al-Qaʿida in Iraq (AQI) had slowly built a capacity to wage full-scale war against conventional armies. At the same time, it had accrued experience in governing civilians on a small scale every time it controlled a town, a village, or even a neighborhood. The point of gravity for AQI before it branched into Syria to take advantage of the chaos brought on by that war was Mosul. The Iraqi roots of ISIS are well-known and well-documented elsewhere, for example in Truls Tønnessen's meticulous history of the group.[4] What is less documented is the degree of control that the movement had in Mosul since the mid-2000s. For years before 2014, militants associated with the AQI, later calling themselves ISI and ISIS, controlled the bulk of the economy, the political life, the courts, the institutions, and the bureaucracy of the second largest city in Iraq. They controlled the city with merciless, targeted violence. The parts of the Iraqi state apparatus that should have clamped down on the group—the police, the security forces, the justice system—were themselves infiltrated to the core. But rather than an alien cancer eating its way into the core of the city, ISIS was in many ways an indigenous creation. It was enabled by the already existing all-encompassing corruption of the Iraqi state, combined with an understaffed and dysfunctional Iraqi security apparatus, especially in Sunni-populated parts of Iraq. In addition, Mosul had gradually become a more conservative place, for reasons that will be elaborated in this chapter. Certain Islamic clergymen in the city were leaning toward strict Salafism, and some were promoting violence as a legitimate means to Islamize society. This does not mean that a majority of Mosul's population supported extremist thought. On the contrary, Mosul's inhabitants were the main victims of the violent acts committed by groups inspired by Salafi-jihadi ideas. However, it does show that the city provided fertile ground for a group like ISIS. A portion of Mosul's inhabitants actively and publicly supported ISIS by pledging a civilian or military allegiance to the group. It would have been impossible for the group to retain control over the city for nearly three years without the explicit support of a large number of Maslawis. The fact that ISIS found supporters in all socioeconomic strata, including wealthy doctors, shows that the motives for supporting the group went beyond economic benefits. Furthermore, there were also risks associated with supporting the group, like the risk of social exclusion and persecution after ISIS's fall.[5] Rather than being purely an import from the Iraqi countryside or abroad, or purely a product of Mosul, it was a combination of exogenous and endogenous factors that coalesced and led to ISIS.

This chapter will give the necessary backdrop to understand how ISIS's governance project became possible. The chapter will then narrow down the focus to Mosul and how the Iraqi government's actions increased the openness to ISIS's extreme ideology in parts of Mosul's population. Building on interviews with businessmen, civil servants, politicians, and others feeling the pressure of the group, the chapter describes how AQI with its mafia tactics became the basis for much of the activity in the city leading up to 2014. ISI and later ISIS were not simply a continuation of al-Qaida in Iraq; the member mass of the two organizations overlapped, but were not identical. For example, some of those who were associated with AQI later joined Jabhat al-Nusra, not ISIS.[6] AQI's influence over ISI gradually diminished as many of the original AQI leaders were killed and replaced by others whose background was in other groups. After the seizure of urban centers like Mosul, a large number of old AQI veterans and sympathizers, and new recruits, swelled the ranks of ISIS. Either way, the early roots in AQI are crucial to explain ISIS and its capabilities at the height of its power from 2014 to 2017.

Heirs of Zarqawi

The group that would gradually evolve into Al-Qaida in Iraq and ISIS was founded by the Jordanian Abu Musab al-Zarqawi[7] in February 2003 under the name *jama'at al-tawhid wal-jihad*. An American invasion of Iraq was imminent, based on accusations that Saddam had weapons of mass destruction and cooperated with al-Qaida. Zarqawi himself was cast in a leading role in the US-led war in Iraq even before the war had started. While before 2003, Zarqawi was unknown outside of Jordan, he was brought to the world's spotlight by the US Secretary of State Colin Powell on February 5, 2003. When Powell made the case for invading Iraq in the UN Security Council, he framed Zarqawi as the link between the Saddam regime and al-Qaida. The evidence was fabricated and the conclusion was wrong. Nevertheless, being used in American propaganda was probably the most fortunate thing that could have happened to Zarqawi and his nascent terror network at that point. When he was depicted in international media as a "terrorist mastermind" who personally beheaded Western hostages, that gave him credibility among people receptive to his message, a credibility that was not necessarily deserved at that early stage of his movement. In hindsight, it might have been a self-fulfilling prophecy. To be sure, the American invasion alone was not responsible for radicalizing all the young Sunni Arab men who would later join Zarqawi's organization. Some of them were radical Salafists before the US occupation. However, the US invasion would be the spark that lit the fire of his movement. It provided useful fuel for Zarqawi's worldview, which was further proven as the American military occupation of Iraqi cities entrenched itself. Zarqawi was killed in an American airstrike in 2006, but he was later hailed as a visionary, and his legacy was and still is a guiding torch for extremist jihadis long after his death. The ideology developed by Zarqawi was the basis for the ISIS "state" that encompassed large parts of Syria and Iraq in 2014.

What is Zarqawi's legacy, then, and why did it have so far-reaching implications? Zarqawi himself has been described as a high-school dropout of few words, with a tendency to drinking, street fights, and petty crimes. He allegedly grew up in a poor Bedouin family in Zarqa, an industrial city in Northern Jordan, in contrast to top leaders of al-Qaida who came from wealthy business families. In his twenties, in 1989, Zarqawi was one of many young Arab men who decided to travel to Afghanistan to engage in "holy war" against the Soviet occupier. Although he arrived too late to fight the Soviets, he allegedly fought the Afghan communist regime that followed in the 1990s.[8] In Afghanistan, he met his first spiritual mentor, the key jihadi ideologue Abu Muhammad al-Maqdisi. Zarqawi returned to Jordan, where a terror plot landed him in jail until 1999. After his release, Zarqawi returned to Afghanistan, where he began his contact with al-Qaʿida. He wanted to bring "jihad" to Iraq, and al-Qaʿida gave him somewhat reluctant support to start a training camp in Afghanistan for jihadis from the Levant. Back in Iraq, he organized suicide bomb attacks targeting Shia civilians and coalition forces. As Truls Tønnessen has shown, when Zarqawi's organization was taken under al-Qaida's wing, it got access to the mother organization's vast networks for recruitment and financial support.[9] It would grow to be the most active branch of al-Qaida and one of the world's most violent terror organizations (ibid). Before it was surpassed by Syria, Iraq was the top destination for foreign fighters, who became an invaluable asset for AQI, partly because foreign fighters were more willing than locals to become suicide bombers. The foreign fighters made their way from Afghanistan from 2001 on, after the American invasion of that country. Others came from various Salafi networks in Jordan, Syria, Lebanon, Saudi Arabia, Kuwait, Yemen, North Africa, and Europe.[10] In 2004, the group officially pledged allegiance to al-Qaʿida under the name *tanzim qaʿidat al-jihad fi bilad al-rafidayn*. Osama Bin Laden then gave Zarqawi, *a posteriori*, the endorsement that Colin Powell and George W. Bush had claimed was there in 2003.

Al-Qaida's support for Zarqawi's project was somewhat reluctant. This skepticism was based on some important differences that would later lead Zarqawi to break with his group's initial sponsor and midwife. Firstly, al-Qaida questioned Zarqawi's strategy for ruthless attacks on Shia Muslims, for both strategic and moral reasons.[11] A widespread view among jihadi-Salafis is that Shia have strayed from the right path, but are still counted as Muslims and can—in theory—be forgiven for their ignorance. In a letter dated July 2005, Osama bin Laden's deputy Ayman al-Zawahiri asked Zarqawi a series of questions, showing a more traditional, lenient view on the Shia. Zawahiri proposed converting them rather than slaughtering them: "[I]f the attacks on Shia leaders were necessary to put a stop to their plans, then why were there attacks on ordinary Shia? Won't this lead them to reinforcing false ideas in their minds, even as it is incumbent on us to preach the call of Islam to them and explain and communicate to guide them to the truth?"[12]

Zarqawi, on his side, was convinced that Shia were servants of the devil and traitors working with the Americans against the Sunnis. His grand plan was to incite sectarian war in Iraq by provoking the Shia. By 2004, the armed opposition to the US occupation was already in full bloom and was estimated to 20,000 men. Some were nationalist Baathist remnants from the old regime, including high-ranking officers in Saddam's military. Others were religiously motivated groups under many different banners: Militant Shias, militant Sunnis, and some groups inspired by jihadi ideas. Zarqawi wanted to use this chaotic scene to his advantage. By targeting Shia leaders, politicians, and civilians, he sought to trigger retaliation attacks against Sunnis and create the necessary space for his group to operate and win terrain. In 2005, his wish became true when Shia militias started to retaliate, and by 2006, a full sectarian civil war had erupted. Key leaders in al-Qaʿida questioned the purpose of this indiscriminate killing of civilians. Atiyya Abd al-Rahman, a close aide to bin Laden, warned in a letter to Zarqawi in 2005 that too much brutality against civilians would make people doubt the justice of their cause. As he put it, "you need all of these people to destroy a power and a state and erect on its rubble the State of Islam." [13] Maqdisi also had a critical view of his pupil's strategy, criticizing both his attempt to incite sectarian chaos in Iraq and his killing of civilians.[14]

Another point of disagreement was the timing for the establishment of a caliphate. While al-Qaʿida supported a step-by-step approach, slowly building support for an Islamic state, Zarqawi wanted to establish a state even before continuous territorial control was secured. Despite these differences, Zarqawi's group was tolerated by al-Qaʿida's leadership, pledged allegiance to bin Laden, and took the name al-Qaʿida in Iraq in 2004. According to writings by Sayf al-Adl, the Al-Qaida military strategist who had helped Zarqawi set up his training camp in Afghanistan, Zarqawi had already aired his vision of establishing a "complete society" *(mujtamaʿ mutakamil)* in 1999.[15] The history of the group shows that it made attempts to secure territorial control already in 2004, and when it did, it was eager to govern the local population in Islamic "mini-states."[16] For instance, following US forces' withdrawal from Fallujah in 2004, insurgents associated with Zarqawi were among those who became de facto rulers over the city for a few months.[17] ISI also tried to found Islamic mini-states in the Iraqi towns of Haditha and Husaybah.[18] Even if these governing attempts were scattered and short-lived, it was a sign of the importance of territorial control and governance for the group's self-image. Already in April 2007, ISI announced that they had appointed ten ministers, including ministers for health, oil, agriculture, and fishing.[19] After military setbacks, the group announced a second cabinet of ministers in 2009.[20] ISI's obsession with declaring statehood did not only irritate the al-Qaʿida leadership, but also fellow Iraqi groups who supported "jihad" as a means to liberate Iraq, such as the Islamic Army of Iraq (IAI). In a 2008 interview with MSNBC, the ISA spokesman Dr. Ali al-Naimi elaborated on his group's opposition to both al-Qaʿida and ISI:

> Although the Islamic State is a great dream and a serious goal, we have objections to this statement [a statement from al-Zawahiri declaring the superiority of ISI in Iraq], and we have our own evidence that has purposely not been published proving that the so-called Islamic State of Iraq is not legitimate. The statement of al-Zawahiri do not obligate us whatsoever, and the errors of al-Qaʿida in regards to spilling the blood of the innocent are more numerous than can possibly be covered in a single response, statement, or interview.[21]

Not long before he was killed in June 2006, Zarqawi had announced that the declaration of an Islamic State was close. His group's governance ambitions became even clearer after his death, when it changed its name to the Islamic State of Iraq under the leadership of Abu Umar al-Baghdadi. It justified the change of name with the fact that it controlled territory as large as the first Islamic state in Medina.[22] The name change went largely unnoticed. Although at that point it was mostly wishful thinking, the group used its declaration of "statehood" to terrorize Sunni Muslims who worked with the government. Most of the Sunni insurgent groups wanted an independent Iraqi state, not the Islamic caliphate that AQI/ISI had as its goal. In the areas controlled by AQI/ISI, it sought to impose a version of Islam that was foreign to most Iraqis: Full-face veils for women, beards, and banning of music. At the same time, AQI disrupted the cross-border trade and smuggling with Syria and Jordan that was an important income for many local tribal leaders.[23] In sum, all this contributed to alienating Sunni tribes from AQI. These tribes played a decisive role in the so-called surge of 2007–8, a period of buildup of American troops in the country in which tribes were given military support by US forces. Together with Sunni militias, this proved an efficient cocktail that rooted out most of ISI's top leadership, and violence dropped.[24]

Iraq, including Mosul, lived through a brief period of relative calm. However, Zarqawi's creation and its affiliates were very much alive beneath the surface, as the next section will show. The policies of Prime Minister Nouri al-Maliki's government, the withdrawal of US forces in 2009–10, the outbreak of the Syrian civil war in 2011, and a wave of popular protests in 2012–13 would unleash the power of the group once more and bring it to the surface in full view.

Repression of Sunni Arabs and popular protests

In 2005, the first democratic elections in Iraq's modern history took place, with the aim of developing and presenting a new constitution. However, many Sunni Arabs of Iraq did not see the new constitution as representing them, and the elections of 2005 left the country more divided along sectarian lines. The process leading up to the new constitution had been secretive and rushed, without real Sunni participation.[25] Many key issues were left unresolved. After invading Iraq, the Americans had chosen to ban members of the Baath party, predominantly Sunnis, from public positions, thereby removing much of the administrative backbone of the state. This decision was popular among large parts of the population, but left 30,000 people without a job. More shocking for Iraqis was the Americans' dissolution of the Iraqi army, intelligence, and security system—taking away the income and pension of another 400,000 families. Ninawa had been a bastion for Baathist generals, and these decisions affected an estimated 40,000 families in Mosul.

Figure 3 *Sunni protesters in March 2013 holding Friday prayer blocking Iraq's main road to Jordan (Photo: Roy Gutman/Tribune News Service via Getty Images).*

Violence marked the period leading up to the first Parliamentary election based on the new constitution that took place in December 2005. The security situation was in free fall, and many were forced to seek protection from sectarian-minded militias. The violence kept many from participating in the election. Sunni Arabs had a fresh memory of US-led military campaigns that had killed scores of civilian Sunni Muslims. The most serious event was the US-led offensive against Sunni insurgent groups in Fallujah in November 2004 which according to some estimates killed up to 6,000 Sunni civilians, in addition to 1,200 insurgents. The city was left in ruins. The year before, in 2003, American forces had shot into a crowd of unarmed protesters in the city, killing seventeen civilians. The lack of trust in the political process led Sunni Arabs to call for a boycott of the 2005 elections. That fateful decision marginalized the Sunni voice in the new political system: They won only 40 of the 275 seats in the new parliament. The Shia and Kurdish political blocks came out as the winners, and key positions went to opposition figures who had been in exile under Saddam.

One of these exile figures was Nouri al-Maliki, the leader of the Islamic Dawa Party with strong links to Iran. Maliki was appointed prime minister in the new government in 2006 and would remain in power for eight years. These years were crucial for shaping power relations in the new Iraq, and would culminate with the invasion of ISIS in 2014. Maliki increasingly portrayed himself as a Shia leader ready to crush the Sunni Arab uprisings against the government. He repressed any attempt by the country's Sunni Arab elites to decentralize power away from Baghdad. In his second term in office, he manipulated various political actors, including Shias, with the aim of concentrating power in his own hands. He issued arrest orders against prominent Sunni politicians in his government, accusing them of links to "terrorism." Peaceful demonstrations against the government first erupted in Anbar in 2012 and spread to Salah al-Din, Ninawa, Diyala, Kirkuk, and Baghdad provinces. Protesters accused Maliki of abusing anti-terror policies and systematically disempowering Sunnis. They demanded a reform of the system and an end to de-Baathification, backed by tribes who had lost influence in the new order. The months leading up to the provincial elections in April 2013, the first since the withdrawal of American forces, saw a rise in violence and tension.

Protests were suppressed with indiscriminate violence throughout 2013. Iraqi security forces were behind outright massacres of unarmed civilian protesters. Hawija South of Kirkuk was a hotspot for the protests and saw the most deadly clashes. For several months, Sunni protesters occupied the central square of the city, Sahat al-Itisam, with tents. On April 19, protesters marched toward an army checkpoint near Hawija and briefly seized control over it. Iraqi forces responded with a brutal crackdown on the tent city, killing at least forty-four civilians aged 13–55. Some were later found handcuffed and executed.[26] Maliki framed the uprising as a continuation of a historic struggle between Shia and Sunnis. By branding as "terrorists" all Sunni Arab groups who resisted his policies, Maliki contributed to the consolidation of ISI, which took the opportunity to craft alliances with Sunni Arab tribes and former Sahwa movement fighters who felt betrayed by the government.[27] After the withdrawal of US forces, many militant Sunni insurgents who had the Americans as their primary target experienced an existential crisis,[28] even if they adjusted their narrative to focus on Iraqi forces as illegitimate and the "new occupiers."[29]

The violence against peaceful protestors in 2013 was as a tipping point in favor of ISI. Many of the survivors were radicalized, and the government's actions served to reaffirm the jihadist group's narrative of being oppressed by the "infidel" Shia. At the same time, the climate for participating in politics, especially in Sunni Arab areas, became almost unbearable because politicians were targeted by ISI or linked groups. A former Mosul politician described the escalation of violence in the city at the time of the protests:

> The way the government dealt with the Sunni uprisings was harmful. Especially when they killed demonstrators in Hawija. This was a big deal in Mosul. I warned [the security authorities in Ninawa] that the violent response in Sahat al-Itisaam was a bad idea, that people who got away from there would go in a violent direction. [...] When there was another term in the governorate council, I did not run. I was convinced that the city was going towards disaster. The ones with money and the ones with guns were the only ones who had any power. It felt useless to engage in politics. I survived five assassination attempts by armed groups who targeted me with bombs. I decided to leave the city.[30]

Fifteen candidates running in the 2013 local elections were assassinated.[31] Seven of them were Mosul politicians running for the Ninawa provincial council.[32] In only two months between April and June that year, around 2,000 people were killed by bomb attacks orchestrated by ISI and other groups throughout the country. ISI also targeted leaders of the protest movement against the Maliki government, indicating that the group was trying to disrupt any rapprochement between the protesters and the government, and to delegitimize the democratic process. The faltering economy affected the level of corruption and created an environment where ISI could easily bribe Iraqi officers and others to facilitate attacks and prison breaks. A wave of jailbreaks that ISI called the "Breaking the Walls" campaign freed hundreds of veteran AQI members from prisons—a certain way of sowing more chaos. By attacking prisons, ISI enabled the escape of more than 500 prisoners from Abu Ghraib prison and more than 100 from Tikrit's Tasfirat prison, in addition to a number of smaller prison breaks elsewhere.[33] With each prison raid, the ISIS army grew as it filled its ranks with more veteran insurgents. This was combined with vehicle-borne suicide bombs against provincial government targets, Iraqi security forces, and Kurdish political party offices.[34]

Despite what many expected, Maliki emerged as the winner of the 2014 election, posing as the only candidate to be trusted to handle the renewed wave of violence in the country. None of the Shia parties, Muqtada al-Sadrs party, and the Islamic Supreme Council of Iraq, wanted to support Maliki as prime minister in a new term. Like in 2010, drawn-out negotiations followed. This time, however, they were cut short by a development that would shock Iraq and the rest of the world.

By 2014, ISI had already done its best to exploit the new civil war in Syria. The Syrian regime had withdrawn from northeastern parts of the country, creating a government vacuum that allowed militants to flourish there. In the beginning, ISI's presence in Syria went under the banner of Jabhat al-Nusra (JN), but that organization soon stood on its own legs. In April 2013, the deep-rooted differences between ISI and al-Qa'ida came to the surface when Abu Bakr al-Baghdadi changed the name of his organization to the Islamic State of Iraq and al-Sham (ISIS), claiming that JN was part of it. Neither the al-Qa'ida leadership nor JN was notified in advance of Baghdadi's expansion plans.[35] The leader of JN, Abu Muhammad al-Jawlani, refused to be part of this new "state," and turned to the central al-Qa'ida leadership to reaffirm his allegiance to al-Zawahiri. As a result of this quarrel, ISIS declared a break with al-Qa'ida. As Syrian rebel groups, including JN, forced ISIS out of western Syria, it consolidated itself in al-Raqqah and the border areas to Iraq.

Masked ISIS militants dressed in beige or black uniforms or jeans, armed with anti-aircraft weapons, and rocket-propelled grenades, swept back across the porous border to Iraq. They sped through the desert in long convoys of Humvees and pickup trucks—each holding up to four ISIS members who shot their way through the checkpoints of the Iraqi army that were there to protect Mosul. Iraqi forces in Mosul were short of ammunition, weapon, and men—the official number of 2,500 soldiers in the city later turned out to be closer to 500. They had nothing that stood up against ISIS's machine guns. By June 10, the group controlled Mosul's airport, its police stations, prisons, and central bank. It was a frenzy of violence. As symbols of the old regime, Iraqi soldiers and Shia Muslims were the first victims. Captured Iraqi soldiers were hanged, set ablaze, crucified.

On June 10, while the last remaining generals of the army fled toward Kurdish region, ISIS massacred more than 600 Shia prison inmates in Badoush prison outside of Mosul, after separating them from the Sunnis. Among the ones executed were also Kurds and Yezidis. The inmates were forced to kneel on the edge of a ravine nearby, while ISIS militants fired rounds at them with assault rifles and automatic weapons. A survivor from the massacre told Human Rights Watch how he pretended to be dead at the bottom of the ravine after being shot: "They kept shooting at us for about 15 minutes. Then they retreated. When they saw that one escaped, four or five of them came back, they shot in the head of anyone who was moving or breathing."[36] Another inmate described how the ISIS militants then put fire to the mass grave to prevent anyone from escaping: "When it was my turn, they set fire to my right leg. But I had to withstand the pain so they wouldn't know that I was still breathing."

Two days later, possibly the deadliest single massacre at the hands of ISIS took place in the military camp Speicher in Salah al-Din governorate. According to the Iraqi ministry of Human Rights, more than 1,566 Iraqi Ari Force cadets were executed near the Speicher camp in Tikrit, Saddam's birthplace and former stronghold. The cadets had been told by their commanders to leave the base by foot as an attack by the jihadis was imminent. The commanders themselves escaped. Walking by foot, the young cadets were met by ISIS militants who separated the Shias from the Sunnis and rounded the Shias up in pickup trucks. The cadets singled out for murder were filmed by ISIS and can be seen in a propaganda video as they are led on gunpoint to the Tigris. One by one they are shot in the head before they fall into the river. The video also shows victims being led to mass graves already full of dead bodies, at the site where Saddam Hussein used to have one of his many palaces, overlooking the Tigris. Mass graves from the massacre were discovered when Iraqi forces retook the area in 2015. There are unverified reports that former Baathists as well as members of Saddam's tribe took part in the massacre in support of ISIS.

ISIS continued their rampage down the Tigris and secured continuous control over parts of mostly Sunni-populated territory. Their convoys pushed on the borders of the autonomous Kurdish region, but were stopped in Khazer, 25 kilometers outside of Erbil. The key oil-town Kirkuk would be seized by Kurdish Peshmerga forces in the heat of the battle, after being barraged by ISIS. Southwards, ISIS controlled areas all the way to Fallujah, which remained a battlefront. 500,000 Maslawis fled immediately when it became clear that their city had fallen to ISIS, although some would later return.

On June 29, 2014, the group's spokesperson Abu Muhammad al-Adnani made a statement titled "This is God's Promise,"[37] which declared the establishment of the Islamic State, a "caliphate" with Abu Bakr al-Baghdadi as the caliph, and the stage was set for realizing ISIS's state-building plans on a larger scale.

Mosul: An occupation from within

The collapse of Iraqi forces protecting Mosul in June 2014 seemed sudden from the outside, but ISIS's occupation of Mosul did not happen in a week. Iraqi insurgent groups of many kinds had long aimed to control cities as useful "safe havens."[38] Mosul had the ideal combination of social, political, and geographical factors in 2014 for an extremist, Sunni jihadi group to grow roots and expand its influence. Unfortunately for Mosul's inhabitants, Zarqawi had an obsession with Iraq and Mosul from early on. For both strategic and more emotional reasons, he saw it as a suitable place to build a future Islamic society. According to Sayf al-Adl's writings, he anticipated that the Americans would invade Iraq after Afghanistan, setting off a spiral of chaos. But he also wanted to reenact an episode in early Islamic history that had Mosul at its center: The military commander Nour al-Din Zangi's campaign to retake the Al-Aqsa mosque from the Crusaders was launched from Mosul.[39] Ninawa's geographical location close to Syria and Turkey was ideal for consolidating Zarqawi's organization in that area. Weapons, money, and recruits flowed freely across the borders.

The Ninawa province is one of the most diverse in Iraq, populated by a mosaic of ethnic and religious groups—some of them exist only in this province. In addition to the Sunni Arab majority (today around half of Mosul's population), there has been a sizeable Kurdish population, as well as Shia Muslims, Christian Assyrians, Armenians, and Chaldeans, Turkmens of different faiths, as well as Shabaks and Yazidis with their distinct beliefs. The historic Mosul was located on the West bank of the Tigris and was a center for international trade and part of "a broad region within which goods, people, ideas, and currencies were exchanged."⁴⁰ Next to Cairo, Damascus, Aleppo, and Baghdad, Mosul was one of the principal administrative centers in the Arab provinces of the Ottoman Empire.⁴¹ When King Faisal was crowned king of Iraq by the British in 1921, it was still unclear whether Mosul "belonged" in Iraq or Turkey.⁴² Representatives from the League of Nations did a census in the city in 1927 to settle the question and found people's understanding of their own ethnicity was in itself fluid, and deemed less important than kinship, religion, or economic ties.⁴³ For centuries, the different ethnic and religious communities had coexisted and created a thriving city where a myriad of languages were spoken in the markets. The city's different communities were interwoven within most neighborhoods. This is in contrast to Baghdad, where neighborhoods have become more and more segregated along ethnic and religious lines since 2003. In Mosul, neighborhoods are still largely mixed.

The complex social fabric in Ninawa later proved easy to exploit for politicians and insurgent groups. Sectarian tension has flared up in periods of conflict. Saddam Hussein, cautious of Kurdish nationalism, forcibly moved Kurds from this city bordering on the Kurdish region in order to "Arabize" it. Hundreds of Kurdish families were forced to abandon their ancestral homes. At the same time, Saddam encouraged Sunni Arabs from the countryside to settle in the city, which led to an influx of people with conservative Muslim, sometimes Salafi, orientation into the city. Following the 2003 US occupation and the strengthening of Kurdish military presence in Ninawa, families were again uprooted as Kurds pushed some Sunni Arabs who had settled in the area under the Arabization campaign to flee.⁴⁴ After the 2005 election, the Kurdish minority in Ninawa dominated local politics and the security apparatus. Both Arabs and Kurds accused each other of trying to exploit the small minorities for their own benefit.⁴⁵ From 2008, Prime Minister Nuri al-Maliki started purging Kurds from Mosul's two army divisions and replacing them with loyal Shiis. The socially fragmented nature of the city made it difficult to govern. It also prevented the development of Sahwa movements there.⁴⁶ Militant groups thrived in this environment, and groups adhering to Salafi-jihadist thoughts gained strength among certain tribes, previous

Baathist generals, and others, as a forceful opposition to the American-installed regime.

The seed of Salafi thought was planted in Ninawa during Saddam Hussein's Faith Campaign (*hamla imaniyya*) in the 1990s, in which the region was especially targeted. The staggering number of public events and meetings organized by Baʿth Party branches gives an indication of the regime's outreach ambitions. As the Faith Campaign proceeded, these events became increasingly religious in nature. For instance, 637 meetings were held in Ninawa during 1999.[47] One of the three institutes for Qurʾan studies that were set up by Saddam—preaching a politicized Baʿth-friendly Islam—was located in Ninawa. The Faith Campaign was a break with the secularism that had underpinned the Baʿthi vision of a modern, Arab, socialist society. Saddam's increased use of religious symbolism and laws, and building Islamic networks and institutions were not motivated by sympathy for Islamism or Salafism.[48] On the contrary, it was designed to co-opt radical Islamist currents that could pose a threat to the regime, by controlling them and attempting to counterbalance the influence of the Iranian revolution. Nevertheless, in the long run it backfired and contributed to a stronger Salafi influence in the country, both those in favor of and those opposed to the Baʿth government.

The economic importance of Mosul made it a natural economic and logistical hub for ISI after the withdrawal of US forces in 2010. It increasingly relied on oil theft and mafia tactics for funding. The inhabitants of Mosul were the main victims as extortion and abductions became part of everyday life. No business was too small or large to be extorted. The public sector, with all its construction projects and contracts, became an inexhaustible source of financing for the militants. Because corruption was so widespread in the city's public institutions, they got a percentage of bribes from officials. But at the same time, they started demanding a percentage of all projects contracted in Mosul. Militants introducing themselves as "al-Qaida," and later the Islamic State of Iraq, demanded 20 percent of large projects from the Ninawa municipality. A contractor for a public building project would often be called up and threatened to give 20 percent of the value of the project to al-Qaida. For example, if a project was worth one million dollars, the militants would demand 200,000. The contractor would then contact the municipality and say that 1 million was not enough to cover the project, he needed 200,000 more. According to my interviews, someone who worked within the municipality and knew about the projects would be working with al-Qaida to communicate these threats. If a contractor, a political representative, or a private business owner failed to deliver, he risked being kidnapped or assassinated by the group, or to have his car or home targeted with bombs.

The militants' tight grip on Mosul's justice system illustrates the level of control the organization enjoyed in the city in the period between 2005 and 2014. Through systematic threats of violence and assassination of anyone who did not comply, AQI had impunity for its actions in the courts. On every level, there were lawyers who cooperated with AQI. If AQI members had been arrested by the security forces, AQI obtained investigation documents about its members from these lawyers, who then threatened judges or other employees of the courts to drop the charges. Mosul lawyers interviewed for this book underlined that this was no secret; all the lawyers knew of someone in their workplace who was connected to al-Qaida. A long-time Mosul lawyer recounts how AQI and later ISI controlled his workplace:

> There were people in my workplace who belonged to al-Qaida with access to very specific and sensitive information within the courts. Among them were [a high-ranking court official], he was sending threats to the judges on behalf of al-Qaida. This was so well-known that people who experienced problems with al-Qaida contacted this man so he could intervene and solve the issue.[49]

Hundreds of witnesses were either killed, tortured, or threatened because lawyers linked to al-Qaida leaked their names to the organization. Tens of judges received threats, but none filed a complaint about it. They knew that the judges and the police were infiltrated by the same militants. So there was no institution that could ensure the protection of witnesses or judges.

For example, two lawyers who worked with al-Qaida were arrested by security forces. Al-Qaida then pressured the other lawyers of the city to go on an open-ended strike protesting the arrests, in order to force their release. All lawyers were forced to participate; if anyone stopped striking, al-Qaida threatened to kill him. In this way, all the lawyers of Mosul were forced to go on strike for against their will, and the strike would only end with a release or the killing of lawyers. After four months of strike, the two lawyers were released.

This, of course, was made possible by the extreme level of corruption already existing in these institutions, where al-Qaida gradually achieved a monopoly on bribes and extortions with their low threshold for deadly violence. The contact with armed extremist groups was not only upheld by people in the city administration, it went all the way to the top of the political establishment. It was not possible to be in a leading position in the municipality without dealing with them. There are signs that the governor of Mosul at the time had close links to groups that would later merge with ISIS, although he has denied such claims. A 2009 letter that is seemingly from an ISI operative in Mosul to the group's central command names Mosul governor Athil al-Nujaifi, Iraq's minister of communication Faruq Abd al-Qadir, and Hajj Riyd in the prime minister's office as officials who agreed to cooperate with the group. In the letter, it is described how some officials yielded after pressure. High-ranking officials in Mosul and beyond probably had various reasons to allow extortions that gradually filled the coffers of ISIS's predecessor. Many did not have any choice, but were protecting their own lives in an environment where the state did not. Some may have done it to enrich themselves or the Sunni community in general, or to weaken the influence of the Kurds.

Most Maslawis saw the underground rulers of the city as criminal gangs enriching themselves. AQI/ISI used extremist religious symbolism and rhetoric, but the Muslim population saw them as being more interested in money than conveying a religious or ideological message. The Christians felt differently about it. Mosul gradually became a more hostile place for groups belonging to other religions than Sunni Islam. AQI and later ISI specifically targeted Christians. Up to 200 Christians were killed by these groups between 2005 and 2014, and many more fled the city. The Christian population in the city is estimated by the Christian community to have been 30–40,000 in 2005. By 2014, the number had shrunk to 3,000 because of threats and harassment from jihadi groups. Christian women were threatened into wearing a hijab in public, and some were forced to fast during Ramadan. Because of several bomb attacks against churches, every church was guarded by Iraqi police or military who searched every person entering. Some churches in Mosul were forced to pay so-called *jiziya* to the group. For instance, a Chaldean bishop in the city was assassinated after churches stopped paying this "religious tax."[50] While historically, *jiziya* was a protection tax imposed on Christians and Jews by Muslim rulers, AQI, ISI, and ISIS used it as a means of extortion. A Mosul priest recounts life for Christians in the period between 2005 and 2014:

> I slept with my clothes on because I always feared an attack against my home or against my church. The people who called themselves the Islamic State of Iraq forced us to write signs outside the churches criticizing the pope. Once there was a church in the United States who had burnt a Quran, that was a big problem for us, we received more threats, we could not sleep. […] Everyone who owned something suffered from extortions. When two priests were kidnapped, I was pressured to pay 200.000 dollars. And the place that I was told to meet the terrorists was in a government building! The directorate for youth and sports. All the people of Mosul was threatened. But Christians were threatened because they were Christians.[51]

Refusing to pay taxes to ISI/ISIS could result in businesses, large and small, being targeted in bomb attacks.[52] According to some estimates, the group got up to 80 percent of its funding from the city after the 2004 withdrawal of US forces from the area.[53] An Iraqi intelligence officer interviewed by AP estimated that ISI drew up to 1.5 million USD from Mosul a month in 2013.[54] In short, everywhere that money was being exchanged or power was being exercised in Mosul, the jihadists had a hand in it. Without payments to the group, the economy would come to a halt, markets would run out of food, and materials and food produce would not be allowed across borders. On the surface, Iraqi army checkpoints and police were present throughout the city, controlling the movement of its inhabitants in a way that made the Iraqi state feel almost omnipresent. In reality, the mafia-like control of ISIS and its affiliates meant that Mosul was outside of state control for years before 2014.

ISIS was not the only group inspired by extremist Salafi-jihadi ideology that plagued Mosul. By 2008, the center of gravity for the Iraqi insurgency had shifted from Anbar and Baghdad to the north. According to Olive Group's databases, violent incidents in Ninawa increased from 463 per month in January 2007 to 685 in January 2008, at the same time as Baghdad saw a sharp decline in incidents.⁵⁵ As the largest urban center in northern Iraq, Mosul became a new focal point for Sunni Arab insurgent groups of various brands, emboldened by the withdrawal of US forces from Iraqi cities in 2009. Weapons became abundant after American ammunition storage depots were looted.⁵⁶ A large number of former Saddam era officers dwelled in Mosul. The lines between ISI, similar *takfiri* groups, and more Baʽthist dominated networks were often blurred. ISI sought to dominate other groups in Mosul including *jaysh rijal al-tariqa al-naqshabandiyya* and *ansar al-islam,* and was behind most of the bombings in the city.

After cuts in defense budgets by the Maliki government the same year because of falling oil prices, Mosul was left understaffed by police officers and security forces.⁵⁷ Locals feared retribution from ISI if they cooperated with Iraqi security forces. This helped keep Mosul out of real control of the Iraqi forces. On their side, Iraqi forces fueled anger against the government by controlling civilians' movement, allowing for and even actively supporting extra-judicial killings of Sunnis by brutal Shia militias. Maliki put Lieutenant General Mahdi al-Gharawi, a former member of Saddam's Republican Guard who was a Shia, in charge of Mosul's police forces in 2011. He got this powerful position despite the fact that he had been accused of supporting extra-judicial killings and torture of Sunnis.

In July 2013, ISI kicked off its so-called "Soldiers' Harvest" campaign with waves of coordinated suicide attacks throughout Iraq. The main targets for these attacks were Iraqi security forces, including ISF targets in Mosul. In Mosul, the provincial elections in June 2013 were marred by repeated attacks on political events and leaders. The elections for the Ninawa provincial council were postponed by two months for security concerns and ended up attracting only half the number of voters as against the 2009 election. The campaign that started in 2013 culminated in June 2014 with the seizure of Mosul, freeing 3,000 prisoners in the city and overrunning key military installations.

Where ideology meets the real world

After many years where their daily lives were in the hands of Iraqi soldiers and police officers, many Maslawis in June 2014 met the new rulers with relief, careful anticipation, and optimism. The ease with which a few hundred ISIS soldiers could invade and seize control over a city of 2 million inhabitants showed how fragile the central government's command over this part of the country was.[58] In the eyes of many Maslawis, it also proved that Sunni lives were dispensable to the government. It confirmed a popular notion that Mosul is somehow an outcast among Iraqi cities because of its historical link to Turkey and because of its Sunni majority population. When ISIS captured Mosul and wrestled the monopoly of force from the central government in a matter of days, it showed with all clarity the hollowness of the government's claim to protect its own population. In Baghdad, a despairing Prime Minister Nouri al-Maliki promised a swift liberation of Mosul from the terrorists. He called the fall of the city a conspiracy by Turkey and the Kurds. Under pressure from both USA and Iran, Maliki was removed from his post the same fall and was replaced by Haider al-Abadi. Under accusations of treason and corruption, Atheel al-Nujaifi fled to Istanbul. He would later be sentenced to prison in absentia for colluding with Turkey.

Rows of Humvees filled with celebrating ISIS fighters rolled through the city center on the day of the fall, while corpses of regime soldiers lay strewn in the streets. Along the street stood Maslawis in disbelief, some filming with their phones, while others joined in shouting "allahu akbar." The morning after, a strange atmosphere reigned in the city. Market streets that would usually buzz with life laid deserted, and people kept indoors. Half a million of the city's inhabitants had fled in a couple of days, and those remaining did not know what to expect. The much-hated Iraqi forces were gone, but what would fill the void they left behind? The Christians and Yezidis of Mosul, having lived through almost a decade of threats, oppression, and murder by jihadi militants, preferred not to wait and see. Most of them fled during the first few weeks and would not return. It was the end of one of the world's oldest continuous Christian communities.

After a couple of days, ISIS removed all roadblocks in the city and proclaimed themselves as the people's saviors. "In the beginning, it was like a dream, we were all in shock," says one man who had watched the convoys parading down the city. "The first time one of them talked to me, he said that they are our brothers who were there to save us from the repression by the government. They said they would not allow anyone to harass us anymore, that they respected us."

In the first couple of months of their rule, the ISIS militants held a low profile. Gradually, through flyers, posters, billboards, and loudspeakers, the ideology of the new rulers—which was to penetrate all the city's institutions and services for three years—gradually became clear to Mosul's inhabitants—now called citizens of the "*wilaya* Ninawa." ISIS presented a new kind of social contract in the form of a "city document," *watha'iq al-madina*.[59] In exchange for obedience to ISIS laws, including paying taxes, civilians were promised justice and security enforced by ISIS courts as well as public services.[60] ISIS had a narrow definition of who was included in their social contract. Yezidis were seen as devil-worshippers and polytheists (*mushrikun*) and those who had not fled were killed or kidnapped and held as sex slaves by ISIS. Yezidis are an ethnic Kurdish minority whose monotheist religion has similarities with Christianity, Judaism, and Islam, but also contains elements from ancient Mesopotamian religions. Specific rules were stipulated for how to deal with Yezidi slaves, reflecting their status as non-citizen residents of the caliphate.[61] In a pamphlet justifying slavery, IS held that

> [T]he captivity and enslavement of the women of the disbelievers at war and their offspring are among the greatest forms of the honour of Islam and its shari'a, as it is a clear affirmation showing the supremacy of the people of shari'a, and the greatness of their affairs, and the dominance of their state, and the power of their might.[62]

Yezidi slaves were shipped around within ISIS-held territories to be bought and sold by ISIS members, sometimes in auctions, in one of the most grotesque parts of ISIS rule aimed at breaking the Yezidi community while also offering slaves as perks for those who migrated to the caliphate. An ISIS ruling allows taking Christians, shi'is, Alawites, Jews, and other "disbelievers" as sex slaves.[63] Although cases where Christians were taken as slaves have been reported, the sex slavery of Yezidi women was by far the most institutionalized and widespread. Estimation of the numbers of abducted Yezidi women ranges from 3,000 to 7,000.[64] In Mosul, auctions were held in a large enclosure in the city center, where Yezidi women and girls wore price tags according to their looks and age. After being sold to ISIS militants, a nightmarish existence followed trapped in houses where they would be raped, abused, and sold again. For many, this went on for several years, driving some to suicide. ISIS's systematic murder and enslavement of Yezidis, killing an estimated 5,000 people, have been recognized as genocide by the UN. Most Yezidi victims were executed in their villages in rural areas of Northern Iraq, some after refusing to convert to Islam. The Yezidis living in Mosul were either forced into exile, killed, forcibly converted, or enslaved, while their property was confiscated.

On paper, Christians had a special status compared to other minorities and were offered the choice of converting to Islam or paying a religious protection tax, *jiziya*.[65] In practice, Christians were forced to flee without having a real option to convert or pay *jiziya*. By the help of local members and collaborators inside public institutions, ISIS had lists of names documenting people's religion, property, and affiliation with the Iraqi army or government. These lists became crucial for the group in the early hours and days of occupying Mosul, and swiftly made the presence of the new "state" felt in every corner of the city. A Mosul doctor who fled to Turkey with his family but returned shortly after had his house confiscated within a few weeks of the ISIS occupation:

> They knew exactly who were Christian and who were not. Why? Because they paid some people generously to gather information, lay people that they recruited from the street. For example, as a doctor I made maybe 2000 USD a month. Daesh would pay, for example, 1000 USD to someone who could not even write his name, as well as a car and a home. Like my home. They took my home because I left, as well as the homes of Christians. They took my new car, and everything in my home. People from Mosul helped them, they gave them information, documents. They had people in *daira al-nufus*, which is responsible for IDs and passports. There are papers there of all the people in the town. They also went to the land registry office. When they came to our hospital, they knew the names of all the doctors, all the nurses, because they had recruited one official in the hospital. They knew that I had a new car, they knew that my wife and daughters had left.[66]

After activating their existing networks in Mosul and persecuting who they defined as enemies of their state, ISIS sought to legitimize its rule to the civilians that it included in its "social contract." It sought to create both what can be called instrumental legitimacy, based on the effectiveness of service delivery, and substantial legitimacy, based on shared values.[67] Creating some level of legitimacy for its governance was not merely ideological, as it was portrayed in the city documents. It was also necessary from a security point of view, because ISIS members were hugely outnumbered by civilians in Mosul, the largest population ever under its rule. Resistance is intrinsic to any political order, and civilians are a two-edged sword for rebels attempting to govern. As Ana Arjona et al. put it, civilians are "an essential source of food, supplies, information, and recruits. But civilians' ties to the incumbent regime put rebels in constant danger of betrayal."[68] ISIS did not have enough manpower to control a potential mass uprising, and had a real fear of sustained local resistance. That fear seems to be well grounded, because there are reported examples of open demonstrations and protests against ISIS in both Iraq and Syria.[69] The public punishments and executions of those accused of treason by ISIS also indicate the need to avert potential resistance.

The city document obliged women to avoid leaving the home and to wear a full cover in public; alcohol, drugs, and theft were banned, and so was the support of or communication with the enemy. ISIS positioned itself as the leader of the entire Muslim community of the world and used the terms *al-raʿaya* and *al-umma* to address civilians. According to the ISIS narrative, there is no authentic Muslim community except the community that lives in the areas under its control. After taking over Mosul and driving out or coopting rival groups, the first priority was to set up courts and a loyal police force. The next step was to deliver basic services like electricity and water, while ISIS education and healthcare was established gradually over the first year. Formally, ISIS set up a range of "*diwans*" or ministries, each in charge of administering different parts of their state: Education, public services, finances and resources, proselytizing, health, tribal outreach, agriculture, and public relations. Specific *diwans* were put in charge of military and defense, intelligence, police, and courts.

As the following chapters will detail, ISIS's ideology was supposed to color every aspect of what was going on in the group's new institutions. The ISIS literalist views on religious texts—including the contempt for foreign cultural influences—are very similar to that of Wahhabism and so-called jihadi-Salafism. ISIS's conclusions and political project, however, are very different from those of most Wahhabi scholars, many of whom see Saudi Arabia as a legitimate Islamic state. It must also be seen separately from the general Salafi current, which in itself is more of a theological or doctrinal trend and does not say much about political preferences.[70] Jihadi-Salafism is a relatively new term for extremist Salafi-inspired groups with an anti-Western and international outlook. There is no unanimous ideological agreement among groups that have been called or called themselves jihadi-Salafi, and the limits for who falls under the term are unclear.

The ISIS brand of jihadi-Salafism goes further than that of al-Qaida, even though the two movements build on much of the same Salafi literature. ISIS makes an effort to "own" the Salafi and Wahhabi heritage, while at the same time redefining its content with the help of its own young ideologues, such as Bahraini Turki al-Bin'ali (1984–2017), who had studied under Abu Muhammad al-Maqdisi. ISIS is more unforgiving than other groups in its understanding of Salafi thought. It calls for the annihilation of all enemies of the true believers—although it theoretically opens a door to "repent" for certain groups. While al-Qaida frames its militant struggle as "defensive," ISIS has no problem with calling its *jihad* offensive. Central concepts in the group's universe are *tawhid*, *takfir*, and *hijra*. *Tawhid* (the oneness of God) in Salafi doctrine means not only monotheism, but also the absence of any pluralism or innovation within Islam, and the elimination of idolatry (*shirk*). *Takfir*, declaring someone an unbeliever, is used to divide ISIS's world into the *kuffar* and the righteous Muslims. ISIS's extensive use of the terms *takfir* and *kafir* stands out among jihadi-Salafi groups. It opens the way for the full-out extermination—ethnic cleansing—of both non-Muslim groups and other Muslim sects. ISIS also widely uses the term *rawafid* (rejectionists) for Shia Muslims, *mushrikun* for Yezidis and others it considers polytheists, and *tawaghit* (tyrants) for "nonbelieving" regimes. ISIS defines *hijra* as the migration every Muslim living outside of the "caliphate" is obligated to make to the territory controlled by ISIS. Its professed puritanism goes beyond religion and bans any cultural or political influence from the outside of the "caliphate." To use Joana Westphal's application of framing theory to ISIS,[71] the group's collective action frame identifies a problem (the war on true Islam) and assigns responsibility for the problem to another actor (the unbelievers). It then presents a solution to the problem (the establishment of a caliphate), and calls for action (migration to its territory and *jihad*, understood as violent struggle against the unbelievers). By appropriating and redefining these normal Islamic concepts for its own use, ISIS links its ideology with the local context in order to rally support. It presented its project as a break with the nation-state, and encouraged its fighters to burn their passports. It avoided the word *muwatin*, the word for "citizen" in Arabic derived from the same root as *watan*, nation-state. However, words carrying some of the same meaning are used by the group interchangeably when addressing the locals: *al-raʿaya* (subjects), *al-nas* (the people), *al-umma al-islamiyya* (community of Muslims), among others. And while ISIS banned any reference to Iraq or Syria, it appropriated many of the symbols and routines associated with modern nation-states, such as a flag, a currency, an unofficial "national hymn," and a bureaucracy with seemingly meticulous documentation of everything from marriage to traffic violations.

In the ISIS worldview, military-strategic goals, territorial control, and governance are intimately linked to ideology. The idea of "liberating" territory and establishing an administration is not new among rebel groups in general. Islamist movements have always had state-building as a mandatory part of their charters.[72] The jihadist movement, which first emerged as radical splinters from the Egyptian Islamist movement, the Muslim Brotherhood, brought these abstract ideals of a new "caliphate" to the ground. As Brynjar Lia has shown, "attempts to form proto-states have been a constant feature of contemporary jihadism over the past 25 years."[73] After the Arab Spring erupted in 2011, jihadi groups have been eager to try to fill the power vacuum that emerged in countries like Syria and Libya. The image of being state-builders with the best interest of the people at heart has become more important jihadist group, even if their proclaimed "state" in fact was nothing more than a neighborhood, a group of prison inmates of part of a town. While some groups have claimed to establish "emirates," and others have seen territorial control as a distant future goal, ISIS was determined to use the term *dawla* or *khilafa*. The word *dawla* has an ambiguous meaning in Arabic and alludes both to the modern nation-state and to early Islamic empires like the Ummayad caliphate (*al-dawla al-ummawiyya*) and the Abbasid caliphate (*al-dawla al-ʿabbasiyya*). ISIS's spokesman Abu Muhammad al-Adnani proclaimed in a 2014 speech that the establishment of a state was a religious duty because they were in the position to do so: "We announced it because—by Allah's grace—we have its essentials. By Allah's permission, we are capable of establishing the *khilafa*. So we carry out the order of Allah (the Exalted) [...]."[74]

William McCants has placed great emphasis on ISIS's idea of the apocalypse to explain its obsession with territory. In the view of Zarqawi and his successors, the sectarian war that had engulfed Iraq, in which "Christians and Jews" allegedly had united with the Shia to fight the Sunnis, was a sign that the end times were approaching. Establishing a caliphate on the ground was necessary to usher in the final battle and the return of an Islamic empire.[75] There is no doubt that this ideological peculiarity has played a role in guiding ISIS's priorities. However, here it is difficult to distinguish between ideology and strategy, a point that McCants also makes. The declaration and broadcasting of its state and the realization of that state were mutually reinforcing. By creating a public image of having a functioning state in Iraq and Syria, the group attracted more foreign recruits to fill its ranks with fighters and its nascent institutions with jihadi bureaucrats. In his call for all Muslims to swear allegiance to the new caliph, Abu Muhammad al-Adnani proclaimed: "If your leaders whisper to you claiming it is not a *khilafa*, then remember how long they whispered to you claiming that it was not a state but rather a fictional cardboard entity, until its certain news reached you. It is a state. Its news will continue to reach you showing that it is a *khilafa*, even after time."[76]

Control of territory facilitates the flow of goods, weapons, and people, and control over oil fields and other resources made it financially possible to substantiate the claim to statehood. When ISIS's forerunners did not spend more than a small fraction of their budgets on institution building and providing social services, this was partly because they had not been economically capable of doing so.[77] An additional factor that probably affected the timing of the caliphate declaration was rivalry with other jihadi groups.[78] Claiming to have fulfilled the goal that other jihadi organizations had worked toward for decades gave ISIS an immediate competitive advantage. It declared all other "Islamic states" and "emirates" null and void. Iraq and Syria were presented as merely the starting point of a caliphate encompassing the entire world. Shapiro and Hansen-Lewis concluded in their 2015 analysis of the ISIS economy that the group's institutions were "inimical to economic growth"[79] and not sustainable. Al-Tamimi, in his account of the various ministries taking shape under ISIS, countered this and predicted that the group's professionalism could indeed make its administration sustainable if it maintained control of its strongholds.[80] Andrew F. March and Mara Revkin in 2015 aired the possibility that the ISIS could become an increasingly "normal" state over time, with bureaucratic administration and positive law, based not only on a reading of early Islamic texts but also on a "long-standing theory of statecraft and legal authority."[81] In hindsight, the most pessimistic predictions about its capacity proved to be true, but the group did manage to keep a continuous territory for longer than most other jihadi rebel groups have done in the past. As with most rebel groups, ideology and pragmatism are deeply interwoven in the political project of ISIS. The footprints of its ideology are clear in many of its actions, both on the battlefield and in its governance efforts. At the same time, the group's leaders have seemingly set aside its proclaimed ideology when practical concerns demand it. The interplay between ideology and pragmatism is important in order to understand how and why ISIS governance of Mosul developed as it did.

3

Policing the Caliphate

Discipline those who do not abstain from crime, subdue the ignorant, prevent clashes, pursue evildoers and seek out immoral persons in their hiding places.
ISLAMIC STATE TEXTBOOK[1]

The Iraq police was bad, but they had mercy. They might arrest you, they might beat you, for nothing, but in the end they would let you go if you were innocent. With daʿish, *if they arrested you, you were done.*
SHOP OWNER FROM MOSUL[2]

For the people of Mosul, the first signs of what it really meant to be ruled by ISIS were the new police forces that appeared in each neighborhood. After a few months of a soft introduction, police patrols walking the streets or driving around in white vans marked "The *Hisba* of the Islamic State" started gradually intervening more in Maslawis' everyday life. It started with encouragements: "You should keep your beard long and follow your religion," "you should cover your head," "smoking is bad for you." Liquor shops were closed. Prayer five times a day became mandatory. Then billboards were put up with pictures of appropriate female dress: Black cover from head to toe, including over the eyes. The time for the colorful hijabs usually dotting Mosul's streets was over. The so-called *khimar* became mandatory, and shop-owners selling women's clothing received large batches of them to distribute. The *khimar* includes a long, two-layered dress, face veil, gloves, and socks—all black. Men were banned from wearing "clothes which resemble those worn by infidels or women," like jeans, chains, or bracelets. Cutting or even grooming a beard or hair was illegal. After

Figure 4 *ISIS banned the depiction of persons, like here in Mosul general hospital (Photo: Mathilde Becker Aarseth).*

a few months, it became illegal for women to go outside the home without a male family member. For most of Mosul's women who remained in the city, three long years began confined between the walls of their homes, with only hurried trips outside the home when absolutely necessary. Punishments for breaking the new laws were gradually announced, and many were shocked when they first realized that beheadings, crucifixions, and amputations in public squares were parts of the ISIS legal code. Minor offences like smoking were punished with lashes. Homosexuals were pushed off tall buildings into their death. Those accused of "adultery" were stoned to death. The executions of those deemed immoral or opposing ISIS became public spectacles that people were forced to watch. The brutality of the Islamic State's police branches in Iraq and Syria quickly became the most broadcast symbol of the group's ruthless methods for civilian control.

Besides the media focus on ISIS police forces' "exceptional" brutality, the ISIS police have often been depicted as a somewhat positive force that provided long-needed stability, predictability, and order in the chaotic war zones that fell under ISIS control. The predictability it offered to the war-fatigued inhabitants was more important than the brutality of the punishments, a number of reports have claimed.³ However, such conclusions often rely on anecdotal evidence and not comprehensive interview-based studies. Moreover, the accounts are most often from Syria, even though Mosul was by far the largest laboratory for ISIS state-building experiment. This chapter challenges the understanding of ISIS police as relatively more legitimate among the inhabitants of Mosul. What did the many day-to-day interactions between Maslawis and officers of the ISIS police mean for civilians' perception of their new rulers—in an environment where the bar for any sense of legitimacy was exceptionally low? This chapter is based on thirty-nine in-depth interviews with civilians who lived in Mosul under ISIS rule, conducted on research trips to Northern Iraq in November–December 2016 and April–May 2018,⁴ as well as interviews conducted on the phone and social media, seen in the light of ISIS documents and other sources.⁵ The main interviews are gathered in IDP camps and in a range of different Eastern and Western Mosul neighborhoods, in an attempt to capture some of the variety in people's experiences.⁶ The neighborhoods include areas that were known to be ISIS strongholds like 17 Tamuz and the Old City; areas that historically have housed many officers in the Iraqi security forces, like Wadi Hajar; central middle-class areas like Muhandeseen; and lower-class suburbs like Al-Zahraa. Informants were chosen on the basis of their home neighborhood and the period of time spent under ISIS occupation.

The ISIS police apparatus is of course part of the group's larger justice system, which included laws, courts, and prisons.⁷ Zooming in on policing is useful for understanding how Maslawis perceived the legitimacy of ISIS, partly because the active role of police in people's everyday lives under ISIS gives ample opportunity to gather rich interview data. The staff of the different police branches—Iraqi or foreign ISIS members—had wide-reaching powers and would sometimes act as de facto judges, in line with their personal interpretation of *shariʿa* and the "interest of the people." A professional police force is key in any successful institution building and governance, also for rebels that want to overthrow the state. Establishing their own law enforcement is often the first priority for rebels who seek to govern, and it is not unusual that these rebel police squads end up being more popular than the national police. A police force that can control small-scale violence is important for rebels to keep a lid on organized resistance, but also to boost their claim as an alternative state authority and service provider. It is the outward face of power monopoly, and needs to prove to the subjects that it does not work arbitrarily. If a rebel group abuses its monopoly on violence and lacks accountability, the result can be a public backlash against it. ISIS strategists knew this from the start: ISIS propaganda often praised the group's own efficiency, professionalism, and accountability, and its police forces were meant to legitimize the new state, not only repressing and controlling its subjects. But what does legitimacy mean in a country with a dysfunctional, corrupt public sector, where its inhabitants have next to no trust in institutions? In Mosul, Iraqi police and security forces were the embodiment of the state's corruption, divisive sectarianism, and incompetence. In the lawlessness of pre-2014 Mosul, the Iraqi security forces were themselves involved in extorting people in the city. Iraqi forces would sometimes drive into the city and enter shops, for example goldsmiths, and take things by force without paying, filling their cars with stolen goods. Anyone who dared to complain risked being put on the government's terror list.[8] How did ISIS perform on this stage? This chapter unpacks the idea of legitimacy in rebel governance by looking closer at how Mosul's population perceived the efficiency, accountability, and predictability of the ISIS police.

Servants of the Caliph

The police forces play a central role in ISIS's "social contract." Its *wathiqat al-madina,* so-called city document, spells out the right to security for people and property and the right to due process according to Islamic law.[9] Security and Sharia justice for the "citizens" of the caliphate was emphasized by Abu Bakr al-Baghdadi in his speeches as well as in other propaganda. For example, a textbook produced by the group describes the role of the police as "servants of the governors [...]: They are the army on which the caliph, the *wali* or the judge depends in order to stabilize security and protect the regime, arrest corrupt offenders, and implement the *hudud* decided by the judge [...]."[10]

Examples of *hudud* punishments are death penalty for blasphemy adultery, homosexuality, "spying in the interest of the disbelievers," apostasy, and murder. Slander, smoking, and drinking alcohol are punished with lashes, theft with amputation of hand or foot.[11] Yet, as already mentioned, police officers not only had the power to arrest people, bring them to the ISIS courts or implement a judge's decision. They also had the authority to decide certain punishments on the spot, so-called *ta'zir* punishments that are not explicitly mentioned in the Sharia unlike *hudud*. Police officers also had the power to make decisions on *qisas*, retributive justice—an eye for an eye in disputes between people. They were supposed to "discipline those who do not abstain from crime, subdue the ignorant, prevent clashes, pursue evildoers and seek out immoral persons in their hiding places."[12] In reality, this meant that although punishments for severe crimes were decided by a judge, the police forces had a large room of maneuver in the system. Part of ISIS's justification for its justice system was that its rulings are "not manmade, not Western, not imposed on us by the West so they can rule us like they want."[13] Ironically enough, Mosul's inhabitants would soon experience that ISIS's hatred of "manmade law" allowed the police to mete out punishments at their own discretion, especially in *ta'zir* cases.

The police branches with the most civilian contact were the general police, *al-shurta al-islamiyya*, and the morality police, *al-hisba*,[14] which cooperated closely with each other. Other police departments were *shurtat al-murur*, which regulated traffic,[15] and *al-jihaz al-amni*, the security police, tasked with preventing vital threats to the group's control.[16] The all-female *al-khansa'* police, directed at women, was featured in many media reports from Raqqa.[17] In Mosul, there was a special "women's team" of *al-hisba*.[18] The general police was in charge of ordinary law enforcement and answered to the ISIS ministry of justice. Because of its important role, the *hisba* had its own ministry and was charged with "promoting virtue and preventing vice," and maintaining a watchful eye on the Muslim community.[19] It was a central part of the propaganda strategy to broadcast the efficiency of the *hisba*, which was underlined in a strategy document.[20] Aaron Zelin's analysis of propaganda output shows that the morality police ranked as the third most covered theme after military and governance.[21] Its tasks included everything related to appearance, clothing, observing prayer times, segregation of women and men, and preventing other "immoral" activities like singing, harassment of women or carrying a device with pictures that violate *shariʿa*.[22] The *diwan al-hisba* was in charge of price control in shops, and administrative tasks like issuing ISIS ID cards or travel permits, much like a regular police office.[23] As life in the caliphate progressed with all its day-to-day challenges, the *hisba* would often issue new, specific bans on everything from decorated clothes or pigeon-keeping to using colloquial expression referring to Allah or Muhammad.[24] In short, the *hisba* was the branch of the ISIS state that was most intimately felt by the population. It was also responsible for the widespread destruction of places called "unislamic" by ISIS.[25] In Mosul, this in included bulldozing and blowing up Shia mosques and holy shrines and tombs, but also destruction of ornaments on Sunni mosques deemed "too creative." Many of the city's ancient churches, monasteries and Christian shrines suffered the same fate. In 2015, ISIS militants were filmed smashing priceless ancient artifacts in Mosul Museum with sledgehammers. Shortly after, the *hisba* oversaw the bulldozing of one of the most important archeological wonders of the Middle East: Nimrud, the capital of the great Assyrian empire 879–709 BC, located thirty kilometers south of Mosul at where the rivers Tigris and Greater Zab meet. The 3,000-year-old winged bull statues with human heads, guarding the entrance of the Nimrud temple, were destroyed along with most of the ancient city in ISIS's quest to wipe out the parts of history that did not fit into their new political construct. The *hisba*'s role in providing a "clean slate" as a foundation for the new state speaks to its importance in the organization.

Spreading safety and security?

U.S. forces withdrew from policing Iraqi cities in 2009, and left behind an understaffed and broken police force. Because of the fall in oil prices and the Maliki government's budget cuts, Mosul had only half the number of policemen it needed by 2014, and the ones who were there were often infiltrated by extremist Shia militias.[26] As described in Chapter 2, The ISIS takeover of Mosul happened at a peak of disorder, at a time when civilians lived their daily lives at the mercy of armed groups in a constant tug of war for influence. As the central government failed to uphold a monopoly on violence, civilians' loyalties were shifting between the groups that vied for power, sometimes along sectarian lines. In a large survey from 2010, half of the respondents in Mosul cited security as their biggest personal problem, compared to 20 percent across Iraq as a whole. Nearly half of Sunnis in the survey had recently observed kidnappings for ransom.[27] Surveys had long shown a lower trust in public institutions among Sunnis than other groups. Often people resorted to tribal courts instead of dealing with the corrupt and ineffective Iraqi justice system.[28] In a Mosul survey published in 2018, 25 percent replied that they had experienced police harassment prior to 2014.[29] Maltreatment by the police and arbitrary detention of Sunnis were the main targets for the protestors' anger in 2013–14 when demonstrations drew large masses in Mosul and other major cities.

In this environment, it is not surprising that Maslawis first were open to ISIS as a guarantor of order and security; a survey showed that 16 percent of Sunnis in Iraq had "confidence" in ISIS in 2016.[30] The organization that was built and cemented on the ideological foundation of al-Qaida, and had much of the same member mass, worked the PR machinery hard to turn its brand around. While al-Qaida had been almost synonymous with criminal and mafia activity in the minds of many Maslawis, its new incarnation portrayed itself as the virtuous savior.

As ISIS took control over the areas surrounding Mosul, it often bragged about its efficient law enforcement and presented statistics showing how "crimes in the people's neighborhoods" had dropped immediately after the establishment of their courts, "spreading safety and security." For instance, the group claimed that 470 *ḥisba* cases had been raised and solved during the first month of its rule in Al-Raqqa, Syria.[31] It is difficult to say with certainty the crime rate in cities under siege. However, for the purpose of this book, how Mosul's inhabitants *perceived* the crime level is an important indicator of ISIS's legitimacy. These factors are interlinked; research shows that people are more likely to comply with the law and cooperate with police when they see the police as a legitimate authority.[32] When asked about the occurrence of crimes like theft, burglary, and violence between civilians under the ISIS occupation, the replies are mixed. Some, like this shopkeeper in Mosul, reported a dramatic decrease in crime because no one wanted to risk losing a limb or being executed for minor crimes:

> The crime level decreased to the level of being almost non-existent. Theft was punished by losing your hand. People were scared; it was not easy to know what could make you lose your life.[33]

ISIS's brutal punishments for crime had a certain deterrent effect in the beginning, but as the occupation dragged on, theft went up as poverty pushed usually law-abiding citizens to steal. According to several ISIS documents, personnel were transferred from the police forces to the military.[34] If this happened on a large scale, it indicates that the group increasingly prioritized military over regular law enforcement—leading to more crime. When asked whether they reported crimes to ISIS, found alternative solutions or simply chose to not act on it, my interviewees were almost equally divided. The two quotations below are examples of the different attitudes:

> Yes, people went to *da'ish* to report crimes when they happened, that's just how it is. For example, a dispute about money, a car crash, a divorce. When the closest person with authority is a tribal sheikh, you go to him to report things. During ISIS, the sheikhs had no authority anymore, so we reported it to the ISIS police. We had no choice if we wanted a solution, we could not just wait for liberation.[35]

> Some people reported crimes to the police, I and people I know did not. What would be the benefit from that? For example, if someone had his motorcycle stolen, who would find it? They didn't have the intelligence or capacity to solve crimes. I don't believe it would give any result. We did not trust them, and we did not want to communicate with them. So it was better to forget about it.[36]

None of these attitudes show a great confidence in ISIS as an upholder of law and order. Interestingly, many of the interviewees who chose not to report crimes did not give disagreement with the brutal ISIS laws as the reason; they simply did not think it would lead anywhere. This is not to say that they supported ISIS laws– most people described them as grotesque—but it shows an openness to new authority in an environment of chronic insecurity. Swift and tangible results were the highest priority, even if it meant that the perpetrator would be killed. This is a common phenomenon in civil war: For example, promises of "harsh, but just" rule as an alternative to a security vacuum have been important to the Taliban in Afghanistan.[37] ISIS claimed in its propaganda that criminal cases that had lingered for years in the previous system were now solved in less than a month under ISIS.[38] Some ISIS administrative documents show that some petty crimes were taken seriously in the group's justice system. For example, prison files from Mosul cite stealing cars or hospital equipment or "stealing money from people" as reasons for detention.[39] New York Times journalist Rukmini Callimachi found nearly 400 files of petty crimes reported to *al-shurta al-islamiyya* office in Tel Kaif, north of Mosul, where locals had reported disputes over a chicken or a few dollars to ISIS.[40] The Tel Kaif police files are too place-specific to draw broad conclusions about the ISIS police. But a dive into the files, systematized and digitalized by George Washington University, reveals a rural community that thirsted for someone with authority to report crimes and quarrels to. When ISIS set up office in town, complaints flowed in from the villagers about money arguments, rude behavior from neighbors, and cows grazing on farmland—often from before 2014. One woman complained to the Islamic police about her abusive and violent husband who used the children's allowance to buy cigarettes.[41] In a different case, ISIS made a husband declare that he would not beat his wife "unless she deserves it [...] and treat her in a respectful manner that preserves her dignity."[42] Although that ruling is hardly championing women's rights, it is interesting that both women and men addressed the extremist jihadi organization with these problems in the first place.

It is clear from the Tel Kaif files that many in the community threatened with reporting someone to ISIS if there was a disagreement. In that sense, the presence of ISIS in itself might have had a disciplining effect. Some also reported people for breaking ISIS moral rules like playing backgammon or grooming one's beard—which is either a sign that they approved of these extremist rules or that they used them to get revenge on their neighbors. An ISIS-produced overview over the reported cases during one month, March 2016, shows that money issues and more or less innocent quarrels between people were the dominating the statistics.[43] Many were reported to the police for swearing, and were let off the hook with a warning—and formally promising to not swear again. An argument over a bicycle ended up in the Islamic Police files, and illustrates how the existence of the police was used as pressure among the locals:

> The Claimant stated that he sold the Defendant a bicycle for (23,000 Dinars) to be paid no later than two days after the date of the sale. After the agreement, the Defendant left, and the Claimant did not see him for a long time. After a while, the Claimant found the bicycle, totally broken, thrown in front of his workplace. Afterward, the Claimant went to the Defendant's father and explained the situation to him; the Defendant's father told the Claimant that it was his problem. The Claimant told the Defendant's father that he would go to the Department of Hisba and report him. The Defendant's father told the Claimant that if he reported them, he would throw him in jail because they were all (the Defendant and his father) in the State [Islamic State].[44]

Theft was also reported: Ten cases during that month in Tel Kaif, out of which only one case was resolved. In general, most cases were not reported to have been resolved. Among the cases that were, a decision was usually made by the Islamic police itself, without the case being passed on to the Islamic court. My interviewees who reported crimes to ISIS in Mosul told of mixed results. Many were left with the impression that crimes that had the potential to stir up opposition to ISIS were quickly dealt with, like smuggling of illegal goods and burglary or theft by undisciplined ISIS members. Reports of disputes and theft often bore no results. One of the few among my interviewees who experienced something resembling a real investigation was a doctor who reported a burglary in his home by purported ISIS members:

> Some people who said they were from *da'ish* came to our home, they accused us of working for the Iraqi army, handcuffed us and took all the money in my house, the phones and the laptop. After that, I went to their police to report it. They answered that they belong to *da'ish* but they are thieves, that they had recently joined the police. They were very polite to us. After that, they brought some suspects to my home twice and asked me if they were the thieves. But I don't think they found them in the end.[45]

In fact, people underlined that they saw ISIS as the biggest crime problem during the group's rule, in the sense that ISIS members committed acts that the interviewees usually would call criminal—even when they followed their own rules and regulations. Even though ISIS defined its own bank robberies, murders, theft, violence, and sexual enslavement as "legal," this did not mean that civilians' sense of justice changed overnight. When Maslawis saw the houses of escaped neighbors being confiscated by ISIS, or civilians being killed for owning a mobile phone, they did not praise the group for consistently following their own rules. The following quote from a Mosul shop owner sums up a common sentiment among my informants:

> At the time of *da'ish*, my area became safer than before, there was hardly any theft, robbery, fighting, killings by regular people. But why was this? Because *da'ish* themselves were doing all the crimes. And those who used to be criminals joined *da'ish* when they came. Others were scared to do any crime because of the harsh punishments.[46]

An important point for ISIS was that it claimed to break with the nepotism that is common in public appointments in Iraq, and to employ people in its administration based on competence and not family or friendship ties.[47] However, no special skills or background was required to join its powerful police force. The police officers that Maslawis encountered in the streets following June 2014 were a mélange of foreign fighters, locals with no police experience, underage boys and well-known criminals from Mosul who had recently joined ISIS ranks. Abu Bakr al-Baghdadi has urged his followers in several speeches to "strive to release Muslim prisoners everywhere," indicating that inmates were seen as a resource for the caliphate. Interviews of ISIS fighters in Syria indicate that many prisoners released by ISIS in Syria joined the group.[48] The police forces had this motley character already at the beginning of ISIS rule, ruling out that it was merely a desperate move by ISIS made toward the end of its rule when resources dwindled. By emphasizing allegiance over other qualities, ISIS was left with largely inexperienced men to police the largest city in its territories, after emptying the existing police system of employees by murdering up to several thousand Iraqi police officers. In theory, Iraqi police officers were promised safety in the "caliphate" after going through *al-tawba* or "repentance." ISIS states this in the Mosul city document:

To the apostates of the army and police and the rest of the unbelieving apparatus, we say that the door of repentance is open to anyone who wants it, and we have designated specific places to receive those wishing to repent subject to conditions. ... For those who insist on remaining apostate, there is no alternative but death.[49]

In Mosul, the repentance process took place in two rounds. Police and army officers—both usually referred to by Maslawis as *muntasibin* or "affiliates"— followed the same repentance procedure. In the first round they were asked to register their names, hand over weapons, and claim allegiance to the Islamic State. In the second round, more detailed personal information was added and a repentance fee was paid.[50] The repentance system was not only a way for ISIS to suppress potential competing organized armed forces, it was also lucrative for ISIS.[51] The repentance fees vary from 1 million to more than 2 million IQD (1,700 USD), and an ISIS document from Mosul lists the conditions for repenting: The repenter was not allowed to move house, he would be killed if he committed any crime, and he had to specify a guarantor who would be punished in case he disappeared.[52] In reality, the repentance option put forward by ISIS was far from a safety guarantee. Iraqi police officers in Mosul were either forced to flee the territories, go into hiding, or risk becoming victims of ISIS extermination campaigns. Staying in ISIS territory meant living in constant fear of their lives. Some former police or military personnel among my interviewees reported having completed the first part of *al-tawba* out of fear for ISIS. Some told that their colleagues who went to complete the second *tawba* disappeared after being rounded up by ISIS. Prison files also mention "police with *tawba*" as a reason for detention.[53] As the liberation of Mosul entered its last months, ISIS went through with mass executions of former Iraqi police and military officers.[54] Many of the victims have later been found in ISIS mass graves.[55] A former army officer described how he, after completing the first *tawba*, stayed in hiding:

> I kept [my army background] secret; most people did not know, only the ones closest to me. I started selling vegetables. Four other officers in the army lived in this area, they were my colleagues in the army, they were killed by ISIS. In the end, when the fighting got closer, I ran away to

another area. [...] They did not start killing police and army officers until after the last repentance. At that point, they rounded up all the men in one neighborhood in a school and checked if they were *muntasibin*, it did not matter if you belonged to the police or army. A part of them were taken by ISIS, a part we don't know what happened to. This was at the time when the liberation operation started.[56]

A new brand of corruption

In Iraq after Saddam, corruption penetrated all levels of the state and hollowed out the police and military from the inside. In November 2014, it was revealed that more than 50,000 "ghost soldiers" and police officers were formally employed by the state—while their salaries ended up in generals' pockets. While it only shows a tip of the iceberg, it is a sign of the extreme levels of corruption and lack of accountability in the country's security institutions. A senior military official told Al-Jazeera that each battalion on paper has 750 troops, but in reality has only 200—the rest of the soldiers being "paid" are either dead, missing, or avoiding service.[57] What looked like a strong military presence in Mosul those fateful days in June 2014, was in fact was a hollow shell. In general, bribes are seen as standard procedure when receiving state services, crossing borders, or securing the release of a detained relative. Sectarian conflicts also mark justice and security apparatus, with police squads used as cover for sectarian militias. Iraq is stuck at the bottom of international rankings when it comes to how inhabitants perceive the rule of law and control of corruption. For a decade, Transparency International's has ranked it among the top twelve most corrupt country in the world.[58]

Since 2003, virtually every Iraqi politician running for office has promised—and failed—to combat corruption. With a population with this low expectations, Mosul's inhabitants were likely to embrace rulers who showed even a minimum of commitment to keeping anti-corruption promises. Iraqi corruption has been credited with enabling the rise of ISIS.[59] How did civilians in Mosul perceive the level of corruption, civilian oversight, and equality under ISIS law? I here use the term "corruption" to describe misuse of public power for personal gain or the benefit of the group, in conflict with ISIS's own laws and regulations.

Iraq's police corruption has on several occasions been used in ISIS propaganda. For instance, a 2015 *Dabiq* article writes about Kurdish Iraqi forces that "their greed and corruption" underscore their inability to effectively wage war against the *khilafa*."[60] In its official documents, ISIS claims to have mechanisms to strike down on corruption and misbehavior by ISIS members. In Tel Abyad, Syria, the group issued an announcement in 2014 encouraging people to bring any complaints about ISIS to their court every Thursday.[61] In a document outlining the structure of the security apparatus, something called the "economic security administration" is charged with investigating financial corruption and embezzlement.[62] It is also responsible for "monitoring the financial situations of the soldiers of the *dawla*, verifying and gathering information about the reasons for the increase of the wealth of a soldier of the *dawla*," as well as preventing looting, smuggling of antiquities, and forging of currency. There are examples of ISIS members being punished or executed for stepping across legal boundaries. Corruption of the more overt or semi-public type so common in Iraq decreased under ISIS; paying your way to better services or to escape trial was not common. Does this mean that there was less overall corruption and more accountability under ISIS? My evidence suggests that instead of disappearing, corruption became more centralized under ISIS rule. As the group seized control over the Mosul's formal economy, it also seized near total control over its informal economy, building on the mafia networks developed under the al-Qaida years. The system that emerged echo Saddam's nepotistic style of corruption during the sanction years of 1990–2003, when smuggling networks controlled by the president's son Uday benefitted the *umana' Saddam*, Saddam's faithful inner circle. The regime ruthlessly and systematically cracked down on graft by anyone outside of this circle.[63] In a similar way, ISIS made clear attempts to crack down on "unauthorized" corruption and misuse of power. At the same time, there are strong indications that the group controlled smuggling of refugees or goods banned by their own rules. This included alcohol, looted antiquities—and cigarettes.

Cigarette trade in occupied Mosul

Officially, smoking was banned by ISIS because it was defined as a form of suicide or self-harm. A few months after the takeover of Mosul, the group started systematically persecuting smokers, punishing them with lashes, fines, and sometimes prison. In media reports, public burning of piles of cigarettes was taken as a sign of the group's ideological rigidity. The level of fines reported by my interviewees vary, but would sometimes reach 150,000 Iraqi dinars (125 USD), a large sum for civilians who often survived off of their savings in ISIS times. The punishment for selling cigarettes could be longer imprisonment and confiscation of property in addition to the cigarettes.[64] A smoker and cigarette seller in Mosul describes persistent crackdowns on smokers:

> I went to the prison three times because of smoking and selling cigarettes. I have children so I had to sell [cigarettes]. The first time, some people told them that I had cigarettes, and some *dawaʿish* came and they arrested me and gave me 40 lashes. The second time someone came to my house and asked for cigarettes, and five minutes after he left, *dawaʿish* came and searched the house and found the cigarettes, and they took them and they took me to the prison for four days and gave me more than 40 lashes. The third time when they came to my house I wasn't home, me and my wife were out shopping but my sons were at home and they beat them both […], and they took a lot of my cigarettes.[65]

When bombs started falling over Mosul daily during the military campaign against ISIS in 2016, the group issued an announcement that smoking was not permitted even during such trying times.[66] It might seem strange to prioritize the smoke ban in a situation with constant military pressure on its borders. However, the cigarette ban not only effectively made the presence of the new police force felt; it also provided a steady source of income for the group, much like the repentance fees. In a country where a third of the adult male population smokes daily, this meant that a large part of my interviewees had been arrested, fined and/or lashed for smoking at some point between 2014 and 2017. A smoker recounts:

They checked for cigarettes everywhere, even inside electrical devices and inside the holes of curtains, because they knew that people were hiding cigarettes there. [...] Someone I know was selling cigarettes illegally. ISIS found out and took his savings, his car, his cigarettes and his motorcycle.[67]

Despite the official zero-tolerance policy on smoking, smokers named ISIS itself as the main source of cigarettes during this period when the group controlled the flow of goods into the city. There are examples of cigarette smugglers working independently from ISIS at great personal risk, but most often ISIS members or middle-men connected to the group were themselves the sources for cigarettes. One man recounts:

I saw that ISIS had a raid and confiscated cigarettes from people. Then they sold them in another area. My brother was a smoker, he got cigarettes from someone connected to ISIS. It was easy to get, you just ordered it and received it after ten minutes. In the beginning, one pack cost 12,000 Iraqi dinars. At the end of the liberation operation the price has reached 75,000 dinars.[68]

A new cigarette brand from Armenia, Akhtamar, became the only brand available in Mosul during the ISIS occupation, indicating that the cigarettes were brought in from Syria. The ISIS cigarette trade gave rise to a standing joke among some of Mosul's inhabitants, recounted in the following way by a man from Mosul:

Da'ish made us proud, they made us hold our heads high and united the people of Mosul. They made us proud [*bayyadu wujuhna*, translated literally as "they made our faces white"] because everyone had the same beard. They made us hold our heads high because we all looked up for airplanes. And they united us because they made all the people smoke the same brand of cigarettes.[69]

By systematically fining smokers, confiscating cigarettes, and at the same time having an unofficial monopoly on selling them, ISIS multiplied the value of each cigarette. The price for a pack of cigarettes increased dramatically after the city was cut off from outside communication, reaching 100,000 dinars

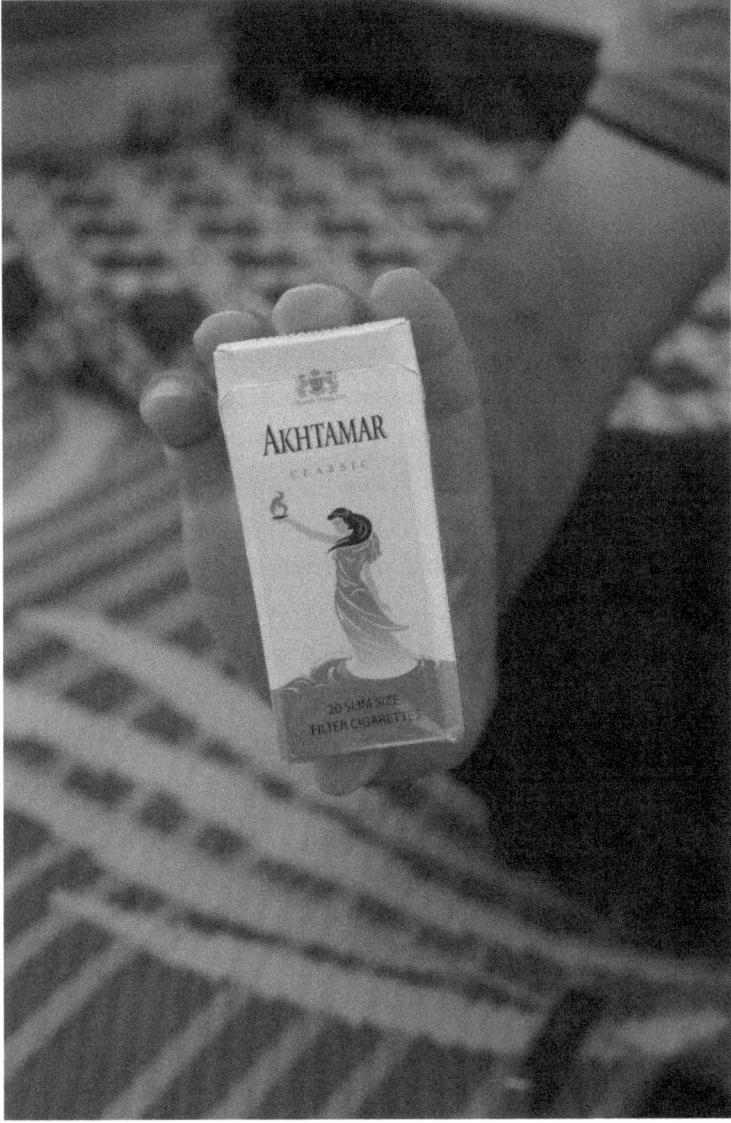

Figure 5 *A displaced man from Mosul shows the cigarette brand sold by ISIS-affiliated men (Photo: Mathilde Becker Aarseth).*

toward the end of ISIS rule, 200 times its original price. It is difficult to establish whether the cigarette smuggling and selling was known by ISIS leadership. A *hisba* ruling from Syria sentenced an ISIS member to prison, a fine, flogging, and exclusion for selling cigarettes,[70] showing that at least occasionally ISIS members were punished for this. In Mosul, the smuggling and distribution was so widely known that the leadership most likely either orchestrated or tolerated it. ISIS members were also known to facilitate smuggling of alcohol and drugs into Mosul—and even civilians out of the city.[71] ISIS is known to take advantage of porous borders for smuggling of oil, weapons, and antiquities. Iraqi intelligence officials and analysts have claimed that the group became deeply involved in growing and smuggling cannabis in Iraq and Syria,[72] and European investigators have discovered a smuggling network from Italy to ISIS-controlled territory in Libya.[73] These and other examples are reminders that terror groups like ISIS are often entangled in organized crime.[74] Traditionally, ideologically and politically motivated groups have been considered the antithesis to organized crime. According to this view, members of a group are either criminals motivated by plundering, or ideologues seeking to change the political and social order.[75] In this logic, a group becomes less of a "dedicated" terror group when it engages in profit-driven crime. However, as Santiago Ballina has noted, many groups are hybrid organizations: "comfortably rooted in both ideology and profit, constantly shifting their strategies and tactics as they evolve."[76] Descriptions of ISIS as rule-based and financially self-sustained have often not taken into account the group's smuggling of goods banned by their own rules. Hardly surprising, ISIS is a deeply ideological movement which simultaneously reaps the fruits of cross-border and internal smuggling of illicit goods and refugees.

Civilian oversight

For a police force to be accountable, civilians need formal avenues to complain about police misconduct. If corrupt and self-serving police officers get free room of maneuver, that will keep people from reporting crime, setting off a negative spiral which leads to more crime. The ISIS police is far from our usual understanding of a democratic police. Still, the inhabitants of the "caliphate" actually had the right—on paper—to file complaints about the behavior of ISIS representatives, including the police. However, a minimum level of trust in the police institution is necessary for civilians to make use of this opportunity in practice. Even if some civilians filed complaints on ISIS police, the level of skepticism in the group's police overall indicates that most civilians were hesitant to file complaints, whether it was out of fear or lack of trust that it would yield any results.

My interviews also revealed that civilians often did not have a clear sense of the lines of command within the ISIS police, and the separation between its various agencies. When asked who had arrested them after breaching a rule, the answer was most often simply *"wahid daʿishi"* (an ISIS person) or the plural *"dawaʿish,"* and often the interviewee was unable to distinguish between a *hisba* officer and an officer in *al-shurta al-islamiyya*. Interviewees used the term *"daʿishi"* to describe both militants working for ISIS and civilians who had pledged allegiance to the group. The unclear distinction between the military and the police in the case of ISIS is not surprising as their "state" found itself in a continuous state of war, which meant that the whole organization was geared toward militarization even as it was trying to govern civilians. Even before ISIS, the distinction between police, military, militias, and criminal groups have been marginal in the minds of Iraqis, as Robert E. Looney points out.[77] The increasing militarization of parts of the Iraqi police after the U.S.-led invasion added to this blurriness. The fact that people saw the divisions and lines of command under their new rulers as blurry, contributed to a sense of unclear accountability.

"Justice is applied evenly"

In its communication, ISIS underlined that there was equality under the law for civilians (in the sense of male Sunni Muslims) and members of the group.[78] "Justice is applied evenly and the Lord of mankind is feared," the viewers were told in a 2016 propaganda video, and the ISIS ministries were described as "places for protecting rights."[79] A number of reports tell of ISIS members being punished or executed in public, including for alleged corruption.[80] Such stories were not uncommon among my interviewees, like this man from Mosul:

> I saw one member of *daʿish* being killed by a gunshot to the head in a public execution because he was accused of stealing from *diwan al-ʿaqarat* [ISIS

real estate ministry]. Another time I saw some *da'ish* members who were arrested because they were accused of trying to take over a house in the name of *da'ish*, without the permission of a judge.[81]

Even if it happened that lower-ranking members were publicly executed, high-ranking ISIS members were commonly seen as immune to prosecution. In general, most of my interviewees claimed, based on their own experiences and observations in public, that ISIS members were treated more leniently in the justice system than civilians. A man from Mosul shared his view:

> It all depended on the rank of the *da'ishi*. If it was a regular *da'ish* soldier in the street, yes, we saw that they were punished. But we never saw a *da'ishi* on a higher level get punished. It was mostly a show to present an image to us "*'awwama*" ["regular folks"] that it was an organization without corruption.[82]

Of course, civilians could only observe punishments and executions that happened in public. There are some reports of higher-ranking members being punished.[83] Yet, my interviewees generally described a strong sense of inequality under the law, which indicates that ISIS failed to project an image to the public of an efficient and accountable regime and police force. The widespread use of public punishments and executions under ISIS in itself highlights the group's need to establish its own authority as the only alternative. As Zachariah Mampilly notes, "symbolic processes that effectively reference the coercive power of the regime may reduce the need for the insurgent government to rely on force to ensure compliance."[84] What ISIS lacked in manpower, it made up for through these public performances of authority and law enforcement. Ana Arjona has suggested that this kind of symbolic violence can have a "freezing" effect on the spectators and help secure obedience even for a rebel group with relatively few members. "It might help to make civilians obey not only because they learn that disobedience carries serious consequences, but also because fear makes them psychologically incapable of reacting in any way but complying."[85] Public punishment of undisciplined ISIS members was an important part of this performance. By moving examples of its law enforcement onto the streets, ISIS wanted to instill fear, but also demonstrate equality under ISIS law and efficiency. If an organization is to keep its eye on the long-term goal and retain internal discipline, it needs to punish disobedient foot soldiers who are tempted by short-term personal.[86] Nevertheless, my data show that many Maslawis were not convinced by these public shows of accountability, mainly because of their personal, negative experiences with law enforcement. My findings support Mara Revkin's suggestion in her analysis of the ISIS social contract, namely that ISIS "selectively punishes its own members only when necessary to appease public demands for accountability."[87] The discrimination between ISIS members and civilians in access to food, housing, and electricity contributed to my interviewees' sense of injustice, even though this discrimination was officially justified by ISIS. Many of the interviewees lamented this, like this man from Eastern Mosul:

> With ISIS, it was justice only in a way that benefitted them and their own interests. At the same time, their emirs were living in big houses with 24/7 electricity, while normal people had nothing. It did not create a sense of justice. There was nothing Islamic about their police or their prisons.[88]

Predictability in law enforcement

Predictability, being able to plan most aspects of life and predict consequences of actions, is a rare luxury for civilians in civil war. This was also the case in Mosul in the years leading up to 2014. From the perspective of an armed group competing with other groups and trying to hold on to territory, acting in a more predictable way means compromising on the flexibility needed in warfare.[89] Even so, for rebels with ambitions for long-term governance, it is necessary to at least display a credible image of predictability. They need to give people a general sense that they know what to expect from life. As Ana Arjona notes in her study of the Colombian civil war, both rebels and civilians have something to gain from some sort of social contract that regulates behavior. Rebels can more easily monitor and control the population, and civilians can more easily adapt their behavior to avoid being harmed.[90] Rebels also have incentives to establish clear rules on *their own* behavior, because it increases civilians' willingness to obey the social contract. In fact, this is at the heart of what building institutions and governing is about. Rebels build or take over institutions because they see the benefits of constraining their own behavior—at least on paper—within a framework of rule-bound institutions, in order to achieve greater benefits in the future.[91] For civilians, institutions mean—at least on paper—that they are better protected from indiscriminate violence by the rebels and by other civilians.

A common assumption is that the use of violence by rebels automatically leads to lost legitimacy. But in a context where unpredictable violence by "roving bandits" is the norm, a more regular rule enforcement can give more legitimacy even though it is brutal and unforgiving. Some predictability in itself gives civilians much-needed room to protect themselves and their families and go on with their lives. Then, brutal laws is an acceptable price to pay. Fransisco Gutiérrez-Sanín describes how leftist militias in Colombia were able to wrestle the power from violent bands by presenting an equally violent, yet more predictable alternative to their rule.[92] In Mosul, ISIS gradually made their new justice code known to civilians through public announcements, starting with written declarations and billboards for their morality code. Although the rules in themselves seem clear enough, a majority of my interviewees describe an inconsistency in how they were implemented. As Douglass North and Barry Weingast argue with regard to state institutions, it is not enough for a government to establish a set of rights; it has to make a "credible commitment" to those rights in order to create meaningful governance.[93] The following quote from a Mosul shop-keeper sums up the most common view:

> If you were arrested by the Iraqi police, you knew that at some point you would be taken in front of a court, you would get a lawyer. With ISIS no, you were dependent on the person who arrested you. For example, sometimes they would cut the hand off someone who stole, but sometimes not, it depended on where it happened.[94]

Rule enforcement is never perfect, and it would be unreasonable to expect a perfect consistency in ISIS's policing of Mosul's population. Even so, rebel groups depend on civilians having a certain respect for their new social contract. In Mosul, ISIS largely failed in fostering respect for their rule, partly because civilians saw it as arbitrary. Moreover, Mosul's inhabitants saw the *hisba*'s intrusion into people's private lives as an invasion of their lives that went beyond what a government should do. This attitude was the same for interviewees in Mosul city center as for those living in the more socially conservative peripheries. The immense number of administrative documents produced by *diwan al-hisba* shows that this part of policing was a major priority for the group. The *hisba* demanded a say in most things in life, including how children could play and how people should mourn their dead.[95] Throughout its rule, the group continued to expand the space for what was being policed, and that was in itself a source of unpredictability and fear:

> No matter how corrupt the Iraqi police was, it cannot be compared to the *da'ish* police. The Iraqi police did not interfere in the personal lives of people, like smoking, shaving, drinking wine, going to the cinema, being dressed in a certain way. It was something strange and foreign to us; it made us feel more unsafe.[96]

The morality rules served only to restrict people's day-to-day life in already difficult times, and when ISIS prioritized that over cracking down on criminals, it created resentment. For ISIS, these rules were not only ideologically important, they were an efficient way to increase social control in a situation where they were hugely outnumbered by civilians. But the group's neverending crackdowns on shaving and clothing, while some experienced a rise in actual crime, weakened civilians' respect for the social contract. Toward the end of the group's rule in 2016, ISIS tightened its grip on civilians, issuing stricter penalties and adding more to its list of banned activities. This was a desperate attempt to strangle opposition, but also to increase its income from fines. As the economic isolation of the city started to be felt, the group imposed higher taxes on people's shrinking incomes. This happened while prices on food sky-rocketed, throwing many into deep poverty. Maslawis saw these as opportunistic moves by the group—a further breach of the social contract. A doctor recounted his experience:

> I lived in Mosul the whole period under ISIS and I saw the rules changing, so it was not predictable. Like with smoking: In the beginning, they would

kick people who smoked. Later, they would imprison them. At the end, they would kill them. It was the same with the internet. The taxes also kept changing. I opened my own clinic during the time of ISIS to earn some more money. They taxed clinics with 2.5 percent of the income each year. In the beginning, they told me that I was exempt from tax because the lower limit was 1.5 million dinar. The next time I went to them, they had decreased the lower limit for taxation to 600.000 dinar. So everything was changing all the time, it was not predictable. They changed the rules according to their needs.[97]

As its finances ran out and military pressure increased from the outside, ISIS was no longer willing or capable of projecting an image of running institutions that served the population. The dwindling money reserves led to even more predatory "taxation"—described by most civilians as extortion—applied in a haphazard way with large variations even within the city borders. The tax regime did not take into account that many Maslawis were left without income after ISIS's occupation of the city.

Conclusion

How did civilians in Mosul perceive the legitimacy of the Islamic State's police branches? In ISIS videos and magazines—directed at an audience outside of the "caliphate"—the group's omnipresent police became an efficient visual proof of a state ruled by *shariʿa*. ISIS went to great lengths to portray its police as efficient, accountable, predictable, and popular among the local population. The bureaucratic documents from the police sector paint a similar picture of a group dedicated to rules, regulation, and documentation. Several media and research reports have suggested that many civilians living under ISIS preferred the group's "brutal, but predictable" rule to the preceding state of anarchy and unpredictability.

This chapter has challenged this view, drawing on interviews with civilians living in Mosul in the period 2014–16. The interviews reveal considerable cracks in the official image of ISIS police forces reproduced in some media and research reports. Legitimacy is a thorny concept, but by dissecting civilians' views on the efficiency, predictability and accountability of the ISIS police, the chapter has aimed to present a more nuanced view of the forces' perceived legitimacy during this period. Civilians appreciated certain parts of ISIS rule, but that did not necessarily translate into legitimacy, even for those who felt betrayed and persecuted by Iraqi authorities. Some Maslawis who experienced a drop in crime in their area saw it as a positive development. However, the overall picture is one of less predictability for Maslawis in their everyday lives.

Firstly, civilians reported arbitrary law enforcement—except in cases that went against important interests of the group. The great variation in civilians' experiences with crime control is a sign of inconsistent law enforcement. Secondly, ISIS's claim of accountability became more and more dubious for many civilians as they experienced corruption and favoring of ISIS members. Thirdly, the group's image of being a predictable alternative suffered because of extreme social policing, opportunistic changing of rules, and a large maneuvering room for individual police officers. In sum, claiming that the ISIS police forces managed to establish a meaningful sense of legitimacy among Mosul's population is a hasty conclusion—even in a city that was a lawless free-zone for armed group. At ISIS's arrival, even the slightest improvement in people's sense of predictability and order could have boosted the group's popularity. The group's failure to live up to its own ideals became one of the reasons why many Maslawis' initial openness to ISIS vanished after a few months of its rule.

4

Resistance in the Classrooms

> "*I saw ISIS soldiers coming with trucks in front of the university library. They carried books and documents out of the library and drove away with them.*"
>
> SCHOOL MANAGER IN MOSUL[1]

> *When Daesh entered our village, my father stopped us all going to school. He said it wasn't safe anymore. [Now] I go to the camp school, but it's hard to catch up. It was a long time ago that my mind thought to study and it's not a serious school. I go because it is something to do. I don't think I will pass my exams, it's too late now*
>
> MOSUL GIRL IN SECONDARY SCHOOL IN IDP CAMP. [2]

Only a few months after ISIS took power, high-ranking ISIS members summoned the city's teachers from all educational levels to a meeting at Mosul university campus.[3] The invitation was issued in letters and in the new ISIS radio station "Al-Bayan" which had been set up in record time. With cautious anticipation many Mosul teachers showed up, some out of curiosity, others out of fear. Although nobody already could grasp the mark that the new rulers would eventually make on the city, there was a strong feeling that this was an important moment that would decide their immediate futures. How did these unknown occupiers view education, which was so ingrained in Maslawis' lives and identity? The city's three universities had a solid reputation in the Middle

East despite the many hardships the city had endured. The Mosul University campus was a lively place where ideas were exchanged freely, and with area close by of cafés, restaurants, and shops where young students would mingle. In fact, the spiritual guide of ISIS-founder Abu Mousab al-Zarqawi, Abu Muhammad al-Maqdisi, was a student at Mosul University early in his life. According to some reports, he found the atmosphere on campus too secular. On this autumn day in 2014, the warm meeting room in the dean's department was packed with teachers, surrounded by ISIS militants armed with rifles. A man dressed in what locals call "Afghan clothes"—the long chemise and short trousers prescribed by ISIS, introduced himself as the education minister of the Islamic State. The nom-de-guerre of this man, an Egyptian holding German citizenship, was Dhu al-Qarnayn, "he of two horns"—a Quranic figure known to have erected a wall between chaos and humanity. This Dhu Al-Qarnayn had a university degree from Germany and had been part of the original Abu Mus'ab al-Zarqawi network in Iraq. After the conquest of Mosul, his hand-written signature could be found at the bottom of important documents issued by the ISIS education ministry. By his side in the meeting room stood Khaled Jamil Muhammad, a Maslawi appointed to be the new president of the university.[4] It was a new time, they declared to the teachers, and the whole education system would soon be restructured to follow ISIS ideology. The teachers gradually understood that their new rulers also wanted input from the teachers for the new education system, one that would produce well-educated, useful and modern Muslims to serve the Islamic State. One teacher who attended the meeting recounts:

> They asked the teachers to propose ideas on how to reform the education system, and some did. One professor, for example, proposed that they could teach more Asian languages, because of the number of Muslims from Asian countries. This suggestion was well received by ISIS; they liked the idea.[5]

The ISIS delegation also informed them of the new principles that would guide education in a "transition period" until the new curriculum was ready.[6] The group introduced school fees, gender segregation, and strict dress codes. All courses teaching art, music, philosophy, social science, literature, history, geography, sports, religious education in Christianity, and parts of the teachings on Islam were shut down immediately.[7] Some of these topics would later reemerge in revised ISIS versions.

As the Ninawa province was turned into "wilayat Ninawa," its 2,700 schools and universities fell under the direct control of the group. They would be cut off from contact with the central ministry of education in Baghdad for three years.[8] By spring 2015, the group had developed its own curriculum for primary and secondary schools and sought to change the content of the entire education system to harmonize with extremist Salafi-jihadi doctrines. The goal was to raise the children of Ninawa to become hardline jihadi fighters protecting the future borders of the state and building the ideal Muslim society. Despite the resources ISIS spent on this reform, it was shelved by the end of 2015, partly due to persistent resistance from teachers, parents, and students. For Ninawa's one million students, it is a story of lost education that will take years to retrieve, and several hundred thousand children were robbed of education even for years after ISIS was expelled. However, as this chapter will show, it was also a story of fierce resistance against all odds.[9] What explains civilian resistance to violent, extremist rebel rule? The chapter investigates the ways in which some of Mosul's teachers, students and parents sabotaged, bargained with, and influenced the implementation of ISIS's planned educational reform. Some parents and teachers, especially from villages around Mosul, explained that they kept away from the schools for security reasons. They were afraid of the coalition air raids and did not necessarily intend to subvert the Islamic State. It is likely that the education reform would have been abandoned regardless of civilian responses, because of the growing military pressure on ISIS and the group's growing financial problems. However, civilian resistance added to these challenges. Before it descended into civil war, Mosul was a proud center of higher education in the province. The chapter suggests that the strength of the educational institutions in place at the time of ISIS's arrival may have made Mosul's civilians more able and willing to resist its wide-reaching reforms. This chapter is based on sixty-three interviews with civilians who lived in Mosul under ISIS rule.[10] These include students, teachers, lecturers, headmasters, professors and administrators, parents of schoolchildren, and high-ranking officials in Ninawa province. It also draws on leaked administrative documents on education issued by ISIS, its new curriculum, its propaganda videos and articles, as well as local and international media and reports by non-governmental organizations (NGOs).

Education in Mosul before ISIS

When rebel groups try to control the education system, it is because it is seen as a crucial arena for long-term ideological influence over a civilian population.[11] The groups that prioritize the lengthy, tricky process it is to reform education often have both a strong ideological commitment and a firm control over territory. According to Ana Arjona's research, when rebel groups try to make such wide-reaching changes, communities with high-quality pre-existing institutions are far more likely to resist the rebel group than communities with low-quality institutions.[12] Measuring the strength of existing institutions is not easy, but there are some features that are crucial. Strong institutions are stable and survive the passage of time and governments, they are perceived as legitimate, and they have the discipline and capacity to enforce rules and regulations.[13] Prior to 1991, Iraq's education system was widely regarded as one of the best in the Middle East, although one that was highly politicized. Education became a top political priority in the 1970s, when the right of free access to schools and universities was stipulated in the constitution. Saddam Hussein spent more on funding education than most other rulers in the region, resulting in the highest enrollment rates in the Middle East and the near eradication of illiteracy in the 1980s. Since then, war, international sanctions, and economic crises have reversed many of these successes. The heaviest blow to education was the US invasion of 2003 and the ensuing war, which destroyed much of the education infrastructure and cut large numbers of internal refugees off from education. The Iraqi curriculum is still a political and religious battleground in some ways, and the education system—like all Iraqi institutions—suffers from years of insufficient funding, corruption, and a lack of modernization.[14]

Despite these hardships, the schools and universities that fell into ISIS's hands in Mosul were relatively strong considering the context. Iraq had managed to reverse some of the setbacks since 2003. Enrollment in primary education had grown at record speed and was back to 90 percent in 2011, while enrollment in secondary education grew from 49.2 percent in 2000 to 79.1 percent in 2013. In Mosul, the main university and most of the schools remained functional throughout the civil war. The teacher informants describe a tightly knit collective of dedicated colleagues organized in teachers' unions. During and after ISIS's hold on the city, makeshift "campuses" were organized by exiled Mosul University staff members in Duhok, Erbil, Kirkuk, and other Iraqi cities so that internally displaced students could avoid interrupting their studies. The fact that education continued even during displacement shows a high degree of institutional stability.

The perceived legitimacy of institutions is also important in assessing their strength; it indicates people's willingness to defend them. Comprehensive data on this are lacking, but my interviewees stressed how the importance of education is a historical part of the identity of Maslawis, even if education had been exploited by changing political regimes.[15] The interviewees from the city center emphasized that this differentiated them from the "simple village people" in rural areas. The informants from rural areas, on their side, underlined that schooling for their children was a top priority, even in wartime. This is not to say that schools and universities were seen as infallible; far from it. But problems like under-funding and politicization did not diminish the general respect for the schools and universities. Mosul's active civil society has often moved in to fill the governance vacuum of the Iraqi state. Mara Revkin has suggested in her studies on ISIS state building that this may have provided more fertile ground for resistance in Mosul than, for example, in Syria's Raqqa province.[16] When the ISIS occupation was a fact, some teachers risked their lives to hide school records and books from being destroyed by the extremists. After the Mosul University's campus was destroyed in the military campaign against ISIS in 2017, a broad grassroots initiative to rebuild the university was launched by civil-society groups.[17] They arranged a book festival on campus, followed by a successful international campaign to collect books and restore the university's looted and burned libraries.[18] The university's faculties resumed their courses while the buildings were still in ruins. Driven largely by students and teachers, without any substantial support from the authorities, this indicates the existence of a potent civil society with the will and capacity to organize despite the authorities in place at a given time. Dozens of similar campaigns were launched in other sectors of society. According to Sarah D. Shields in *Mosul before Iraq*, the adaptability of the city's population to political realities has characterized Mosul since the Ottoman period.[19] Many of the informants mention this historical legacy when explaining their resistance to ISIS's education reform.

The ISIS plan

Schools and universities were central to the ISIS narrative of being not only a group, but a state-builder. ISIS propaganda describes education as more important than military efforts for keeping effective long-term rule:

> And the education system is of no less importance than the military sector, but actually is greater in influence than the military sector, for the military sector has been put in place to subjugate the people to the *taghut* [tyranny] by iron and fire, while the education system has been put in place to do away with the signs of the religion, make people support the *taghut*, and ingrain its ideas and principles through persuasion and instruction.[20]

In the announcement cited above, education is described as "the gate through which organizations enter to spread their principles, establish the pillars of their rule and secure the loyalty of the people and their support for them." Education under the old Iraqi and Syrian regimes is described as godless indoctrination ruining the future generations.[21] This is contrasted with the new ISIS education system, where children's only stated wish is to become *mujahidin* for the Islamic State, learning to fight infidel rulers.[22] In the new ISIS schools, there is no room for "nationalism, racism, pseudo-historical events, or geographical divisions that also contravene Islamic *shariʿa*."[23] Educational institutions are seen as an important arena of unwanted ideological and political ideas, such as Baathism and nationalism, to be replaced with ISIS's brand of jihadi-Salafism. At the same time, education is ultimately seen as a tool for the "caliphate's" military survival and expansion, a fact that Dhu al-Qarnayn also was open about toward the teachers.

The curriculum reform was overseen by the *diwan al-taʿlim*, the ISIS education ministry in Mosul. ISIS painted a picture of running a full-fledged ministry of education in Mosul, and encouraged people to submit applications for jobs under the *diwan al-taʿlim*.[24] My interviews reveal, however, that the education administration was reduced to its very basic functions under the group's rule. This was partly because many employees fled Mosul or boycotted the new rule, and partly because ISIS itself shaved off most of the tasks. An employee in the education directorate of Mosul described how their workload shrunk after ISIS arrived:

> [M]ost of our normal tasks stopped, and they replaced the name with *diwan al-taʿlim*. Other than that, they just came and went now and then, just a few people, around 20, they did not stay there all the time. They were just supervising us and showing that they were in control; they did not replace us or move us.[25]

This echoes the situation in other directorates taken over by ISIS, which were either shut down or reduced to a minimum. Most of the directorates—with the exception of those in charge of health, education, water, electricity, and sewage—were closed down and their buildings repurposed as jails or storage rooms. Both ISIS propaganda videos and administrative documents show that ISIS intended to enroll all teachers in their territories in mandatory "repentance" sessions, where each teacher was forced to pledge their allegiance to ISIS and its principles.[26] An ISIS announcement reads:

> The repentance will be carried out for all those who worked in the prior education system (director, supervisor, deputy director, temporaries, fixed, non-fixed, retired, employment of youth, employee, guard). And similarly for teachers in the universities and institutes.[27]

None of my interviewees reported that they had been called to a formal repentance session. This is supported by the absence of such sessions in propaganda directly mentioning Mosul. The informants describe how ISIS representatives briefly visited each primary and secondary school in the weeks following the takeover and gave general instructions to focus the teaching on religion and abolish certain subjects. New deans sympathizing with ISIS were installed in the two university faculties that remained open for some months: The medical faculties (medicine, pharmacy, nursing, dentistry) and the science faculties (chemistry, physics, biology). The rest of the university was shut down immediately. ISIS needed a stable supply of doctors to treat wounded soldiers, and the many doctors who had been among the first refugees to flee the city, had already created a shortage. In its propaganda, the group claimed to have completely restructured medical education in Mosul and Raqqa, removing "superfluous subjects that are irrelevant to a physician's day-to-day work"[28] and reducing the length of medical studies from six to three years. This "restructuring" was in reality an amputated version of the existing medical studies. ISIS's reformed medical studies never materialized in Mosul, because the medical faculty was closed in 2015. In general, ISIS showed little interest in university studies. It was mostly on the primary and secondary levels that the group had grand plans.

One of the first changes made in lower education was that ISIS shrunk the length of primary and secondary school from twelve to nine years. Five years in primary school would be followed by two years in an intermediate level, and two years in a secondary level before graduation at age 15. An announcement from ISIS spells out the grades needed to continue studying after that, either in specific Sharia institutes or other studies.[29]

Until the fall of 2015, after what ISIS called a "transitional school year," teaching continued with a reduced, "Islamized" version of the old curriculum and only limited supervision by ISIS. During this period, an ISIS-appointed committee of around fifty local teachers developed more than sixty schoolbooks under the strict supervision of Dhu al-Qarnayn. ISIS also developed several educational videos and mobile applications for children.[30] According to interviewees who were present at the university in this time, most of the teachers in the committee participated against their will—but some sympathized with the ISIS ideology and educational project. When the curriculum was completed after nine months, books were given to teachers in PDF format on CDs for the pupils or teachers to print at their own cost. The purpose of the books is spelled out in the introduction to each copy:

> We hereby lay down the first building block of an Islamic education, based on [this] curriculum, guided by the prophecy and the understanding of the first righteous ancestors and their original flock, and a clear vision which is not eastern nor western, but Qur'anic and prophetic, far from the whims, the untruths and the errors of calls to socialism in the East or capitalism in the West, or the agents of the [political] parties and errant curriculum in various corners of the Earth.[31]

The books paint a picture of promoting a holistic worldview, with references throughout to the group's ideology, militarism, and political project. Most of these books never saw the light of day in any classroom. They do, however,

Figure 6 *ISIS schoolbooks in Quran studies, mathematics and history for elementary school.*

provide a window into ISIS's educational ambitions and its vision of what an idealized inhabitant of its state should learn. The religion books make up a large part of the curriculum, revolving around direct reading of the Qur'an. Throughout the books are instructions to the teachers to recite verses from the Qur'an. *Anashid,* or hymns composed by ISIS, are an important part of the readings. One of the texts for the second grade hails the children of the "caliphate" as "cubs," the next generation of fighters.[32]

Most of the textbooks have a clear militaristic stamp with pictures of Kalashnikovs, guns, and tanks even in sections such as geology that are unrelated to combat. In mathematics, the pupils are taught to multiply tanks and guns; recognize the shape of fighter jets, rockets, and bazookas; and count bullets and ISIS flags. ISIS has its own textbook for the secondary level to teach the visual programming language Scratch, with examples of how to create videos of fighting scenes.[33] Physical exercise, history, and Islamic studies were replaced with new ISIS versions, and physical exercise for boys changed to military training.[34] Like in other ISIS propaganda, much effort was put into the books' visual design, with some teachers describing it as "more modern-looking" than the official Iraqi curriculum.[35] The content does not fall short of the state curriculum in terms of complexity and progress for the different levels. In fact, the religion books intended for six-year-olds were deemed too complex for their age level by teachers interviewed. Young children learning to read are expected to read complex Qur'anic texts and delve into the concepts of Islamic jurisprudence. The timetable for six-year-old first-graders contains the subjects the noble Quran, the Prophetic Hadith, physical fitness, Arabic calligraphy, Mathematics, Science, Reading, the Life of the Prophet, and Muslim creed.[36] Each subject had a book, which meant that ISIS doubled the usual amount of books used on the primary level. Many of the teachers criticized what they saw as ISIS's lacking understanding of pedagogy, as these comments from a Mosul headmaster show:

> A pupil in the first class can hardly read the letters, how can he read long paragraphs from the Qur'an? It is beyond the children's abilities; it doesn't do anything for them and is just a waste of time.[37]

Most of modern history is scrapped in the new curriculum in favor of a focus on the Prophet Muhammad's lifetime.[38] History is portrayed as naturally culminating in the Islamic State. Several of the books are less clearly tied to the ISIS political project. In the course *al-adab al-shara'iyya*[39] the children are taught good manners according to the *shari'a*. The course *al-'ulum* (science) encompasses subjects as diverse as the organs of the human body, family structure, mosques, housing, healthy food, animals, plants, illness, and how to brush your teeth with a *mishwak*, a wooden pick.[40] Other topics are environmental awareness and the importance of eating enough vegetables. The course *al-jaghrafiyya* (geography) focuses on topography and natural phenomena, staying clear of today's political geographical maps[41] The schoolbooks are characterized by piecemeal use of various Islamic and Salafi sources. They target nationalism and democracy as un-Islamic and dismiss the traditional Sunni schools of law, promoting one monolithic Islam devoid of independent reasoning. All subjects are written with the clear aim of justifying and legitimizing the building of the "caliphate" and the use of violence against deviants, including Muslims, as explained in the context of the apocalypse. In sum, the ISIS educational reform plan in Mosul was ambitious and wide-ranging. A letter to schools dated September 15, 2015, is titled "handing over of books." In the letter, all school administrations are demanded to gather all the books printed under the "infidel government" and stored in the schools' storage rooms. "Any administration that fails to do so shall be held accountable. May God reward you abundantly," the letter ends.[42] On the ground, these ambitious plans soon ran into an obstacle: An overwhelming majority of the teachers refused to spread this curriculum in their classrooms. Civilian resistance to the new ISIS educational program took different (and overlapping) forms that can be categorized as everyday resistance, engagement, and defiance. Defiance is open opposition to the rulers, while everyday resistance and engagement are more subtle forms of resistance.[43]

Everyday resistance

The vast majority of the resistance to ISIS's education system was what I call everyday resistance, where decisions to act were taken either by individuals or by small groups in discrete conversations with colleagues and friends. The term everyday resistance was coined by James C. Scott, and means a covert form of defiance that does not require coordination and carries less risk than overt defiance.[44] Everyday resistance is quiet subversion of the rule without direct confrontation. Charles Tripp has described different acts that can constitute everyday resistance: "Whether this happens in the sphere of property (through pilfering, quiet encroachment and alternative economies) or of education (through alternative forms that escape the dictation of the state) or of culture, broadly defined (through reaffirmation of values that resist the mainstream), all these activities can feed into a politics of resistance."[45]

Already in the first month after ISIS started interfering in the teaching, the number of students in the classrooms plummeted. The majority of the teachers report that most of their colleagues did not go to work unless they were directly threatened by ISIS. Exact teacher attendance numbers are difficult to establish. However, statistics from the Ninawa educational directorate underline this trend. For example, in the ISIS-held village of Qayyara, the directorate reported that only four out of more than 700 teachers kept working under ISIS.[46] Mosul's classrooms started emptying during the transitional school year, while the teachers still received their salaries from Baghdad. This indicates that the boycott was motivated by more than lacking salaries. In 2015, the Iraqi government decided to cut public servant salaries to areas controlled by ISIS in an attempt to strangle the group economically. A small number remained on the job after the transitional year. Several thousand teachers decided to retire early after ISIS took control of the city, and that way avoided working for the group.[47] By 2015, mostly children of ISIS members or sympathizers were left in the classrooms, while the rest stayed in their homes. Teachers who were directly approached by ISIS and forced to work told students they trusted not to come to class. There are also reports of teachers organizing secret private classes in their own homes to avoid teaching the ISIS curriculum. Several teachers went out of their way to save the old curriculum, as well as records of their schools and institutes from the group's destruction. The headmaster of a school North of Mosul described his colleagues' reactions to the brutality:

> After we saw the new curriculum, we stopped teaching. All the teachers refused to come to work, but Daesh forced some of them to come to the

school, they threatened to kill them if they refused. One female teacher, Lailah Al-Zuibaidi, was killed because she refused the ideas that Daesh introduced. This teacher was very well-known to the people in our town, so Daesh killed her to make an example for other teachers who wanted to refuse. We hid all the administrative documents of the school and the old curriculum in a storage place underground.[48]

Journalist and writer Hélène Sallon has described a similar story in her book on Mosul; how the dean of a technical institute scanned all the administrative documents of the institution as well as the students' grades and saved copies on external hard disks.[49] The originals he meticulously put into plastic tubes that he secretly buried in the faculty's garden over the course of two months. In this way, the administrative record of the institute survived ISIS rule, despite the faculty being burned during the battle for Mosul.

As the number of pupils and students fell, teachers used this in meetings with ISIS as arguments for shutting down the schools and faculties. A former medical student at the university recounts:

> The teachers told us not to care about ISIS, to just focus on our old curriculum and keep studying and go home, keep away from ISIS. They told us that they were forced to teach us, and they intended to leave at the first opportunity. And many did.[50]

The teachers who decided to stay at home did so without directly confronting ISIS. Teachers described it as a "closed circle":

> Our opposition to *da'ish* was secret, it was a closed circle between the teachers, the pupils, the supervisor and the headmaster. We only told the pupils who we trust to not come to school. If that information was passed on to *da'ish*, they would have beheaded us immediately. They used to hang people they had killed from the bridge.[51]

These acts of silent resistance were not established through any formal agreements, but agreed upon in private conversations in homes of school corridors. The account of a primary school teacher on the outskirts of Mosul is representative of my informants' description of this process:

Most of the teachers in our school and the other schools in our district agreed to stop teaching. How can I teach the son of a friend how to kill and how to bomb himself? We did not have a meeting about this among the teachers, but we talked about it. We did not say it directly to *da'ish* of course, because, as you know, they are not human. Everyone said that they would not teach. I would not do it even if they killed me. I will not commit their sins.[52]

ISIS was met with a similar response in schools and universities alike. After ISIS's initial meeting for teachers on campus, several meetings were held in the university library to plan the new ISIS curriculum. But only a handful of teachers showed up, despite the threat of sanctions if they did not. One of the university teachers present at one of the meetings recounted:

Some [of my colleagues] did not attend the meetings, and some had already fled the city. [ISIS's president of the university] asked the scholars and the teachers to give their advice on how to develop the education and the schoolbooks. In the beginning, they were friendly toward us teachers. At first, they tried to co-opt us and make us cooperate. They sent someone who was a professor and who had joined *da'ish*; he went to all the teachers and tried to convince us to work for them. He argued that it was important for the sake of our children's future.[53]

This friendliness soon faded when it became clear that none of the teachers would volunteer to develop the new ISIS curriculum. The result was that ISIS officials appointed some teachers to work on the books. On several occasions, ISIS officials scolded teachers who skipped classes, threatening to kill them and burn their homes with their families inside.[54] From time to time, the group posted written warnings threatening the teachers who did not show up for work with execution for treason, specifically listing the names of teachers.[55] The teachers who were personally threatened with punishment most often followed orders and returned to school for a while, and then stopped attending again.[56] In some cases, ISIS would withhold part of the salary of the teachers who did not come to work. An employee in education administration in Mosul recounts:

Deciding not to teach was a tough response, also economically—*da'ish* cut the salaries of those who did not go to work, by fifty thousand dinar. The economic situation of the teachers was already very bad, so they suffered because of their tough response to *da'ish*. But we did not want to do what they wanted and take their money.⁵⁷

Dhu al-Qarnayn called Mosul's primary school teachers to a new meeting in the *diwan al-ta'lim* at the beginning of November 2015.⁵⁸ Here, he repeated that it was mandatory for all teachers to keep teaching, threatening to decapitate those who refused, a message that was repeated several times in mosques and on posters in the city. Several dozen teachers were arrested during this period because the classrooms remained empty.⁵⁹ Later in November 2015, Dhu al-Qarnayn also invited the parents to meet with him. The tone was now more stern. Al-Qarnayn warned the parents and reminded them that it was a religious duty to send their children to the ISIS-run schools.⁶⁰ In an attempt to lure pupils back to school, the group agreed to meet the parents of the school-skipping children half-way and give them a "failing amnesty" on the condition that they signed up immediately. A letter signed Dhu al-Qarnayn from March 14, 2015, refers to a meeting with parents where pupils who had failed to meed were given a second change.⁶¹ These increasingly desperate attempt to force compliance shows that ISIS was well aware of the teachers' and parents' boycott. They were equally aware of the possibility that university students could organize against their rule, so they recruited informants as spies to prevent that from happening.⁶² One medical student, a representative in the student council, tells how she was taken to an ISIS court and accused of plotting against ISIS on Facebook:

> *Da'ish* said the people in our Facebook group were likely to organize a rally against them and I was one of the accused. [...] It was just a regular group, but *da'ish* was scared and wanted to stop all gatherings of students. They arrested some members of our group, who were imprisoned and tortured for 11 days. I managed to avoid getting arrested. I was only taken to a *da'ish* court and questioned by a judge. He looked very nervous. He did not find proof against me, and my position was somewhat strong. Then he tried to get out of me any information about opposition to *da'ish* among my colleagues. [...] They were scared of us because we were young men and women and they often heard talk against *da'ish*. They thought that if this continued there was a risk that we would rise up against them.⁶³

Engagement

As Tripp notes, the everyday resistance described above does not necessarily lead to—or may not even be intended to lead to—overturning the order of power. However, they may prepare the ground for a more public and active resistance.[64] When teachers or students were personally confronted by ISIS officials in formal meetings or in school and campus corridors, many actively engaged and bargained with the group's officials to avoid complying with their rules. Instead of succumbing to ISIS demands or flat-out refusing them, they used persuasion and excuses. Sometimes it would lead to small victories. One professor argued with ISIS officials that he was not competent to write the new schoolbooks like they asked him to:

> I said, "No, I cannot do it because I am a researcher, a teacher, I am not someone who writes books for students." In the end, they let it go. They forced some of the other teachers to do it.[65]

In a primary school, the teachers argued against the group's imposition of the hijab on first-grade girls. The arguments led ISIS to relax the rules for the youngest girls. The headmaster of the school in question recounted:

> We tried to negotiate in a clever way. For example, we said that it is difficult to make the small girls wear the hijab; they would only take it off. So [ISIS] agreed that the first and second class were exempted from the hijab. Of course, we knew that it was not right to force the hijab on the older girls either.[66]

Several teachers were approached by ISIS members and asked to use the education for the group's military purposes on the battlefield. The leader of a high school described one such meeting:

> They tried to pressure us into making changes, but we tried to respond in a clever way. For example, if they tried to make us use some machine or electricity for their purpose, we said: "This is not possible, the machine has limits, we cannot do anything about that." We blamed it on the science and said that it was not in our hands. And ISIS accepted this, they had no other

choice, because most of the ISIS people had a low level of education and did not really understand anything of science.[67]

The few students who remained on Mosul University had little direct contact with ISIS except when they were berated for violating the dress code or for mingling with the opposite sex. When students were arrested on campus, usually for these reasons, they and their fellow students often tried to escape by bargaining. A medical student recounts:

> One time a man from the *hisba* came into the cafeteria and arrested a student for wearing too-tight trousers. The student tried to convince him that it was his body that was fat, not the trousers that were too tight. When someone was arrested by the *hisba*, other students would try to negotiate with them and say that they did not break the rules, or complain that their rules changed every day. Some told them that our Prophet did not like the color black that they imposed on us.[68]

Sometimes the negotiation attempts were successful, other times not. Nevertheless, these and other examples indicate that the teachers and students did have some influence on ISIS rule. They knew the inside of the educational system better than ISIS and took advantage of their personal relations with colleagues and friends. Some of the high-ranking ISIS managers, like Dhu al-Qarnayn, were highly educated. Still, ISIS was depending on the local teachers' goodwill in administering the education. They had neither the personnel nor competence to run a large university only with their own staff. Similarly, while it was achievable for ISIS to change the curriculum for primary and secondary levels, especially with the help of local teachers, creating new content for the range of subjects taught at the university level was next to impossible—neither was it part of ISIS plans. Knowing this, the university lecturers ignored ISIS's instructions as long as they were not personally threatened with sanctions.

With some exceptions, the content of university classes was left untouched by ISIS. Even though ISIS officials were installed in leading positions at the university, they were rarely appointed as teachers. ISIS advertised in mosques for university lecturers, which indicates that they intended to replace some of the academic staff.⁶⁹ The few attempts that were made to install ISIS-friendly lecturers were not respected by the academic staff. One Mosul University lecturer described the group's attempts to run a university as "a laughing matter."⁷⁰ The headmaster at a technical college lamented that one of his former students, who had failed almost all his courses, had returned to the school as an ISIS member and was put in charge of a whole department.⁷¹

When the group brought in cattle and sheep to graze at the university's lawns, teachers saw it as the final proof of ISIS's lacking respect for the university. Eventually, all the faculties except medicine were closed and the University looked more and more like a military headquarters. The university chemistry lab became the possible best-equipped bomb-making facility in ISIS territory. The weapons manufactured in Mosul University included peroxide-based and nitrate-based chemical bombs, and explosives used in suicide vests. An Iraqi explosive expert interviewed by Wall Street Journal called the campus "the best Daesh research center in the world."⁷² In April 2015, Iraqi forces fighting to retake the city of Tikrit recovered a hydrogen peroxide drum filled with a

Figure 7 *The central library of the university, burnt by ISIS before retreating (Photo: The Asahi Shimbun via Getty Images).*

homemade chemical explosive, for the first time on an Iraqi battlefield. After that, similar explosives that were possibly produced in Mosul University were found other places in Tikrit and Anbar. This us of the university made it a target for aerial bombing by the coalition against ISIS, and the university's buildings were bombed several times in the course of 2016. At the time when the university was closed following several rounds of bombing in November 2016, only a handful of students and lecturers were still attending—lecturers who ISIS forced to attend and students who sympathized with the group. The university remained closed after November 2016. Most of the remaining facilities were looted, destroyed and burnt by retreating ISIS militants toward the end of the battle for Mosul.

Defiance

The most visible and risky form of resistance is defiance: direct confrontations to challenge the group and mobilize public opinion.[73] There are documented examples of such resistance against ISIS leading to small victories in both Iraq and Syria. In July 2014, after a prominent imam and his followers refused to pledge allegiance to ISIS leader al-Baghdadi, a large number of the imam's supporters marched to the mosque where he preached to demonstrate solidarity.[74] ISIS detained some of the protesters but did not kill any of the religious leaders, who had large followings. The same month, it refrained from demolishing a Mosul mosque after residents formed a human chain around it. In July 2013, the Raqqa teacher Suad Nofel marched onto the streets alone every day for three months, protesting in front of the ISIS headquarters. Her handmade signs read messages such as "Don't tell me about your religion, but show it in your behaviour!" and "No to oppression, no to unjust rulers, no to atonement, and yes to thinking!." Reports say that ISIS agreed to free a number of prisoners after more citizens joined her protests.[75] In January 2015, the Islamic State closed one of its courts in Mosul after growing local opposition to its harsh judgments.[76] Many university students in Mosul describe direct confrontations with the *hisba* on campus, for example concerning the dress codes. One medical student described how he and his friends went many times to protest the rules, but were shrugged off:

> The female students had problems doing the studies because they had to wear a *niqab* and gloves. We went to the *hisba* on campus and told them that this was not right, we have our rights, they should not force people to behave in a way they did not want. They told us to not worry about this and focus on our studies.[77]

Open resistance that bore fruits are rare glimmers of hope in a rule which most often showed zero tolerance to open defiance. According to a UN report, a number of teachers were killed for refusing to change the curriculum to conform to ISIS ideology. For instance, four teachers were abducted from a college in Mosul in January 2015 because they opposed the ISIS reform—they were never found. A primary school teacher in Tel Afar was executed for the same reason.[78] The persecution of noncomplying teachers was not systematic, but it was widely announced when it happened as a public show of force. Several of the teachers interviewed for this book recounted stories of colleagues who were killed for their open opposition to ISIS. One of them was primary school teacher Ashwaq al-Naimi, who was publicly executed by ISIS on September 17, 2014, for refusing to follow the teaching instructions.[79] After she was killed, Ashwaq al-Naimi was referred to on social media and in the news as a martyr and an icon of Mosul's resistance.[80] According to my informants and news reports of the incident, she criticized ISIS's teaching instructions in front of her pupils in the girls' school where she worked,[81] refusing to teach what she called racist thoughts. A university friend and colleague of al-Naimi described the incident in the following way:

> She told her students: "This curriculum is not suitable for the people of Mosul. The people of Mosul are educated (*muthaqqafa*), we love life, and we live together, all the different sects side by side, with our Christian brothers and our Yezidi brothers."[82]

Al-Naimi's classroom speech soon reached ISIS ears after one of her pupils reported it to her parents, who then informed the ISIS police. Al-Naimi was arrested and publicly executed by a gunshot to the head a few days later; it was filmed and broadcast online. She had been given the opportunity to repent in front of an ISIS court, but declined. Al-Naimi's colleague describes the impact of the killing among the teachers:

> It was a very painful event, bringing everyone into a state of strong grief. This turned many people against *da'ish*. They kept this event in their hearts. It showed what the true path of *da'ish* really is: Killing.[83]

These and other examples show that some individuals and groups are willing to go to great lengths and risk their own lives in order to influence how rebels govern. However, my interviews confirm that these kinds of acts are exceptions because ISIS was notorious for violently repressing any sign of defiance. The group relied on public spectacles of brutal force—executions, torture, and display of dead bodies—in order to prevent further resistance. As mentioned before, these brutal spectacles can have a freezing effect on civilians. But it can also have the opposite effect and lead civilians to disobey because they are outraged—an awakening effect. Ana Arjona writes that "people may feel the need to react, to partake in their own defense, and to look for support in others in order to endure hardship. Uniting may not only provide actual protection but also the sense of responding to injustice; it may help to build a sense of self-ownership, of belonging, and of self-worth."[84] From my interviews, it is clear that ISIS's violent spectacles in the streets and squares of Mosul could have both a freezing and an awakening effect on civilians, depending on the individual. Some teachers recounted how the experience of watching rebellious colleagues being executed was a reason why they decided to more actively resist ISIS rule. Others used these spectacles as an explanation for the opposite, why they chose not to openly defy the group—it was simply too dangerous.

Resistance in strong institutions

In their interviews, Maslawis expressed a clear rationale for opposing ISIS education. Parents and teachers rejected the idea that ISIS's ideas, which they describe as immoral and un-Islamic, should be planted in their children's and students' minds. They argued that the ISIS educational system did not represent the values of the people of Mosul. University students saw ISIS as an anti-intellectual movement that because of its ignorance and incompetence would only have a destructive effect on their education. The stated goal of these acts of resistance was clear: to subvert the ISIS attempt to control education, even if it meant that the whole system would grind to a halt for the foreseeable future. At the time that ISIS introduced its new curriculum, approximately one year after the takeover, little of the initial support for ISIS was left in Mosul. This quote from one Mosul professor is typical of how the informants narrate the turn of events and their own role:

> When ISIS went into Mosul, this ancient city known for its uniqueness, its traditions, and especially its scientific traditions, with its rich educational environment, it took them by surprise. They decided to use all these things and invest them in the construction of their caliphate. They thought these existing institutions and organizations were ideal to spread their thoughts. But they did not count on the response of Mosul society to their plan—from the inhabitants, from the educational staff, from the students themselves, even from some children, and especially from the families and the parents. Maslawis' tough response turned ISIS's plan to use the educational system into a failure.[85]

Considering the group's brutal crackdown on opposition in Mosul, it would have been reasonable to expect a fear of collective action in the realm of education. Even though there was a consensus among the interviewees that teaching ISIS ideals would be destructive, one might expect that no individual was willing to risk imprisonment or execution.[86] Research suggests that paying the costs involved in collective resistance is justified when armed groups significantly threaten the institutional status quo that civilians want to preserve.[87] Strong institutions give some bargaining power; civilians can threaten, even implicitly, with the possibility of collective action against the group.[88] Teachers, students, and parents in Mosul reported that they were influenced by the acts of others. As a manager at the education directorate in Mosul recounted:

I did not let my son go to school, because I knew how their education was. It is racist thought, it is about forcing everyone into one path. They were teaching children how to use weapons. Because of this, the parents kept their children at home. I was working in the education directorate, so people were influenced by my decision to not let my son go. Then they decided to do the same.[89]

The findings suggest that the strength of Mosul's educational institutions and traditions was greater than ISIS's capacity and organizational strength to change them. How its rules in the education system were enforced was dependent on which ISIS member was set to enforce them. This was true in clothing rules, in dealing with opposing teachers, and in implementing changes in the classroom. Both Iraqis and foreign fighters had a wide range of reasons for working with ISIS. While some were driven by ideological and religious conviction, others worked with the group for economic gain or power. As Barbara F. Walter has shown, average citizens may be inclined to support an extremist group if they believe it will win the war, regardless of their own convictions.[90] The mix of foreign and local recruits with different motivations creates organizational challenges for the group.[91] This underlines the problems of seeing it as a monolithic organization, when in reality it is a broad and complex movement with more dividing its followers than what unites them. It also suggests that extremist organizations risk running into civilian resistance when they try to control relatively strong and locally grounded institutions. Rather than gradually changing the education curriculum and involving the teachers, ISIS violently imposed its all-encompassing plan, erasing the institutional culture and many years of carefully developed curricula with the stroke of a pen in order to realize its imported idea of a caliphate. Both teachers and parents feared that ISIS's indoctrination plans could have immediate and irreversible effects on the children.

Conclusion

By restructuring the educational administration, changing the content of classes, and militarizing instruction, ISIS set out to turn Mosul's educational institutions into a vehicle for their own political and military project. This chapter has detailed how ISIS was confronted with civilian resistance from parts of Mosul's population in its attempt to implement this in the city's classrooms. The civil war context and the group's worsening financial situation are also important factors in explaining why the reform came to a halt. My data suggest that civilian resistance in the education sector also influenced ISIS's implementation of its reform to some degree. The findings support Ana Arjona's theory that the success or failure of rebel institution building is influenced by the strength of institutions in place when a rebel group arrives. The educational institutions in Mosul have maintained a level of strength and popularity despite difficult circumstances under shifting regimes. This, along with the scope of the ISIS reform, may have created fertile ground for civilian resistance in the classrooms and school corridors of the so-called caliphate.

5

A Reign of Terror in Mosul's Hospitals

"As doctors we do not discriminate between pepople. In the Iran-Iraq war, I treated Iranians. ISIS forced us to discriminate".

DOCTOR FROM MOSUL [1]

As Mosul suburbs were being invaded by ISIS, doctors and nurses treating patients in Mosul's hospitals were faced with tough decisions. Dr. Khaled, a doctor at one of the hospitals on the West bank, was on a day shift in the maternity ward when he heard that a curfew was announced. Like most other people in Mosul, he did not give it much thought, but his colleagues started leaving the hospital out of fear that the bridge to the East would be closed off. Because Dr. Khaled was in charge of the premature babies in incubators, he could not leave. He thought the curfew would only last some hours, so he stayed in the hospital to look after the newborns and their mothers. But the curfew did not end, and he was stuck for three days in the hospital. Then reports came in that a militia had taken over the neighborhood next to the hospital, and most of the hospital staff left. "I could not leave the babies, they are very fragile. So I convinced an ambulance to come and move the incubators with the smallest babies, 14 of them, to a hospital in the East bank together with their mothers," Dr. Khaled says. The ambulance came and brought the babies to safety, and he finally went home to his wife and children in the East.

Like everyone else, he was shocked when two days later they heard that a jihadi group calling itself the Islamic State had occupied entire West Mosul. All his neighbors fled to Kurdistan, and Dr. Khaled and his family followed. But they would return only two days later, when his mother called and said that his father had suffered a stroke from the shock.

> I decided to go back to stay with my family and look after my father. The mentality of my mother is that she never wants to leave Mosul, she wants to die in her own home. And if I left, ISIS could come and take all my things. It is difficult to lose everything you own, your house, your things, your memories. So we decided to stay, and he thought the situation would be over soon. We thought the Iraqi army would come back.

When he returned to work, one of his colleagues had suddenly become a member of ISIS and he was now in charge of the hospital. Dr. Khaled was told he could not work in the maternity section anymore because it was *haram* for a man. Three long and harsh years would follow where he was moved around to different clinics and hospitals at the whim of ISIS health officials. Most communication with the health ministry in Baghdad was cut off, and by March 2015 it had completely stopped. Instead of official Iraqi letters, letterheads with the logo of the Islamic State health department came into circulation. Mosul's health system was promoted in ISIS propaganda as a proof of the group's successful state-building. The reality was that the health system in Mosul quickly deteriorated on Islamic State's watch. This chapter will have a closer look at how ISIS managed the health sector in Mosul. The findings highlight the many conflicting interests that a rebel group attempting to govern must grapple with.

Rebel groups have often been described as geared either toward short-term exploitation of civilians and resources, or toward long-term construction of institutions and ideologies. Various explanations have been given for which trajectory a rebel group takes. For instance, Jeremy Weinstein distinguishes between opportunistic and activist rebellions, positing that the resources available to the rebels determine the future nature of the movement. "Where the economic resources are available to meet the start-up costs of rebellion, the extended process of shaping identities, mobilizing networks, and building ideologues is often cut short."[2] William Reno has argued that so-called predatory rebels do sometimes engage in state-building, as in his case of the Liberian NPFL, but they do so exclusively for their own immediate economic and political benefit. The "institutions" they run are hollow shells intended to create outside recognition and ease the exploitation of civilians.³

By examining ISIS governance of Mosul's health system between 2014 and 2017, I seek to nuance the dichotomy between predatory and state-building rebels. Running institutions means giving up some of the flexibility that a militia needs to win terrain in a civil war.⁴ Like all rebels who aspire to govern civilians, ISIS had to balance ideological purity, the wish to garner civilian support, military needs, and the pragmatism needed to efficiently administer its "proto-state." Despite their seemingly apolitical character, hospital wards, and corridors, surgical theatres, pharmacies, and doctors' offices became deeply entangled in ISIS's political and military project. The findings presented here suggest that rebels can combine predatory rule with substantial governance of civilians. On the one hand, ISIS kept health services open for civilians for long stretches of its rule, which gives an impression that it channeled significant resources to the benefit of the civilian population. On the other hand, discrimination against non-ISIS members and predatory behavior to serve military needs were also characteristics of ISIS's health system, resulting in the suffering and death of an unknown number of civilians. The chapter is partly based on thirty-eight interviews with informants who lived in Mosul under ISIS rule, fifteen of which are in-depth interviews with doctors and other hospital staff who worked in Mosul city the entire duration of ISIS rule in their neighborhoods. The remaining twenty-three informants are civilians who were in contact with the health system as patients or relatives of patients, employees in the Mosul doctors' syndicate, the leader of the health directorate, hospital managers, and members of NGOs who treated civilians from ISIS-held territories during the liberation of Mosul. Furthermore, the chapter builds on a comprehensive analysis of propaganda and leaked ISIS administrative documents from the health sector, complemented by a range of secondary sources.⁵

As the military pressure on the group grew, providing services gave way to pure predation. In the last half year of ISIS rule, the health system became purely an instrument for the group's armed forces, leaving the several million inhabitants of the Ninawa province without adequate services. Mosul's supply lines were blocked, an estimated one third of the doctors fled the city, and hospitals became military targets toward the end of the operation against ISIS in the spring of 2017. As in any case of rebel governance, it is difficult to measure the impact of rebels' policies versus outside factors. Nevertheless, I argue that ISIS's destructive mix of ideologically motivated micromanagement, lack of overall planning, and exploitative behavior at the expense of civilians accelerated the breakdown of the health system and reinforced the public discontent with ISIS governance more generally. I will detail three central characteristics of ISIS health services as described by patients and health workers: a rigid religious regime inside hospitals, systematic discrimination against non-ISIS members, and exploitation of medical personnel. These characteristics highlight how micro-level governance was entangled with clear predatory behavior within one sector of the ISIS proto-state. The chapter will first describe the state of affairs in Iraqi public healthcare in June 2014, and outline ISIS's official approach to healthcare in their vision of the state.

Health as state-building in Iraq

The history of healthcare in Iraq in many ways symbolizes the making and unmaking of the modern Iraqi state as a whole. The basis for the country's public health infrastructure was laid down by the British mandate rulers, guided by a growing belief that better medical services to the civilian population would yield political and economic advantages.[6] During the mandate period and the following thirty-eight years of British-backed monarchy (1920–58), the health system became a symbol of the modern nation-state, built on Western-oriented science, progress, and respect for hierarchy. Following the Baʿth Party's ascendance to power in 1968, oil nationalization and administrative reforms led to a golden decade in terms of social and medical services, which ranked among the best in the Middle East. The eight-year war with Iran from 1980 had a devastating impact on the country, but at the same time consolidated the state apparatus and led to unprecedented progress in the health sector. In 1990 the downturn began, with the Gulf War and US-led sanctions regime officially designed to cripple Iraq's military capabilities. Instead, it resulted in the degradation of Iraq's social and material infrastructure.[7] The US-led invasion of 2003 and the ensuing war were a decisive blow to Iraq's once-respectable health system, leading to mass-scale displacement, extensive damage to hospitals and education, and an unprecedented exodus of health workers. The full long-term health effects of US warfare in Iraq are yet to be documented.[8] Sanctions and war have deeply changed the health ecology by creating multidrug-resistant bacteria[9] that Iraqi authorities will grapple with for decades to come.

Despite its rises and falls of fortune, Iraq's universal healthcare system, staffed by a proud cadre of medical professionals, has deep roots—precisely because health was an instrumental part of various regimes' visions of the state. In Mosul at the beginning of 2014, the city's hospitals were experiencing something of a new spring. Relative calm had led to the return of a number of exiled health workers. The government had boosted the health budgets after more than a decade of neglect.[10] Forty-seven primary health care centers and 14 hospitals existed in Mosul at the time of ISIS's arrival in the city, and there were a total of 199 primary health centers and 22 hospitals in the Ninawa governorate.[11] Iraq's health system had a lower technical and scientific level than most countries in the region in 2014. However, within Iraq, Mosul was a crucial medical center, and Ninawa's two medical colleges made the governorate an important provider of medical staff. A number of large-scale projects for new health facilities in Ninawa were under way in 2014, but had not yet been inaugurated at the time of ISIS's arrival.[12] Furthermore, smaller hospitals were being built in Ninawa's rural population centers. A project for better equipping the existing health facilities was also ongoing, making CT scanning, ultrasound and ECG machines available in primary health centers. A new medical compound with a range of specialized clinics was under construction in West Mosul,[13] as well as a privately funded 600-bed hospital. According to the World Health Organization (WHO) in Iraq, not all of them were put into use under ISIS rule over the city.[14] During the military operation to liberate Mosul, many of these new constructions were ruined or damaged.[15]

Some level of public healthcare has become an intrinsic part of the social contract between state and citizens in modern states. In states, rulers' ability or inability to provide healthcare has very direct and visible consequences for civilians' lives and is often closely linked to a rule's perceived legitimacy. Research

Figure 8 *A woman in Mosul dressed in the khimar that ISIS forced all women to wear including a veil covering the eyes (Photo: Martyn Aim/Corbis via Getty Images).*

has shown that formal statehood is less decisive for the effective provision of services than is often presumed.[16] In many weak or fragmented states, service delivery by sub-state entities instead of or alongside the state is the norm rather than the exception.[17] In her broad study of rebel governance between 1950 and 2006, Reyko Huang found that 25 to 35 percent of all rebel groups establish health clinics along with other essential institutions like legislative bodies, police forces, and schools.[18] Rebel groups do not need hospitals only to treat wounded soldiers and retain potency on the battleground. They also need to take into account the great symbolic significance of a working health system in order to minimize the risk of popular resistance. Rebel institutions exist because rebels recognize the fact that greater reward can be reaped by the rebel group in the long term if it constrains its behavior today.[19] As Ana Arjona notes, armed groups have incentives to establish institutions because "doing so helps them to both gain territorial control and strengthen their organizational capacity."[20] This incentive is particularly strong for rebels with long time horizons.

Managing a modern health system is a complex operation, demanding specialized personnel and a constant flow of supplies that can be hard to come by in a war economy. Health services are easily affected by changes in the security level. Studies document the link between insecurity, worse health services, and greater risk for healthcare providers.[21] Patients and health workers can be deterred from reaching healthcare facilities; normal communication is disrupted, making outreach campaigns difficult; supply routes are disrupted; and populations are displaced. Added to these challenges are poor sanitation, contaminated water, and inadequate shelter, which quickly escalate the effects of a crumbling health system by facilitating the spread of diseases. Health workers in civil wars often find themselves in the line of fire as their services are vital for rebels and civilians alike. In Iraq, doctors also have become targets of organized violence, and are murdered or kidnapped because of their past affiliation with the Baʻath party or to cause further destabilization.[22] In a 2012 survey 80 percent of Iraqi doctors reported having been assaulted by a patient or their family members, and 38 percent had been threatened with a gun.[23]

Despite the context of an ongoing civil war, ISIS had a relatively solid starting point for providing health services to the population after the group's takeover of Mosul on June 10, 2014. The city had the most sophisticated hospitals of all ISIS-held areas, and a large number of educated medical staff remained even after an initial brain drain in 2014. In addition, an unknown number of foreign fighters arrived to work as health staff. Most salaries were being paid by the central government until the summer of 2015. Although hospitals were cut off from contact with Baghdad in March 2015, many of their services were self-sufficient. ISIS had better economic means than most other rebel groups,[24] as well as more continuous territorial control, which provided a degree of stability needed for efficient service delivery. Despite these resources at the group's disposal, the health system would become among its least successful attempts at governing.

"Serving the Muslim populace"

According to ISIS propaganda, its *diwan as-sihha*, health ministry, was responsible for "developing the health sector, and providing any means essential for preventing and treating sickness and disease."[25] ISIS specifically urged doctors and medical students to migrate to Islamic State–held territories, underlining that migration is mandatory for Muslims who have skills needed in the "caliphate."[26] In a document issued in Ninawa, it gave a "final warning" to medical personnel, pharmacists, and teachers of medicine and nursing who had fled the area.[27] Those who did not return within thirty days would have their property confiscated. A clause left the door open for health personnel to "repent their sins" if they did return. ISIS mentioned the plight of civilians, especially children, on several occasions in propaganda videos on health. One video, describing the so-called ISHS, Islamic State Health Services, gave virtual tour of an ISIS-run hospital, including departments for newborn and pediatric care. In one scene, the now-infamous Australian ISIS doctor Tareq Kamleh showed the empty bed of a severely injured girl who had been shown in a previous scene. "Unfortunately, this girl died because of the *kuffar* bombs. We need you in the caliphate. What are you waiting for?" he asked, turning toward the camera.[28] Boasting of healthcare that has no immediate military function could, in theory, be taken as a proof that ISIS seeks to legitimize its rule among locals. However, these messages were mostly addressed to potential new recruits and foreign fighters. The plight of civilians was presented as an argument for emigrating to the Islamic State, where meaningful job opportunities allegedly abounded in the modern hospitals and clinics of the "caliphate." While ISIS material on education directly addresses civilians and urges locals to enroll their children in ISIS-run schools, there is little effort to directly advertise the health system to the inhabitants of the "caliphate."

Administrative documents for use in the territories can give a more untainted picture of ISIS's priorities on the ground than propaganda tailor-made for recruitment. ISIS produced a large quantity of administrative documents related to health in its various provinces or *wilayat*. This include public announcements, medical reports for militants, travel permits for medical reasons, fatwas, birth certificates, and vaccination cards for children.[29] Some public declarations refer to the needs of civilians as a motivation for a strong health sector. Doctors are called upon to "serve the Muslim populace"; exiled doctors are threatened to either return or have their property confiscated.[30] Administrative documents, often mimicking Iraqi regime documents, often give the impression of a streamlined, accountable, and universal health system. On the ground, however, ISIS did no real effort to promote this image in their interaction with civilians. The following section will detail three central characteristics of ISIS health services as described by patients and health workers: a rigid religious regime inside hospitals, systematic discrimination against non-ISIS members, and exploitation of medical personnel. These characteristics highlight how micro-level governance was entangled with clear predatory behavior within ISIS-run health institutions.

"Let her die and God is responsible"

In the eyes of Mosul's doctors, the most estranging aspect of ISIS health care in Mosul was the strict implementation of gender segregation and clothing rules that sometimes cost Mosul's inhabitants their lives. Although Mosul is a Sunni Muslim–majority city that has become increasingly conservative, its inhabitants describe the rules imposed by ISIS as extreme and foreign. All direct contact between female employees or patients and male employees or patients was banned.[31] ISIS rules for *shariʿa* attire applied to medical staff like everyone else: Females had to perform their tasks wearing a two-layered cloak, *ʿabaya,* thick gloves, and full-face veils covering the eyes. Males had to wear ankle-length trousers and keep their beard long and their hair short. These rules disproportionally affected female staff because they severely hampered their movement and examination of patients.[32] Women had to be transported to work by a male family member. When a female doctor was seen talking with a male colleague, her father or husband would receive a warning and sometimes be punished with lashes. The constant bickering by patrolling *hisba* groups about their clothes led many female employees to stay at home because they felt unable to do their work properly. This resulted in a severe shortage of female doctors, who were already underrepresented in the hospitals. This in turn affected female patients because they could only be treated by women. A female doctor described the psychological stress and the physical limitations created by the clothing regime:

> It affected our work very much, the first month I could hardly breathe, and we could not see anything through the veil, we could not sow [the wound of] a patient well. [...] Sometimes the things they said were very painful. Like you are an immoral woman trying to excite men, not just a doctor trying to make a schedule for your work.[33]

Although men and women were allowed to work in the same place, all communication between them was banned, and they were not allowed to be alone together. In some hospitals, female and male staff had separate workdays. The segregation created a range of obstacles to efficient treatment: A male doctor would not be allowed to ask a mother about her child's medical background and condition. A female doctor could not report to a male colleague about the current state of the patients when her shift ended. A male hospital manager could not issue direct instructions to a female staff member about how to prioritize patients. In pediatric wards, child patients were frightened by the fully veiled nurses and doctors and could not easily identify their female family members. Two male doctors described how these rules overshadowed the tasks they were set to do, in a context where they were already overworked because of the lack of staff:

> Because of the black masks—we called it the mask of Zorro—I did not even recognize many of my colleagues [...]. We could not communicate, not even stand for a few seconds together. When handing over a patient, I could not say anything, so I tried to write it down on a note and pass it secretly to my colleague. We lost the joy of work; we just did what we had to, without interest, and then returned home.[34]
>
> ―
>
> When I am working to prepare a report about a critical case, for example leukemia, it is a very stressful situation for me as a doctor to make decisions about the patient. And then they come and ask me "Why did you not shorten your trousers? Why did you shorten your beard?" This made me very angry, and many times I would go home to try to calm down, and then go back to write the report.[35]

ISIS gradually moved childbirth and obstetrics to a designated women's hospital, al-Battoul hospital in West Mosul. The employees there reported more freedom as they were working in all-women zones. However, this hospital lacked the capacity to cover the needs of the entire female population, and its services were prioritized for ISIS members' wives, according to my interviewees.[36] The rules for clothing and segregation were identical for private and public clinics and medical practices across Mosul. A male doctor in a public clinic recounted:

> I am the only surgeon in my center, so I had to reject all female patients who needed surgery. [...] The woman would return to her home without treatment, unless we managed to direct her elsewhere. This was very strange for us. Usually there are female doctors all over Mosul treating male patients and vice versa.[37]

In a *fatwa*, religious ruling, ISIS allowed for women to be treated by a man if no female doctor was available.[38] While on some reported occasions ISIS lifted the segregation rules, overall they were strictly enforced regardless of the seriousness of the patient's condition.[39] It was incomprehensive and frustrating for patients when they were told to wait many hours with severe pain even if treatment and doctors were available—only because of ISIS's gender rules. A patient described his experience at the entrance of the hospital guarded by ISIS members:

> I had a gout attack under ISIS, they had to take an x-ray of my foot. At that time, the male doctor was missing. The so-called *hisba* did not let a female doctor examine my foot, so I had to wait. [...] I said it was very painful, I needed an examination as soon as possible. He said it is not possible. This is something not related to religion. It is in Islam that a male patient is preferred to be examined by a male doctor. But it can be critical and a matter of life or death. For me it wasn't, but what if? For us this is completely weird and out of this planet.[40]

With a civilian population suffering from mounting airstrikes against ISIS targets, the segregation rules increasingly did become a matter of life and death. It was underlined in an ISIS announcement that the military campaign was no excuse for disregarding the clothing rules.[41] If a female patient was brought to an emergency room, it was not uncommon for her to be sent away or left to die because there were no available female doctors or surgeons. If a female patient was not wearing the appropriate clothes or shoes, she would often be sent away to get new ones regardless of how critical her condition was. A male doctor described his feeling of helplessness in such situations:

> I could not measure a woman's blood pressure because she could not uncover her arm. One time a teenage girl, about 16 years old, was brought to the emergency room after an airstrike. I rushed to treat her, and [ISIS]

stopped me. I argued that I wanted to save her life, they said that I was not allowed because I was a man and there were no female doctors present. I said that she might die, they replied "Let her die in peace and God will be responsible." This girl died, every time I think about it I want to cry for her. Because of their beliefs, she died in front of me. I feel like I did not do my job.⁴²

Because the hospitals were used actively by ISIS's fighters, hospital workers were among the few outsiders who got insight into the most grotesque part of ISIS rule: The sex slavery of captured Yezidi girls and women. The captives were sometimes taken to a hospital for treatment because of traumas to their bodies following mass rape. There are also reports of Yezidis being raped inside the hospitals. As so-called *sabaya* or slaves they were not forced to wear veils, and with their bare faces they clearly stood out among the other women in hospital corridors. Many of them had been kidnapped from the Yezidi heartland of Sinjar, and some wore traditional Yezidi headgear with sequins. A female doctor cried when she described encounters with Yezidis in her clinic:

> We would check them and they had bruises all over their bodies. When no ISIS people were there we would ask what had happened to them. They said they were kept in houses full of Yezidi girls, they would take one every day and rape her. One said that if any ISIS militant would try to get close to her, she would scream and try to escape, but she couldn't escape because they were stuck in a room. We wish we had the power to do anything to help them, but we didn't. It broke my heart when I saw these beautiful, young girls being raped by ISIS. I imagined myself or my daughter in their place. It was really, really hard to see those young girls in ISIS' hands. Their families had all been killed.⁴³

Fearing for their own lives, health workers could not do much more than examine and medicate the deeply traumatized girls. In the gynecologists' offices, horrendous injuries to the girls' bodies bore witness to what they were experiencing in captivity.

> As a man, I was not allowed to go to the gynaecology hospitals. But I heard from colleagues there that they treated Yezidi women who had been "married" 20 times in a month [...] Women came in with severe vaginal

bleeding. When one was asked what had happened to her, she said that more than ten people had attacked her last night. One of the times I went to Ibn Sina hospital, I saw some of the Yezidi women. Some of them were older, fifty, sixty, some were holding children. Daesh brought them to the hospital for treatment. Some of them were crying, they were afraid of Daesh even when they were in the hospital. I asked the older one if she was ok. She said "yes, why not?" I said, "Daesh killed your family." She said "My family are *kuffar*. Daesh told us the truth about our religion, now we can become Muslim and go to *jannah*." But they would say anything to avoid punishment [...] Big crimes happened to this people. I heard from one colleague that a Yezidi girl was brought to the gynaecologist, and her uterus was outside her body, after something had been put into her vagina. We had never seen such shameful crimes in our lives.[44]

Because of the constant surveillance of employees inside the hospitals, there was little organized resistance against ISIS within the health sector.[45] However, some tried to work around ISIS restrictions in order to treat civilians. On other occasions, doctors were killed for refusing to follow orders, according

Figure 9 *Jumhuri hospital in West Mosul was destroyed during the liberation battle in 2017 (Photo: Sebastian Backhaus/NurPhoto via Getty Images).*

to some reports.⁴⁶ My interviewees reported several incidents where doctors were lashed after refusing to treat wounded soldiers at the expense of civilians.

"Ikhwa or ʿawwama?"—"Brother or civilian?"

ISIS did not explicitly say in written form that the group's members should be prioritized in the health institutions under their control. This was nevertheless the unwritten rule in all hospitals in Mosul, including pediatric hospitals, where ISIS soldiers' children were prioritized over other children regardless of their condition. Both ISIS fighters and those who pledged a so-called civilian allegiance to ISIS—a declaration of support without having a military role—were given priority over other civilians.⁴⁷ The discrimination between ISIS members and non-members took various forms. The most overt form was that ISIS members or their families were allowed to skip the hospital queue and, protected by ISIS guards, demand immediate treatment. The ISIS guards would often ask if the patient was an *"ikhwa,"* a "brother," meaning ISIS member, or *"ʿawwama,"* "regular folks," the term they used for civilians, in order to prioritize the "brothers" and their families. Queue skipping in a situation of immense pressure led to arguments and friction between the local doctors and ISIS guards, because some doctors would insist on treating the most urgent patients first. ISIS tasked some of the administrative staff in hospitals to be mediators in such disputes—which could get violent. After the ISIS takeover, many of the administrative staff members had become superfluous as the bureaucracy shrunk. The downsizing of the bureaucracy was partly done by ISIS, and partly a result of the isolation of the city from the Iraqi state apparatus, which meant that some employees no longer had any tasks. One of these redundant staff members redeployed as an mediator described a kind of scene that would often recur between doctors and ISIS members:

> Sometimes they started arguing and then I had to solve it. Sometimes it escalated to weapons. For example, one child was brought to the hospital but he was already dead by the time he came. So the parent, a Chechen

foreign fighter, blamed the doctor for the child's death and he pulled a gun on him and knocked the gun on his head.[48]

When an argument of this sort escalated and brought a lot of attention, it was brought to the ISIS commander in charge and sometimes settled in the doctor's favor. Other times the doctor would be chastised for refusing to prioritize ISIS members, but harsh punishments against the doctors were not common. That would risk pinning the valuable doctors even more against ISIS—and increase the brain drain out of the hospital.

A more subtle form of discrimination was when ISIS withheld medicines from civilians while they were available in separate storage rooms or field hospitals for ISIS members. The separate storage rooms were well known because they were used by doctors when they treated ISIS members. Some local doctors were also sent to the front lines to treat wounded ISIS soldiers with makeshift "clinics." During the second year, hospitals started running out of medicines because the existing governmental storages were running low. Doctors and patients report that new drug brands from Syria started appearing in the pharmacies, indicating that ISIS imported medicines via the open road between Raqqa and Mosul until the last six months of the occupation of Mosul.[49] These medicines were sold in pharmacies or sometimes directly from Syrian-registered trucks. However, they were too expensive for most civilians, many of whom had their salaries cut and were surviving on savings or help from relatives. The medicines were free for ISIS members, but could cost up to five times the regular price for civilians. Added to this were the new fees imposed by ISIS on civilians for all health services—including cancer treatment and childbirth—a break with the long history of publicly financed healthcare in Iraq. ISIS gradually charged for more services in order to finance the hospitals after salaries stopped and medicines became scarce. As the group's finances were increasingly channeled to military spending, the health sector became more self-financed, depending on civilians' payment. The money collected from patients was spent on providing a minimum of services and salaries for hospital staff. The salaries were only a fraction of those before ISIS, and barely covered travel expenses. The skyrocketing prices for healthcare were the main concern among civilians. According to my interviews, in the last year of ISIS rule in Mosul, medical treatment had become a luxury that only the few who still had savings could afford. Even civilians who could afford it were denied treatment if medical staff was told to prioritize the "brothers." During the last months of the liberation battle, medical services were almost exclusively reserved for wounded fighters and their families.

Al-ikhwa and their families had their own, exclusive supply line for medication, which was well known and highly institutionalized. When an ISIS member or his family needed a drug, including expensive and rare medicines, they got a permission letter from a doctor or from the *diwan al-sihha* that granted them the right to free medication from the hospital storage rooms. They could also go to the "Brothers' pharmacy," an ISIS-only pharmacy set up in the Ibn Sina hospital. In addition to using the government stores of medicines and those imported from Syria, ISIS filled its medicine stocks by looting pharmacies that belonged to people who had fled the city. The group practiced tight control on pharmacies, and only authorized pharmacists could sell medicines.[50] In a letter addressing pharmacists of Mosul, ISIS blamed them for increasing the prices for medicines. The letter listed fixed prices and called for a "spirit of love and cooperation among the Muslim populace" to ensure reasonably priced medicines for civilians with chronic diseases.[51]

This stands in stark contrast to realities reported by patients and doctors in my study. They report skyrocketing prices in pharmacies controlled by ISIS and medicines for the chronically ill being prioritized for ISIS members. One doctor recounted:

> We had a very expensive drug that would usually be imported from Germany [...], it cost 3,000 dollars. It is only supplied by the government because it is too expensive for normal people. After ISIS occupation, we would send a patient to them who needed that drug, because they controlled the drug stores. They told us they did not have it. The next day, one of their brothers needed the same, and he got a paper from the *diwan al-sihha*, he went to the storage and he got it. [...] We reached a point where the medical staff collected money from each other to give to a patient who needed it to buy drugs.[52]

A third form of discrimination was the stricter enforcement of dress codes and segregation for civilians than for ISIS patients. Officially, gender segregation and clothing rules were universal and absolute, but the rules were sometimes ignored when ISIS members were treated. A female doctor recounted her experience of the different practices:

> The clothes restricted our movements. If I want to enter a needle in the back of a baby, I want to see the area clearly. With the cover on my face, I don't see anything clearly. I asked them to please let me uncover at least my eyes, because I risked paralyzing the patient. I asked, what if I was treating an ISIS soldier, do I also put the needle in his body blindly? They said no, then you can uncover your eyes. I said "No, this patient is the same as that patient," but they didn't listen.[53]

Lastly, during most of ISIS rule over Mosul, civilians were not allowed to leave the city to get necessary treatment, even for life-threatening conditions. ISIS members, on the other hand, would regularly be transferred to other parts of the "caliphate" and even to high-quality hospitals in Turkey if the treatment was not available in Mosul.[54] A fatwa was issued declaring that travelling to *dar al-kufr* [the abode of the infidels] was permitted if it was necessary for health reasons.[55] There are examples of civilians in Mosul obtaining such permission during the first year under ISIS. As the military struggle intensified, this became an option often reserved for the group's members. An unknown number of civilian children and chronically ill patients died because of these policies. A man in Mosul told of how his grandson was denied permission to travel for lifesaving treatment:

> My grandson had a chronic illness and he needed some special medicine. [...] The medicine was not available under ISIS. I tried to get the medicines from outside, but it was impossible. He stayed three months in the hospital in Mosul. ISIS told us to pay 5,000 IQD per day, but I did not have any money because I did not get my salary. A doctor helped me secretly and transferred my grandson to intensive care, which was free. But he got sicker, and I kidnapped him from the bed and left Mosul. We managed to escape to Erbil, but my grandson died after a month.[56]

Similar stories were common among my patient-informants.⁵⁷ As the blockade on Mosul began to suffocate the supply of food and money from the outside, the mortality rate started rising among patients. Patients with weakened immune systems were most vulnerable to the lack of food, and the sporadic supply of electricity made the hospitals unable to run lifesaving equipment. Children and old people suffered disproportionally from the lack of both medicines and food. ISIS often used the civilians' medical needs as a means to pressure civilians into joining them or sending one of their sons to fight for them. A staff member in a children's ward recounted:

> The most difficult was to see children die of leukemia because they did not receive the necessary treatment. […] I know that they died because of *da'ish* because *da'ish* had chemotherapy medicines, and they would be given to *da'ish* people who had a sick child who brought a permission from *diwan al-sihha*, and that child would live. Some people joined *da'ish* just to get medicine for their children. Other people made the decision to let their child die rather than join *da'ish*.⁵⁸

Managing health personnel

Approximately one third of the doctors disappeared from work during the summer and fall of 2014. After ISIS closed the city borders, crossing them was only possible with the help of smugglers. This was both costly and risky, so many were forced to stay in the city until it was liberated. Some chose to stay in hiding to avoid working under ISIS. Medical staff were a valuable asset, and ISIS members would routinely come to doctors' homes and pick them up by car if they failed to show up for work. Administrative employees in the hospitals were tasked with informing on their colleagues if they did not show up for work. In some cases, ISIS would also send young scouts around to doctors' offices to report any absence. An atmosphere of fear and suspicion took over the workplaces. Staff members not only had to stay on the alert toward the newly installed ISIS-run management and the *hisba* patrols roaming the corridors. Many doctors were shocked to see when they returned to work that some longtime colleagues had joined the ranks of the extremists. The previous colleagues in the hospitals had rapidly been split in distinct sub-groups: Those who fled or never showed up for work, those who remained as a matter of responsibility for the population, and those who sympathized with the ISIS project. The sense of trust between hospital workers had vanished overnight. The ones who saw themselves as occupied by extremist terrorists had to suppress every sign of unhappiness with their new rulers. ISIS sympathizers could be everywhere; anyone who aired any discontent with a colleague, a patient, or even a cleaning lady, risked being reported for treason. Although exact numbers are difficult to confirm, it is beyond doubt that many local doctors and medical staff members did pledge formal allegiance to ISIS. Doctors who joined ISIS did get some advantages compared to other doctors, such as the occasional promotion and more lenient treatment by the *hisba*. However, as locals they were still ranked below the foreign fighter doctors. Most of the pro-ISIS doctors and medical staff were arrested or killed during the liberation of Mosul. One doctor recounted:

> The sector where I least expected to see people joining *da'ish*, pledging a civilian allegiance, was the health sector. I could not believe my own eyes when I saw that some of them had joined. [...] One doctor was very wealthy. [...] His family was living the high life, I could not understand why he would join. He appeared in a *da'ish* propaganda video. [...] A doctor I know was in his last year of specialization in surgery; he left his specialization to go with *da'ish*. I talked to some of them and asked why; some would not give a straight answer. Some joined them, and maybe regretted later; as soon as you had joined there was no way back, you would be killed. Some of the doctors had family members killed by the Iraqi army, or had been arrested or tortured, and they wanted revenge. Some were kicked out of Baghdad in 2004 because they were Sunni. Each person had his or her reason to support *da'ish*.[59]

However, the large majority of the staff in the hospitals was still locals who had not pledged allegiance to ISIS, and they were shuffled around to different hospitals at the will of ISIS officials. Gearing the health system to serve its military advance, the group prioritized the largest hospitals in Mosul as well as smaller hospitals near the frontlines, like Qayyara. In the largest hospitals, administrative directors were replaced with those loyal to the group. Usually, medical management positions were occupied by the same locals as before. Because ISIS members were favored for important positions, those positions sometimes ended up being filled by inexperienced people. ISIS members who lacked the necessary education and training were hired as doctors, nurses, and managers, which had some bizarre results. For instance, ISIS put a former gasoline seller in charge of the emergency department in one hospital, while a foreign fighter with only two years of education was hired as a dentist.

ISIS's attitude toward doctors was two-faced. On the one hand, doctors were invaluable assets to the group and were treated with a softer hand than other civilians. Killing a doctor was something of a "red line." But they were often threatened at gunpoint when the tense atmosphere in the hospitals reached a climax. Doctors were routinely threatened with execution if they did not show up for work, but there are no examples in my material of such threats being carried through.[60] When disputes happened between local doctors and ISIS members, the group's seniors made an effort to solve the conflict without antagonizing the doctors. The group's warfare and the consolidation of its power were dependent on keeping the hospitals open and keeping a sufficient number of doctors working. On the other hand, doctors were more exposed to confrontations with ISIS than many other civilians because they were working alongside its members in locations used as headquarters. With less than half of the staff remaining, and a steady stream of wounded civilians and fighters incoming due to airstrikes, the working conditions for medical staff deteriorated until it became nearly unbearable under ISIS. In the most intense periods, up to eight times the normal number of patients would come in, according to my interviews. twenty-four-hour shifts were not uncommon, and ISIS would routinely punish doctors who had skipped work by forcing them to stay working in the hospital for weeks without returning home. As the coalition forces drew closer, many doctors became de facto hostages in the hospitals because they were not allowed to leave for the liberated areas. In addition to the huge workload, the medical staff worked for free during most of the period. In general, ISIS governance of the health sector bears few signs of active governance. ISIS did not introduce new work plans during their rule, but in practice relied on existing frameworks put in place by the Iraqi health authorities. The group advertised hospitals refurbished by the regime prior to 2014 as their own "new Islamic State hospitals."[61] In reality, in most cases its rule represented instead a reduction of the services available prior to 2014. The group cut the training time for medical students in order to keep the supply of new medical staff flowing.

The parts of the health system with no strategic or military value for the group—like vaccination of children—were met with indifference. Before 2014, an extensive vaccination program was in place in Ninawa that made vaccinations universally available in all cities and rural areas. This kept running for about six months after the takeover, but came to a halt because importing vaccines and employing doctors to implement these programs were not prioritized by ISIS. BCG and measles vaccines were not available; polio and hepatitis were only in limited supply.[62] The result was an explosion of diseases that had been eradicated in the country, some imported by foreign fighters: Measles, scabies, and other communicable diseases like meningitis started spreading. One Mosul doctor working with prevention and protection against communicable diseases lamented the lack of guidelines under ISIS:

> The guidelines from the ministry remained the same; *da'ish* did not have their own guidelines. They did not have any plans, nothing, it was just random. They did not have any humanitarian or scientific rules to work by. It depended on the *da'ishi* [ISIS member], whatever he feels like at that time becomes the rule. We were shocked about what was going on. Usually, if someone suffers from a communicable disease, we put them in isolation units, take tests, send them to Baghdad and get a quick answer. Under *da'ish* we could not do that, we were completely dependent on ourselves. This, of course, affected our work severely. *Da'ish* did not have any program or policy on communicable diseases; we tried to keep working with the old system but it was very limited what we managed to do. We did our best to overcome the limitations, by way of teamwork.[63]

The old health directorate of Mosul remained open, with its staff reduced to a handful of employees. In general, public offices and directorates that ISIS saw as superfluous were cut to a minimum or shut down. Because of Mosul's relatively well-developed health infrastructure, Mosul became the main medical hub for ISIS throughout their territories. New laboratory equipment from Mosul medical college was transferred to the group's new medical school in Raqqa, according to the group's newsletter *al-Naba'*.[64] Al-Jumhuri hospital in West Mosul was known to be one of the top surgical hospitals in Iraq, and its operating theatres had recently gone through a costly modernization. It soon became the center for treatment of wounded ISIS soldiers, and fighters were brought there from all across their territory. Civilians started associating the hospital with ISIS, and because of this, many tried to avoid seeking treatment there. Similarly, local doctors tried to avoid being assigned there by ISIS because it would make them more open to accusations of collaborating with terrorists. Because the hospital was essential for treating ISIS soldiers, it was strictly prioritized at the expense of civilians, with patients being screened by guards at the hospital entrance. Similarly, because of its military importance, Jumhuri was the destination for many of the foreign doctors and medical personnel who came from abroad to work for the group. Doctors and health workers from all over the world walked the corridors of Jumhuri: Australia, Germany, Turkey, Saudi Arabia, Kuwait, Russia, Serbia, Netherland, Iran, Sweden, Sudan, Brazil, France, Somalia. There was a lot of friction between the local doctors and the foreign fighters who had become their colleagues.

> We were suffering from the ISIS doctors from Russia, Tunisia, and Morocco. They were very extreme in their views. [...] When I was working alongside them, I had to agree with everything they said; they intervened in my work.[65]

Jumhuri became the group's most important administrative center for healthcare throughout its territories, even though there were local branches called *diwan al-sihha* also elsewhere in Syria and Iraq. The *diwan al-sihha* was located on the lower floors of Jumhuri hospital and was responsible for administering hospitals, field hospitals, and distribution of medicines. On July 4, 2014, the day before ISIS leader Abu Bakr al-Baghdadi gave his famous speech in Mosul's al-Nouri mosque, Baghdadi was spotted by doctors in the Jumhuri hospital. Surrounded by a large entourage of armed guards, the mysterious leader of the nascent state had a tour of the hospital—which attests to the military significance it was seen to have from early on. It is well documented that ISIS used medical facilities as military bases, effectively using the patients and doctors as human shields because they considered hospitals to be safer from air bombardment than purely military targets. A public announcement banned gatherings in front of hospitals during the military operation, in an attempt to divert attention away from these de facto military bases.[66] The car mechanic units for ambulances in the basement of each hospital were used to prepare suicide bombs. As the coalition against ISIS closed in on the group and reclaimed East Mosul, Jumhuri hospital became even more important as a sniper position, as it was located on a hill on the West bank of the Tigris. Doctors who spent time in Jumhuri hospital confirm other reports that the hospital's basement was used for weapon storage and preparations for suicide bombs. One young doctor tells of a grim event in al-Salam hospital toward the end of the military battle:

> I saw ISIS militants going down to the basement to get their guns, they were shouting "allahu akbar." We also saw ISIS driving out of the hospital with a suicide bomb car, and after a while we heard a big explosion from the car, it had been hit by an airstrike. The ISIS militants next to us were cheering and shouting.[67]

Such events put on full display the unbearable and conflicting position that Mosul's remaining healthcare professionals were put in. They had chosen to stay behind to save civilians' lives, often without pay, motivated by a sense of responsibility for their city's population. They worked alongside ISIS militants who justified murdering civilians, they witnessed suicide bombers driving onto the streets from their workplace—and then they tried their best to patch together the random civilian victims of the same bombs.

The mixed civilian-military nature of the hospitals did not keep them from being targeted by the coalition against ISIS. Jumhuri was completely destroyed by airstrikes in the final days of the military operation against ISIS in July 2017. By that time, most of the civilians and staff had managed to escape the building. In total, nine out of Mosul's thirteen hospitals were damaged or destroyed in the battle, slashing the healthcare capacity by 70 percent.

Conclusion

The tension between ISIS's ideology, its ongoing military campaign, and its ambitions to provide public services became clear in the group's administration of Mosul's health system. It is to a large extent what Aymenn Jawad Al-Tamimi in his analysis of ISIS has called "parasitic co-optation"[68]—preying on the resources already present in the territories, relying on existing medicine stocks and salaries still being paid by the central government, while merely rebranding the institutions as ISIS's own. In this sense, the health system represents a clearer case of predatory rebel rule than other parts of the ISIS administration. Predatory rebels may give the impression of running institutions by changing key positions, names, and administrative documents. However, as William Reno notes, such measures are intended to "achieve outside recognition, not serve local inhabitants."[69] ISIS presented its health system as a modern, innovative, and well-functioning part of its new "state," offering universal services. In reality, existing plans for crucial health functions were ignored. Planning, organizing, and innovation were practically non-existent, and the group preyed on the available resources in an unsustainable way. Their management style caused many civilians' deaths, waves of infectious diseases. Many doctors were horrified by the group's actions in the hospitals and decided to escape the city, leading to even more pressure on the remaining doctors. ISIS members were given preferential treatment, which made the public's initial support for the group dissolve quickly.

The group's self-serving behavior indicates a short time horizon in which immediate military gains trumped the long-term interests of both civilians and the group itself. Interestingly, this predatory behavior was combined with a strong fixation on ideology, to a point where it interfered not only with the treatment of civilians but also with the treatment of fighters, whom the health system was geared to serve. The fact that ISIS provided some level of healthcare to civilians and actively used hospitals as spaces for ideological indoctrination of the population indicates a long time horizon. In conventional "new civil war" literature, modern civil wars are often described as purely criminal, predatory, and depoliticized.[70] ISIS's entire project can hardly be dismissed as a purely predatory endeavor. Instead, the findings presented in this chapter demonstrate how rebels' predatory practices can coexist with ambitions for substantial, long-term governance. The case of Mosul's health system under ISIS serves to highlight the complexity in rebels' approaches to civilian institutions.

6

Conclusion

"If Allah (the Exalted) causes the khilafah to remain and gain strength, then it is thanks to Allah alone, for victory is only from Him. And if it vanishes and weakens, then know that it is because of ourselves and our deeds."
ISIS SPOKESMAN ABU MUHAMMAD AL-ADNANI, JUNE 2014[1]

"Every day for three years we said to ourselves that the next day liberation would come. Can you imagine living like that for three years?"
A DOCTOR IN A MOSUL HOSPITAL[2]

Thousands of Iraqi soldiers, Kurdish Peshmerga forces, and a range of different militias took part in the military operation to liberate Mosul from ISIS, dubbed "We are coming, Ninawa." These forces were backed from the air by warplanes in a US-led coalition, dropping thousands of bombs on the city during the months that followed. The operation started in October 2016, but would last until July the following year because of unexpectedly fierce resistance from the ISIS war machine. ISIS protected its borders with suicide bomb trucks rammed into enemy lines, anti-tank missiles, anti-aircraft launchers, and self-propelled artillery. The heavy machine-gun fire that killed scores of Iraqi and Peshmerga soldiers originated from those soldiers' American ally—looted by ISIS. The group had entangled itself deeply in the civilian infrastructure of the city, which raised serious challenges for the advancing coalition against ISIS. Not only did ISIS use schools, universities, and hospitals as military bases and weapon factories. They also forced civilians to stay inside these buildings while the city was being bombarded, using them as human shields to avoid being targeted. The result was heavy bombing of hospitals, bridges, universities, power plants, and other infrastructure crucial for civilian life. The military campaign killed more people than ISIS had done during its three-year reign of terror and mass murder in the city. When Prime Minister Hayder al-Abadi declared Mosul liberated on 10 July, it was a broken city that had been freed. The Old City that had survived even the Mongol invasion of the thirteenth century was now in rubbles after indiscriminate bombing to win this important and symbolic victory against ISIS. Underneath the rubbles were the dead bodies of thousands of civilians who happened to live in the "wrong" neighborhoods.

As Iraqi forces and its allied militias advanced quarter by quarter, pale men in long beards, women in black gowns, and malnourished children emerged from the ruins, with their hands above their heads, escaping toward government-held areas. Most of them had lived through three years of hell, with little or no income, starvation, and abuse—all brought on by the so-called governance of the Islamic State. Most people had lost someone close: A sick child who did not get medicine from ISIS, a brother who was killed for carrying a mobile phone, friends disappeared forever in ISIS prisons, colleagues later

Figure 10 *Civilians escaped from Mosul's ISIS-held Old City during the liberation battle in 2017 (Photo: Laurent Van der Stockt for Le Monde/Getty Images Reportage).*

found in ISIS mass-graves, entire families wiped out by coalition bomb raids. A ruthless "justice process" followed, where Shia militias and Iraqi forces were behind countless extrajudicial killings, sexual abuse, and torture of suspected ISIS sympathizers, in an environment of bloodthirsty revenge.

For ISIS, its main stated end-goal had been to govern a community of "righteous" Muslims while waiting for the apocalypse. Compared to its forerunners AQI, ISI, and ISIS, the Islamic State, following its announcement in June 2014, made a stronger effort to cater to the local population in Mosul, at least during the first few months. However, many Maslawis' initial support quickly waned as they experienced that it was not able or willing to provide the security, predictability, and public services that they desperately needed. Why did one of history's wealthiest jihadi rebel groups, with an abundance of local resources and a professional military machinery supported by foreign fighters, fail to achieve its stated goal? A large part of the explanation lies, of course, in the mounting military onslaught from the outside. But ISIS's inherent contradictions, which have been highlighted throughout this book, contributed to tearing apart the group's ambitious governance project even before the military campaign made it impossible to run government institutions effectively. Some of these contradictions are specific to ISIS, while others are common to rebel governance situations in ongoing civil wars.

The failure of ISIS governance was partly due to the near-impossible balancing act between ideology and pragmatic concerns. This study gives some support for hypotheses that jihadi rebel groups sacrifice pragmatic state-building to keep their image of ideological purity. The chapter on healthcare shows that the efficiency of vital institutions like hospitals was undermined by ideological micromanagement, to the detriment of both civilians and ISIS members. The ideological convictions explain many of the group's actions and are crucial to explain the appeal of its propaganda and the effectiveness of its recruitment machinery. However, the reasons behind the failure of ISIS governance are more complex than just an overzealous commitment to ideology. ISIS governed the health sector with dogmatic micromanagement, but also predatory behavior to serve the organization's immediate military interests and the individual interests of ISIS commanders. Its initial plan for educating the Mosul's children shows an uncompromising ideological line.

Yet, the failure of that plan was due to a range of factors: The strength and legitimacy of existing local institutions, civilians' agency, and military assault from the outside. Finally, the fact that ISIS police failed to create a sense of legitimacy in the population was not primarily because of its hardline ideological commitment. Civilians' main objection to ISIS police was that it was corrupt, unpredictable, opportunistic, and discriminatory. ISIS's bending and breaking of its own rules throughout its reign was one of the most common criticisms against it.

Zachariah Mampilly notes that "[m]ore often than not, the proclaimed values of an insurgent command fail to harmonize with its actual treatment of civilians on the ground."[3] It is important to keep in mind that ideology is not a constant, and ISIS adjusted fundamental parts of its official ideology to fit realities on the ground. For instance, the Syrian town of Dabiq long played a central role in the group's narrative of the apocalypse. ISIS claimed that the final battle between the "crusaders" and the "true believers" would take place in the town and named its English language propaganda magazine after it. In 2016, however, as Turkish-backed forces closed in on the town, the group launched a new magazine named Rumiya.[4] ISIS lost control of Dabiq in October 2016. Adjusting ideology to practical concerns could also be about financial convenience, as when the group allegedly sold oil to several of its declared arch enemies, such as Syria and Turkey.[5] ISIS's "fatwa" justifying sex slavery of Yezidi girls and the justification of burning a Jordanian pilot to death are other examples. ISIS professed that it was against any "innovation" in Islam, but there is no doubt that its interpretation of existing Islamic sources is full of innovations.

It is difficult to know for sure when ideas really matter to a rebel group and when they are used as a cover for other motivations.[6] In addition, a group is not a monolithic entity where all the members have the same motivation and end goal. This is especially true for a group with members from a wide variety of socioeconomic backgrounds and countries as diverse as Belgium, Saudi-Arabia, Uzbekistan, and China. It might be convenient to portray a military enemy as homogeneous and monolithic, but it obscures more than it helps us understand a group. There is also not necessarily a causal link between certain (extremist) beliefs and violent behavior on an individual level. Most people with extremist views never turn their ideas into violent acts, and terrorists committing violent acts are not necessarily motivated by their extremist beliefs.[7] Not all members of ISIS are motivated by the group's official ideology. Many of them are not even aware of important tenets in the ideology.

Is it possible to draw a line between the ideology or a rebel group and its military strategy? With its propaganda machinery, ISIS exploited the dynamics of Western mass media and completely overshadowed the more amateurish propaganda of other, competing jihadi groups—most of which had focused on military activities and criticizing the status quo. A state's authority is constantly constructed and justified through language and communication. ISIS's media strategy made it the most widely covered jihadi organization in history, and this strategy, combined with spectacular terrorist attacks in the West, is much of the reason why Western media has framed ISIS as an existential threat. To use Charlie Winter's classification, the group's propaganda combined warfare with Sunni Muslim victimization and description of a full-fledged society in the "caliphate."[8] In his study of propaganda output during one month in 2015, 53 percent of the ISIS media output was about the utopian state, including governance, social life, religious life, justice, economics, and nature.[9] By the end of 2016 the Islamic State had lost a third of its territory and almost half of Mosul. From 2015 to 2017, its media production dropped by a half, with the exception of a spike in media production by the Ninawa Province Media Office during the Iraqi government's military campaign to recapture Mosul.[10] When the territorial control started dissolving, the propaganda focus shifted away from governance and more toward warfare. This is not surprising; it is difficult to make propaganda about territory and governance without controlling the territory, and important media centers and media leaders were hit in airstrikes. Still, it is yet another sign of how ideology and pragmatism are interwoven. The expansion of the "caliphate" had built-in limits from the beginning, landlocked as it was by the American-supported Kurdish government to the East, an interventionist Turkey to the North, Iraqi government forces to the South, and the Russian-supported Syrian regime to the West. After ISIS was decimated as a territorial power, its propaganda no longer emphasizes the importance of territory, but instead focused on its global agenda. In a clever spin, Abu Bakr al-Baghdadi even insisted in a September 2017 public statement that the group's loss of territory in Syria was in fact a blessing, and that its patience and steadfastness had spread fear among the "infidel nations."[11]

ISIS's political project was from the beginning plagued by contradictions without obvious solutions. The group wanted to construct a state on Earth in the service of the *umma* and God, but at the same time, it tried to usher on the end of the world. On the one hand, the group justifies its actions and its state-building as a favor to the worldwide Muslim community, *al-umma*. On the other hand, it promotes an individualistic focus. Jihadis see themselves as fighting a defensive war, and jihad is *fard al-'ayn*, an individual duty for every capable Muslim. This means that each individual has the right to act on his or her own, and defy or topple authorities when deemed necessary. The motivation for martyrdom is equally focus on the individual's personal gain. Yet another contradiction is found in its view of authorities: ISIS calls for the revolt against political and (the wrong) religious authorities, and it wrestled power from old political elites and tribal leaders, turning existing hierarchies on their heads in cities like Mosul. Many of the ISIS members who ended up dominating Mosul came from the countryside around the city, which many Maslawis saw as a "revenge" by the marginalized countryside on the privileged city people. Against Iraqi culture, teenage ISIS fighters—some of them did not even speak Arabic—threatened elderly men and women with guns and forced tribal leaders to cooperate or flee.[12] At the same time, the new structures put in place by the organization were no doubt extremely authoritarian. Criticizing the decisions of high-ranking militants was risky. A near-godlike aura surrounded the elusive Abu Bakr al-Baghdadi. He was introduced by its spokesman in 2014 as no less than the "mujahid, the scholar who practices what he preaches, the worshipper, the leader, the warrior, the reviver, descendent from the family of the Prophet, the slave of Allah, Ibrahim bin Awwad bin Ibrahim bin Ali bin Muhammad al-Badri al-Hashimi al-Husayni al-Qurashi by lineage, al-Samarri by birth and upbringing, al-Baghdadi by residence and scholarship."[13]

This book has underlined the risk of taking ISIS's own paperwork at face value, and showed the sometimes glaring contrast between the impression given by bureaucratic documents and civilians' accounts. It shows the importance of analyzing jihadi rebel groups in light of their local context, especially when a group involves itself so deeply with the local population. The findings show that ISIS is not exceptional in how it dealt with civilians. The social and material havoc wrecked by ISIS in Mosul may be unique in the city's history, and some of its methods were particularly ruthless and cruel, some amounting to genocide. At the same time, Mosul's inhabitants saw parts of ISIS rule as a continuation of what previous governments had done under different brands: Using repressive tactics to enrich individuals at the expense of society. After Mosul's liberation, the extortion tactics so familiar to Maslawis have continued—this time under the flag of Shia militias supported by the government. In future research it is important to consider both the local context and the wider literature on rebel governance to enrich our understanding of jihadi groups, instead of willingly adopting their propaganda message of being exceptional.

For many Maslawis today, the ruins of parts of Mosul are reminders of ISIS's failed attempt to govern near two million people, and the military campaign brought on by its governance experiment. Many of the destroyed buildings—including hospital, universities, and police stations—are still not cleared or rebuilt years after the end of ISIS rule.[14] This points to some of the underlying reasons that allowed for ISIS to take over the city in the first place: widespread corruption, bureaucratic inefficiency, and a divisive, dysfunctional Iraqi government. Iraqi politicians' lacking willingness to change this means that Iraq is still a fertile ground for extreme groups like ISIS to grow and consolidate themselves again. In 2019, Iraq was shaken by the largest and most resilient anti-government popular protests since 2003. The tactics used against today's protesters in Baghdad and Basra seem to have be taken from the same book that were used against the protest tent cities in Hawija and other Iraqi cities in 2013: Meeting peaceful protesters with bullets and violence. Security forces have shot into crowds of unarmed protests, an unknown number have been kidnapped and tortured, and Iranian-backed militias have been behind violent attacks on protest camps. All to terrorize people from showing their anger and disillusionment with corrupt and incompetent politicians. "Activists, journalists, academics and anyone suspected of supporting the protest movement logistically or morally started receiving death threats before they were kidnapped," an official of a human rights organization told the Guardian.[15]

More studies based on interviews with civilians in conflict zones are needed to deepen our understanding of ISIS, jihadi groups, and rebel governance more broadly. Many accounts from ISIS-held areas have left the impression of civilians as either passive victims or supporters. Such simplistic dichotomies are not only deeply unfair to the inhabitants of these areas, many of whom actively resisted and affected the way in which ISIS ruled. These simplistic accounts of civilians can be used to justify military action or extra-legal persecution of civilians, as has been the case in Mosul. More micro-level studies of the dynamics in rebel governance situations can help us see civilians as the individual agents they are.

Notes on Sources and Methodology

Interviews, administrative documents, and propaganda material produced by ISIS are the main sources for this study. ISIS produced immense quantities of administrative documents of all sorts: birth certificates, ID papers, medical certificates, speeding tickets, police files, and so on. Documents show that ISIS had ambitions to regulate agriculture, prices on food and medicine, local disputes, and crime. Moving beyond these realms that are usually regulated by states, the group spent considerable resources and paperwork on governing the private sphere down to the tiniest detail. Restrictions on clothing, haircuts, children's play, social interaction, mourning costumes, language, and other matters that are usually considered private make up a large part of bureaucratic paperwork produced by ISIS.

As mentioned in the introduction chapter, the unusual amount of documents produced by the group has been the source of a number of research articles and media reports. The fact that an extremist jihadi-Salafi group with a declared aim to bring about the apocalypse invests so much effort in bureaucratic micromanagement of civilians is puzzling. However, violent rebel groups often produce a wide range of bureaucratic documents. Some of the media and research coverage of the ISIS administration has demonstrated the risk of conflating paperwork and bureaucracy with successful state-building. Even though documents give valuable insight, seen in isolation they primarily document the group's ambitions and self-projected image rather than actual

Figure 11 *Children from Mosul in Debaga camp for displaced persons (Photo: Mathilde Becker Aarseth).*

implementation. On many occasions, the existence of a record that documents a function in the ISIS administration has been taken as a sign of efficiency and rigor. As this book has shown, there are many possible pitfalls to such conclusions.

Because of the limited access to ISIS documents, ten or even a hundred documents showing the implementation of a policy say little about systematic implementation in a meaningful way in a city of nearly two million inhabitants or a "caliphate" of up to eight million. Thousands of complaints filed in some ISIS-controlled police stations tell us that these complainants had some confidence in the group as an upholder of order, but do not shed light on all the crimes that went unrecorded for various reasons. Furthermore, large parts of the available papers document ambitions rather than actual implementation. Documents describing educational plans, announcements of school start, exam dates, and reorganizing of university departments[1] were distributed in areas where education was at a standstill for most of the period under ISIS. Lastly, many documents are not about governing civilians per se, but document military activities. For example, regulations on the use of internet and satellite

TVs were put in place to keep intelligence from leaking out,² and a clothes factory in Mosul was reorganized to produce military uniforms.³ Several (undated) documents show the transfer of personnel from various ministries to the military, illustrating how military concerns always trumped civilian governance.⁴ Lastly, much of the paperwork on "governance" activities in fact documents activities that serve no public purpose. At best, it documents a bizarre prioritization of resources while fundamental public institutions were left to wither away. Forms that register mosque attendance and other activities by the *hisba* are examples of this.⁵

Administrative documents referred to in this book are predominantly taken from trusted open online sources, in particular Aymenn Jawad Al-Tamimi's online repository of ISIS documents. Some files referred to in the chapters on policing and education are taken from George Washington University repository of ISIS files. I have evaluated and translated the original in each document that I refer to. The propaganda material used in this book is gathered online, often via websites like Jihadology, which post links to videos and other material that are accessible even if the original posting has been removed. In terms of propaganda, I have focused on the group's officially recognized and most widely disseminated propaganda because I consider this the most central arena for ISIS to present its vision for governance, even though social media and personal messenger applications are also important vehicles for ISIS propaganda. The study draws on propaganda videos in Arabic and English, the English language magazines *Dabiq* and *Rumiya*, the Arabic language newsletter *al-Naba'* and various textbooks in Arabic produced by the group. I supplement my analysis with reports from Arabic-, English-, French-, and Scandinavian-language media and existing research, as well as public reports from national and international NGOs.

I conducted interviews for this study during three four-week research trips to northern Iraq in 2016, 2018, and 2019, in addition to interviews conducted on the phone and social media. My main aim was to interview both providers and users of public services under ISIS rule between 2014 and 2017. In the realm of education, this included teachers from primary school level to university level who had taught in schools and universities in Mosul or the surrounding villages, as well as administrative employees in the education sector. On the "user" side, I interviewed students from Mosul University who had been enrolled under ISIS rule, and parents who had children of school age during this period. In the healthcare system, interviewees include doctors of various specializations and administrative health employees who had worked under ISIS, as well as patients and relatives of patients who had been in ISIS-run hospitals, and managers and political representatives in the relevant areas. For the chapter on policing, I did interviews with people in internally displaced people (IDPs) camps and in the streets of various Mosul neighborhoods. Some were interviewed on more than one of the three topics. In addition to interviewing specific professionals, I interviewed a large number of civilians selected only on the criteria that they lived in Mosul for a longer period between June 2014 and the liberation in 2017. I conducted some interviews alone, but most in the presence of my Iraqi assistant who assisted with translation when necessary. I conducted the interviews in Arabic, recorded them, and translated the parts quoted in the articles. When interviewees spoke fluent English or French, the interviews were conducted in those languages.

My selection of interviewees was partly based on "snowball sampling" in which informants introduce other informants. All my civilian interviewees experienced at least seven months of ISIS rule, and most were Sunni Muslim Arabs or Kurds. Added to this were interviews with persons who had fled in the first day or two of the takeover, but who nevertheless shed light on aspects of ISIS governance. These include political, military, and administrative leaders from Ninawa provincial council, NGOs who received IDPs from Mosul,[6] and Christian families from the town of Qaraqosh. Additional interviews were done by my assistant after my departure. He followed my instructions about the questions and choice of interviewees and recorded the interviews.

During the first trip, because of security issues described in the next section, I focused on interviewing IDPs within the autonomous Kurdish region (KRG): in Erbil, Duhok, and the three IDP camps Debaga, Baharka, and Ankawa. For interviews on the education system, I contacted IDP camp schools because some professionals tend to take on the same work inside camps as they had in their place of origin. In this way, I tracked down schoolteachers, university teachers, and school managers in the camps. Similarly, I contacted clinics in the camps to locate doctors from Mosul. Through contacts that I made in the camps and in Erbil, I tracked down more teachers and students, which again led me to others. By phone, I interviewed students from Mosul University who had fled Mosul and continued their studies in Kirkuk. To expand the pool of possible interviewees I went to Avro City, a neighborhood in Duhok where many relatively affluent IDPs from Mosul have settled since 2014. In Erbil I interviewed more students, and exiled political and administrative leaders from Mosul, like the director of education in Ninawa and the governor of Mosul.

At the time of my second trip, the most recently displaced people dwelled in camps outside of the KRG. Because of that, I went to Hassan Sham and Khazer IDP camps between Erbil and Mosul to conduct interviews for the articles on health and policing. When I arrived in April 2018, ISIS no longer held territory in Ninawa and internally displaced persons were slowly returning to their hometowns. Because the security situation allowed for trips to Mosul at this point, I made eight-day trips together with my assistant to Mosul, where I interviewed civilians and employees in the health sector who had worked there under ISIS rule. For interviews on civilians' experiences with the ISIS police, I went to various central neighborhoods in Mosul. Building on my existing network, I was able to locate a handful of relevant interviewees who then introduced me to others. Most of these interviews were pre-arranged and conducted in people's own homes or in private offices in their workplaces, while other appointments and interviews were made by traveling to various neighborhoods and approaching people in the streets.

In the education sector, I did thirty-three interviews lasting between thirty minutes and two hours with students and employees in the education sector, as well as thirty interviews with civilians lasting between fifteen minutes and one hour. In the health sector, I did fifteen in-depth interviews with medical staff lasting between one and a half and three hours each, in addition to twenty-three interviews with civilians. Chapter 3 is based on thirty-nine interviews with civilians. The interviews for this study were a combination of semi-structured and open-ended, departing from a pre-determined set of questions but leaving room for the interviewees to bring focus to what they deemed relevant and ascribe meanings to it. This approach was necessary because my aim with the interviews was two-fold. On the one hand, the interviews were a way to obtain a fuller description of the workings of ISIS administration, which required that

I include certain specific questions about these structures in all interviews. On the other hand, I wanted interviewees to give their own, subjective opinion on the administration, and this required an open-ended approach.

Security context during field trips

Security considerations and the political atmosphere at the time of my field trips meant that I did not have complete freedom in choosing my informants. For security reasons, and because a battlefield is not an ideal place for qualitative research, I did not enter Mosul during my first stay, but did interviews within the KRG. The military campaign led to heightened security measures because of the increased chance of suicide attacks inside the Kurdish region, but this had little negative impact on my work within the KRG. The wave of displaced people who ended up in the Kurdish region presented an opportunity to do research interviews among people who had recently fled from Mosul and had experienced the majority of ISIS rule. Because of visa limitations, I was not able to stay in Iraq at the peak of the IDP stream during spring 2017 when civilians from Mosul city started entering the camps in large numbers. KRG was a refuge for people of all socioeconomic backgrounds, and nearly all Iraqi districts that had been under ISIS control were represented there. Using the approach described above, I managed to interview civilians with a range of professional backgrounds from a variety of neighborhoods in Mosul as well as rural areas outside the city. I had the freedom to choose my own interviewees within the camps.

At the time of my trips to Mosul in April–May 2018, the security situation was relatively good; the Iraqi army and its affiliated militias had re-established their presence and checkpoints were controlling the entrance of each neighborhood. However, raids to arrest suspected ISIS supporters still happened regularly in the city, and several suicide attempts by sleeper cells had been foiled in the months following liberation. Both physically and socially, the city bore scars of ISIS rule and the military campaign to expel it. Large parts of west Mosul were in rubble after intense air bombardment by the coalition against ISIS, and many of its inhabitants were still lingering in camps.

ISIS's divisive rule had disturbed the general sense of trust among inhabitants of Mosul, which had been one of the most ethnically and religiously diverse cities in Iraq before ISIS's genocide against certain groups. After the liberation of Mosul, many Maslawis that I interviewed felt collectively accused by Iraqi security forces of having supported ISIS. At the same time, in their view they had been betrayed by Iraqi forces who had left the city in ISIS hands. Maslawis' general distrust of the central government was deepened by ISIS occupation of Mosul. This was expressed in a general wariness about being interviewed about ISIS-related issues, especially among certain groups. While internally displaced persons in the relative safety of the Kurdish region had shown a great willingness to be interviewed, those still residing in Mosul were more skeptical to be interviewed. Many doctors worked in close proximity with ISIS members and directly followed their orders within the hospitals. I visited several hospitals and contacted hospital managers and the Ninawa doctors' syndicate. Those interviewed in hospitals or clinics, with colleagues or supervisors around, seemed to speak less freely about their experiences and avoided going into detail. On two occasions, the current managers of hospitals contradicted their subordinate doctors' accounts. While the doctors described ISIS interference in almost every aspect of the hospitals, managers of the same hospitals described less contact with the militants. Because they answered directly to the health directorate, hospital managers had significant personal incentives to avoid that any of the hospital staff was being associated with ISIS. In the end, the large majority of my interviews on healthcare were done in peoples' own homes after making an appointment in their workplace or on the phone. In my experience, the interviews conducted in private in peoples' own homes provided the richest and most detailed accounts. The context described here naturally affected my freedom to spend as much time as I wanted in each location, have informal conversations, and freely pick my research subjects.

Strengths and weaknesses of method

The combination of open, closed, pre-determined, and improvised questions resulted in rich accounts providing unexpected details. Most of the telling details about everyday ISIS rule in the hospitals were brought up by the informants themselves. When a new piece of information was mentioned, I followed it up in interviews with others. I also conducted follow-up interviews with most of the informants to solicit their feedback on my conclusions, either in person, on the phone or via social media. This strategy, sometimes called respondent validation, helps to rule out misunderstandings about informants' accounts and their interpretations of events, as well as to identify my own biases.[7] Particularly because the topic of my research is understudied, it was fruitful to approach the interview with a tentative plan, but retain flexibility. This active listening approach makes it possible to achieve "rich data," data that are detailed and varied enough that they provide a fuller picture of what was going on.[8]

I strove to collect as broad a selection of interviews as possible, reflecting different socioeconomic strata in Mosul and the rural areas surrounding the city. Iraq is a country with considerable internal differences in education and income levels, and for the articles on education and health, the combination of well-educated and less-educated sources gave important insight. While doctors and teachers are in the best positions to describe the workings of the system in detail, members of the general public are important sources to describe the services from the perspectives of the parents, students, or patients, regardless of their education level.

Unfortunately, female interviewees are underrepresented in my data for two main reasons. Firstly, the ISIS regime strictly limited women's freedom to move outside of their homes. Walking outside without a male guardian or failing to comply with the clothing rules could have severe consequences, which confined most women to their homes for most of the time. Women's participation in working life decreased dramatically. Thus, men have more hands-on experience with the workings of ISIS governance practices and are able to share richer information on the topics relevant for my study. This is particularly true with regards to policing. Secondly, I found that men were willing to be interviewed more often than women, and willing to share more detailed information. When possible, I strove to include women among my interviews. The overrepresentation of men is nevertheless an inherent weakness in my data, and women's experiences deserve more scrutiny in future research.

The main sources in this study—interviews, text study of ISIS sources, and secondary sources—all have inherent biases and sources of invalidity. I here use the term "validity" to refer to the correctness or credibility of a description, without implying the existence of one "objective truth" to which an account can be compared.[9] Interviewees may have personal, psychological, professional, and security reasons to give certain representations of the events and leave out certain other representations. Interviews are often invaluable when trying to shed light on subjective experiences and attitudes, and are a convenient way of overcoming distances in time and space.[10] Nevertheless, even descriptions of seemingly mundane structures and events are imbued with interpretation and colored by personal experiences. Interviews are "retrospective accounts that often explain and justify behavior."[11] In post-ISIS Mosul, it is reasonable to expect that interviewees may seek to justify their own behavior in their retrospective accounts. To minimize this effect, I strove to make the interview situations as comfortable and private as I could, conducting the interviews in the informants' own homes when possible. I made it clear early on that I anonymize all informants, leaving out their name, age, and workplace. Furthermore, I tried to diversify the informants' backgrounds as much as I could within the given limitations. For example, I interviewed health personnel from all the main hospitals as well as smaller clinics and private practices. Although new details emerged from each interview, the descriptions of the most central aspects of the healthcare system were consistent.

Propaganda sources have the obvious bias that they are created to increase recruitment, fear or public appreciation of their rule, most likely leaving out anything that will affect any of these in a negative way. As such, they are not reliable as sources for the workings of institutions on the ground. However, they are valuable as documents describing in detail the group's official narrative. Administrative documents that are meant for external distribution are also geared toward creating an image of a functioning state vis-à-vis civilians, and the line between an administrative document and propaganda is not always clear cut. Sometimes documents indirectly show deficiencies, for example in the declarations threatening doctors who do not return, suggesting that working conditions for doctors were not optimal in the "caliphate" and that hospitals were lacking staff. In a November 2015 declaration, ISIS urged students to re-register in other departments if their original department had been shut down,[12] revealing the group's deficient capacity in the university sector. However, many documents are declarations distributed among locals to justify the new rule, often written in a victorious and grandiose language and describing an ideal situation rather than facts on the ground. Administrative documents that are meant primarily for internal use within the organization and its bureaucracy are, in theory, more reliable in their descriptions of ISIS institutions. Yet, it is important to keep in mind that they are written to address members in time of war, and the strategic aim to boost the internal morale may obscure the image of what was actually happening on the ground.

It is important to be aware of the limitations of using online sources collected by third parties. Only a fraction of the total output of administrative documents are available online, and third parties may have their own reasons for selecting of documents to be made available online. While many documents were destroyed by the group before retreating, many remained and are still being uncovered, and a comprehensive analysis of these documents is an important avenue for future research.

One of the main aims of my study is precisely to show the discrepancy between the image created by the documents and the reality lived by civilians. Nevertheless, although civilians are the most valuable sources in my study, they too have inherent biases and their accounts cannot be taken as the last word. Triangulation of different data selection methods allows a broader and more secure understanding of the issues that are being investigated.[13] It reduces the risk of systematic biases due to a specific method, and allows for "a better assessment of the generality of the explanations that one develops."[14] Triangulation, however, does not automatically increase the validity of conclusions. My aim has been to distinguish the credible accounts from the not credible accounts by considering the possible validity threats. In practice, this means that I have left out information provided by only one source, and focused on the accounts that recurred often among the interviewees. Often these accounts have been confirmed by external sources like NGOs or independent researchers.

Ethical considerations

In addition to raising methodological challenges, the research context raises important ethical issues concerning my own security, the security of the research subjects, and possible unforeseen negative consequences of the research results.[15] At the time of my visits to Mosul, spending long periods in public in Mosul as a foreigner entailed certain security risks. A plethora of armed militias were charged with controlling the various neighborhoods of the city. Although the security situation in general was good in central neighborhoods, the existence of sleeper cells made kidnapping a small but real threat for foreigners in the city. In western Mosul, unexploded mines left behind by the group were still a real risk even though the main streets had been cleared. For these reasons, I tried to minimize the time spent in public and returned to Erbil before dark. The help of my Iraqi assistant was invaluable in minimizing security risks and in gaining access to Mosul, which was separated from Erbil by five checkpoints manned by Kurdish soldiers, Iraqi soldiers, and the Popular Mobilization Forces. I decided locations for interviews in Mosul based on my assistant's security recommendations, as well as conversations with international organizations working in the city and staff at the Norwegian embassy in Jordan with responsibility for Iraq. With a few exceptions, we did not visit western Mosul, and stayed away from peripheral neighborhoods whose inhabitants sometimes can be more skeptical to the presence of foreigners.

Because of fear of persecution by the government or remaining ISIS sympathizers, many Maslawis had real concerns for their own security during interviews. Many of my interviewees, especially doctors, stressed that they spoke on the condition of anonymity so that no quotes could be traced back to them. I chose to anonymize all civilians, including those who did not ask to be anonymized, because it is difficult to determine the possible negative consequences that the information shared might have for the interviewees. Exceptions are representatives of the Iraqi government or organizations who were interviewed in their official capacity. Most interviews were conducted in homes, offices or shops to avoid unnecessary attention toward both the interviewees and myself.

When interviewing vulnerable groups like refugees and victims of violence, it is important to keep in mind the risk of re-traumatizing the subjects. Nearly all of my interviewees had been victims of violence or had experienced close friends or relatives being harmed or killed, either at the hand of Iraqi regime soldiers or ISIS members, or as a consequence of the 2016–17 military campaign. For instance, a majority of my male interviewees had been lashed for breaching rules, and many had been imprisoned or had family members imprisoned. Doctors were traumatized from seeing patients die when treatment was readily available, and gynecologists saw the devastating effects of sex slavery when treating kidnapped Yezidi girls in their clinics. Many interviewees had lost their children or other relatives in coalition airstrikes, and all refugees interviewed in camps had experienced traumatic flights, including seeing other refugees starve to death. Because of the aim of my interviews, I often did not delve into these traumatic events in detail because they were often not related to my questions, which focused on governance practices. I included few members of the religious and ethnic minorities who were most systematically persecuted—Shia Muslims, Christians, Yezidis, and others—among my interviewees because they had not experienced contact with the governance structures I investigated. When interviewees described such events, it was often on their own initiative. I avoided interviewing displaced people who had just arrived in a camp, focusing instead on those who had had the chance to settle there. The camps that I visited were managed by Kurdish authorities and international NGOs and were known to have relatively good living conditions. I clarified the aim of the interview and ensured interviewees that it was anonymous.

The aim of this study has partly been to describe the preconditions for, and the obstacles to, efficient governance for an extremist jihadi group. The results presented here may raise ethical questions in themselves. As Baele et al. note, research findings in political violence may "trigger violent dynamics or help contestable actors increase their efficiency and enhance their ability to reach their goals, without necessarily directly impacting either researchers or subjects."[16] In recent years, research on terror groups has diversified, often producing information on very concrete dynamics and structures that can be of direct use to terror groups. Some examples are radicalization processes, financing of terror groups, or counterinsurgency strategies. On the other end of the spectrum, research into these topics can be used by governments in ways that are beyond the researcher's control, for example as justification for military action. Funding for certain projects researching ISIS propaganda has been conditioned on sharing the research methods with the intelligence services.[17] Increasing demands that research should have impact can make these problems more prominent. Researchers cannot put constraints on their work to prevent their results from being exploited in unwanted ways in the future, but it is important to be aware of these mechanisms.

Notes

Chapter 1

1. In reality, the bomb was the self-detonation of the Islamic State's military leader in Iraq, who had been cornered by security forces and blew himself up rather than surrendering.

2. The International Organization of Migration estimated 375,354 displaced persons from Mosul and surrounding areas in June 2014 alone. See https://www.iom.int/files/live/sites/iom/files/Country/docs/IOM-Iraq-Mosul-Crisis-.Activity-Report-3.pdf. The military operation to retake Mosul that started in October 2016 displaced a further 400,000, putting the total number of people displaced from Mosul and the surrounding areas at more than 800,000.

3. The estimates of ISIS's territorial control vary, and depend on how one defines "control." 100,000 square kilometers is a rough estimate of the areas where ISIS was the dominant power, although for a short period.

4. Brynjar Lia, "Understanding Jihadi Proto-States," *Perspectives on Terrorism* 9, no. 4 (2015): 36, http://www.terrorismanalysts.com/pt/index.php/pot/article/view/441. The use of the terms jihadi-Salafi, jihadism, and jihadi is the object of debate. The political orientation of groups that are called jihadi-Salafi varies. In this book, the term is used to describe extreme groups that have anti-Western and internationalist outlook and draw on Salafi/Wahhabi religious tradition or discourse. Jihadism/Jihadis have in common with jihadi-Salafis the acceptance of violence as a legitimate means to fight the perceived occupation of Muslim countries worldwide by "infidel crusaders" and apostate local regimes. Importantly, in this book, the use of Jihad/Jihadi/Jihadism/Jihadi-Salafi must be seen as separate from the religious concept of jihad as a peaceful and spiritual struggle as it is used by many Muslims.

5. The Islamic State, July 2014, Audio message from Abu Bakr al-Baghdadi, https://ia902501.us.archive.org/2/items/hym3_22aw/english.pdf (English version).

6. The Islamic State, July 2014, Audio message from Abu Bakr al-Baghdadi, https://ia902501.us.archive.org/2/items/hym3_22aw/english.pdf (English version).

7. Stephen M. Walt, "ISIS as Revolutionary State," *Foreign Affairs*, November/December 2015, https://www.foreignaffairs.com/articles/middle-east/isis-revolutionary-state.

8   A few examples are Richard Barrett, *The Islamic State*, The Soufan Group (2014), http://www.soufangroup.com/the-islamic-state/. Patrick B. Johnston et al., *Foundations of the Islamic State*, RAND Corporation (2016), https://www.rand.org/pubs/research_reports/RR1192.html.

9   Fawaz A. Gerges, *ISIS: A History* (Princeton, NJ: Princeton University Press, 2017); Joby Warrick, *Black Flags: The Rise of ISIS* (New York: Anchor Books, 2015); Michael Weiss and Hassan Hassan, *ISIS. Inside the Army of Terror* (New York: Regan Arts, 2015); Patrick Cockburn, *The Rise of Islamic State: ISIS and the New Sunni Revolution* (London: Verso, 2015); Jessica Stern and J.M. Berger, *ISIS. The State of Terror* (London: William Collins, 2015).

10 Cole Bunzel, *From Paper State to Caliphate: The Ideology of the Islamic State*, The Brookings Institution (2015), https://www.brookings.edu/research/from-paper-state-to-caliphate-the-ideology-of-the-islamic-state/. Hassan Hassan, "The Sectarianism of the Islamic State: Ideological Roots and Political Context," June 13, 2016, https://carnegieendowment.org/2016/06/13/sectarianism-of-islamic-state-ideological-roots-and-political-context-pub–63746; Craig Whiteside, "A Pedigree of Terror: The Myth of the Ba'athist Influence in the Islamic State Movement," *Perspectives on Terrorism* 11, no. 3 (2017). Truls Hallberg Tønnessen, "Heirs of Zarqawi or Saddam? The relationship between al-Qaida in Iraq and the Islamic State," *Perspectives on Terrorism* 9, no. 4 (2015), http://www.terrorismanalysts.com/pt/index.php/pot/article/view/443/874; William McCants, *The ISIS Apocalypse: The History, Strategy, and Doomsday Vision of the Islamic State* (New York: St Martin's Press, 2015); Aaron Y. Zelin, "Picture or It Didn't Happen—A Snapshot of the Islamic State's Official Media Output," *Perspectives on Terrorism* 9, no. 4 (2015), http://www.jstor.org/stable/26297417; Tore Refslund Hamming, "The Al Qaeda–Islamic State Rivalry: Competition Yes, but No Competitive Escalation," *Terrorism and Political Violence* (2017), https://doi.org/10.1080/09546553.2017.1342634; Loretta Napoleoni, *The Islamist Phoenix: The Islamic State and the redrawing of the Middle East* (New York: Seven Stories Press, 2014). Cockburn, *The Rise of Islamic State: ISIS and the New Sunni Revolution*.

11 Jamie Hansen-Lewis and Jacob N. Shapiro, "Understanding the Daesh Economy," *Perspectives on Terrorism* 9, no. 4 (2015).

12 Efraim Benmelech and Esteban F. Klor, "What Explains the Flow of Foreign Fighters to ISIS?" *Terrorism and Political Violence*, no. October (2018), https://doi.org/10.1080/09546553.2018.1482214.

13 Aymenn Jawad Al-Tamimi, "The Evolution in Islamic State Administration: The Documentary Evidence," *Perspectives on Terrorism* 9, no. 4 (2015), http://www.terrorismanalysts.com/pt/index.php/pot/article/view/447.

14 Charlie Winter, "Apocalypse, later: a longitudinal study of the Islamic State brand," *Critical Studies in Media Communication* 35, no. 1 (2018), https://doi.org/10.1080/15295036.2017.1393094. Brandon Colas, "What Does Dabiq Do? ISIS Hermeneutics and Organizational Fractures within Dabiq Magazine," *Studies in Conflict & Terrorism* 40, no. 3 (2017), https://doi.org/10.1080/1057610X.2016.1184062.

15 Bart Schuurman, "Research on Terrorism, 2007–2016: A Review of Data, Methods, and Authorship," *Terrorism and Political Violence* (2018), https://doi.org/10.1080/09546553.2018.1439023.

16 Schuurman, "Research on Terrorism, 2007–2016: A Review of Data, Methods, and Authorship."

17 Yoram Schweitzer, Omer Einav (eds.), *The Islamic State: How Viable Is It?*, Institute for National Security Studies, Tel Aviv University (2016), http://www.inss.org.il/publication/the-islamic-state-how-viable-is-it/.

18 See for instance Charles C. Caris and Samuel Reynolds, *ISIS Governance in Syria* (Institute for the Study of War, 2014), http://www.understandingwar.org/sites/default/files/ISIS_Governance.pdf

19 One exception is Mara Revkin, who has produced articles and reports on various aspects of ISIS governance. See for instance Mara Revkin, *Does the Islamic State Have a "Social Contract"? Evidence from Iraq and Syria*, Yale University and University of Gothenburg (The Program on Governance and Local Development, 2016). Mara Revkin, "To Stay or Leave? Explaining Migration Decisions in Islamic State-Controlled Mosul" (Revkin, Mara Redlich. "Competitive Governance and Displacement Decisions Under Rebel Rule: Evidence from the Islamic State in Iraq." *Journal of Conflict Resolution* 65, no. 1 (January 2021): 46–80).

20 *Mosul: ISIL's Economic Engine*, RAND Corporation (September 13, 2017), https://www.rand.org/nsrd/projects/when-isil-comes-to-town/case-studies/mosul.html#population.

21 Nelson Kasfir, "Rebel Governance—Constructing a Field of Inquiry," in *Rebel Governance in Civil War*, ed. Ana Arjona, Nelson Kasfir, and Zachariah Mampilly (Cambridge: Cambridge University Press, 2015), 24.

22 Anthony Richards, "Conceptualizing Terrorism," *Studies in Conflict & Terrorism* 37, no. 3 (2014): 213, https://doi.org/10.1080/1057610X.2014.872023.

23 Kasfir, "Rebel Governance—Constructing a Field of Inquiry," 24.

24 Ana Arjona, Nelson Kasfir, and Zachariah Mampilly, eds., *Rebel Governance in Civil War* (New York: Cambridge University Press, 2015), 1.

25 Arjona, Kasfir, and Mampilly, *Rebel Governance in Civil War*, 6.

26 Angel Rabasa et al., *Ungoverned Territories. Understanding and Reducing Terrorism Risks* (Santa Monica, CA: RAND Corporation, 2007), Anne L. Clunan and A. Harold Trinkunas (eds.), *Ungoverned Spaces* (Stanford, CA: Stanford Security Studies, 2010).

27 Florian Weigand, "Investigating the Role of Legitimacy in the Political Order of Conflict-torn Spaces (working paper)," (2015): 7.

28 An interesting edited volume in this respect is Stathis N. Kalyvas, Ian Shapiro, and Tarek Masoud, eds., *Order, Conflict, and Violence* (Cambridge: Cambridge University Press, 2008).

29 See for instance Elisabeth J. Wood, *Insurgent Collective Action and Civil War in El Salvador* (New York: Cambridge University Press, 2003). Laia Balcells, *Rivalry and Revenge: the Politics of Violence during Civil War* (Cambridge: Cambridge University Press, 2017). Alexander B. Downes, *Targeting Civilians in War* (Ithaca, NY: Cornell University Press, 2008).

30 Some examples are Michael Jerome Wolff, "Building Criminal Authority: A Comparative Analysis of Drug Gangs in Rio de Janeiro and Recife," *Latin American Politics and Society* 57, no. 2 (2015), https://doi.org/10.1111/j.1548-2456.2015.00266.x; Jennifer Keister, "States within States: How Rebels Rule" (PhD University of California, 2011); Zachariah Cherian Mampilly, *Rebel Rulers. Insurgent Governance and Civilian Life during War*, 1st ed. (Cornell University Press, 2011), http://www.jstor.org/stable/10.7591/j.ctt7zfvj; Stathis N. Kalyvas, *The Logic of Violence in Civil War* (New York: Cambridge University Press, 2006); Jeremy M. Weinstein, *Inside Rebellion* (New York: Cambridge University Press, 2007), 47–9.

31 Mampilly, *Rebel Rulers. Insurgent Governance and Civilian Life during War*, 14.

32 For an extensive literature review on civilian agency in conflict, see for example Shane Joshua Barter, "Unarmed Forces: Civilian Strategy in Violent Conflicts," *Peace & Change* 37, no. 4 (2012), https://doi.org/10.1111/j.1468-0130.2012.00770.x.

33 See Bethany Lacina and Nils Petter Gleditsch, "Monitoring Trends in Global Combat: A New Dataset of Battle Deaths," *European Journal of Population/Revue Européenne de Démographie* 21, no. 2/3 (2005): 159–60, http://www.jstor.org/stable/20164300.

34 Lia, "Understanding Jihadi Proto-States," 38.

35 Nelly Lahoud, *The Jihadis' Path to Self-destruction* (London: Hurts & Company, 2010), 1–26.

36 For simplicity, I use the term "ISIS member" to describe militants, including foreign fighters and their families, and those who made a civilian pledge of allegiance to the group. The term "civilian" is used to describe inhabitants of Mosul who did not pledge allegiance to the group.

Chapter 2

1 Peter Chambers, "Abu Musab Al Zarqawi: The Making and Unmaking of an American Monster (in Baghdad)," *Alternatives: Global, Local, Political* 37, no. 1 (2012).

2 The Islamic State, July 2014, Audio message from Abu Bakr al-Baghdadi, https://ia902501.us.archive.org/2/items/hym3_22aw/english.pdf (English version)

3 During Saddam Hussein's regime, the Nujaifi family was involved in horse trades with Saddam's sons Uday and Qusay. While the family stayed out of politics during Saddam,

Athil's father and grandfather were members of parliament in the monarchist era. Athil's brother Osama has served two terms as vice president of Iraq.

4   Truls Hallberg Tønnessen, *The Origins of the Islamic State* (forthcoming).

5   Mara Revkin, *The Limits of Punishment. Transitional Justice and Violent Extremism* Institute for Integrated Transitions, United Nations University (2018), 66.

6   Tønnessen, "Heirs of Zarqawi or Saddam? The relationship between al-Qaida in Iraq and the Islamic State," 49.

7   Born Ahmad Al-Khalaylah.

8   Joas Wagemakers, "Invoking Zarqawi: Abu Muhammad al-Maqdisi's Jihad Deficit," *CTC Sentinel* 2, no. 6 (2009).

9   Truls Hallberg Tønnessen, "Al-Qaida in Iraq: The Rise, the Fall and the Comeback" (PhD thesis, University of Oslo, 2015), 259.

10 Mohammed M. Hafez, "Suicide Terrorism in Iraq: A Preliminary Assessment of the Quantitative Data and Documentary Evidence," *Studies in Conflict & Terrorism* 29, no. 6 (2006): 596, https://doi.org/10.1080/10576100600790878.

11 McCants, *The ISIS Apocalypse: The History, Strategy, and Doomsday Vision of the Islamic State*, 13.

12 Quoted in Guido Steinberg, "Jihadi-Salafism and the Shiʿis. Remarks about the Intellectual Roots of anti-Shiʿism," in *Global Salafism: Islam's New Religious Movement*, ed. Roel Meijer (London: Hurst & Company, 2009), 123.

13 McCants, *The ISIS Apocalypse: The History, Strategy, and Doomsday Vision of the Islamic State*, 14.

14 Wagemakers, "Invoking Zarqawi: Abu Muhammad al-Maqdisi's Jihad Deficit." J.C. Brisard and D. Martinez, *Zarqawi: The New Face of Al-Qaeda* (Polity, 2005), 129. https://books.google.no/books?id=F6SNDMjJW4YC.

15 Muhammad Al-Ubaydi et al., *The Group That Calls Itself a State: Understanding the Evolution and Challenges of the Islamic State*, Combatting Terrorism Center (Westpoint, 2014), 11, https://ctc.usma.edu/the-group-that-calls-itself-a-state-understanding-the-evolution-and-challenges-of-the-islamic-state/.

16 Truls Hallberg Tønnessen, "The Group that wanted to be a State: The 'Rebel Governance' of the Islamic State," in *Islamists and the Politics of the Arab Uprisings. Governance, Pluralisation and Contention*, ed. Hendrik Kraetzschmar and Paola Rivetti (Edinburgh: Edinburgh University Press, 2018), 55.

17 The extent of AQI's role in Fallujah is questionable, even though the Americans focused on AQI in justifying their siege on the city. See for example Roel Meijer, "'Defending our Honor': Authenticity and the Framing of Resistance in the Iraqi Sunni Town of Falluja," *Etnofoor* 17, no. 1/2 (2004), http://www.jstor.org/stable/25758067.

18 Tønnessen, "The Group that wanted to be a State: The 'Rebel Governance' of the Islamic State," 55–6.

19 Al-Ubaydi et al., *The Group That Calls Itself a State: Understanding the Evolution and Challenges of the Islamic State*, 14.

20 Al-Tamimi, "The Evolution in Islamic State Administration: The Documentary Evidence," 119.

21 As quoted in Lahoud, *The Jihadis' Path to Self-destruction*, 221.

22 Tønnessen, "The Group that wanted to be a State: The 'Rebel Governance' of the Islamic State," 60.

23 Phebe Marr and Ibrahim Al-Marashi, *The Modern History of Iraq*, 4th ed. (Boulder: Westview Press, 2017), 242.

24 For a discussion of the effect of the various components of the "surge," see Stephen Biddle, Jeffrey A. Friedman, and Jacob N. Shapiro, "Testing the Surge: Why Did Violence Decline in Iraq in 2007?" *International Security* 37, no. 1 (2012), https://doi.org/10.1162/ISEC_a_00087.

25 *Unmaking Iraq: A Constitutional Process Gone Awry*, International Crisis Group (September 26, 2005), https://www.crisisgroup.org/middle-east-north-africa/gulf-and-arabian-peninsula/iraq/unmaking-iraq-constitutional-process-gone-awry.

26 See for example Tallha Abdulrazaq and Gareth Stansfield, "The Enemy Within: ISIS and the Conquest of Mosul," *The Middle East Journal* 70, no. 4 (2016): 526–7.

27 See for instance Stern and Berger, *ISIS. The State of Terror*, 44.

28 Truls Hallberg Tønnessen, "Motstand og politikk i Irak," *Babylon* 8, no. 1 (2010): 24.

29 Myriam Benraad, "Iraq's Enduring al-Qaeda Challenge," *The Washington Institute*, November 18, 2009, https://www.washingtoninstitute.org/policy-analysis/view/iraqs-enduring-al-qaeda-challenge.

30 Interview conducted in Erbil, 01.11.19.

31 Marr and Al-Marashi, *The Modern History of Iraq*, 284.

32 "Another Iraq candidate killed ahead of provincial polls," *The Daily Star Lebanon*, June 14, 2013, http://www.dailystar.com.lb/News/Middle-East/2013/Jun-14/220395-gunmen-kill-election-candidate-in-iraq.ashx#axzz2X550kr6J.

33 "maṣdar yuʾakkid hurūb 600 najīl min sijn abū ghrayb baynahum akhṭar al-irhābīn ('Source confirms the escape of 600 prisoners from Abu Ghraib prison, among them dangerous terrorists')," *Almada Press*, July 22, 2013, http://www.almadapress.com/ar/news/15489/مصدر-يؤكد-هروب-600-نزيل-من-سجن-أبو; Aki Peritz, "The Great Iraqi Jail Break," June 26, 2014, https://foreignpolicy.com/2014/06/26/the-great-iraqi-jail-break/.

34 Michael Knights, "Al-Qaʿida in Iraq: Lessons from the Mosul Security Operation," *CTC Sentinel* 1, no. 7 (2008), https://ctc.usma.edu/al-qaida-in-iraq-lessons-from-the-mosul-security-operation/.

35 Aaron Y. Zelin, *The War between ISIS and al-Qaeda for Supremacy of the Global Jihadist Movement*, The Washington Institute for Near East Policy (2014), 4, http://www.washingtoninstitute.org/uploads/Documents/pubs/ResearchNote_20_Zelin.pdf

36 *Iraq: ISIS executed hundreds of prison inmates* Human Rights Watch (October 30, 2014), https://www.hrw.org/news/2014/10/30/iraq-isis-executed-hundreds-prison-inmates.

37 Audio message by Abu Muhammad al-Adnani, June 2014, "hādhā wa'd allah" ("This is God's Promise"), https://azelin.files.wordpress.com/2014/06/shaykh-abc5ab-mue1b8a5ammad-al-e28098adnc481nc4ab-al-shc481mc4ab-22this-is-the-promise-of-god22.mp3

38 Truls Hallberg Tønnessen, "Training on a Battlefield: Iraq as a Training Ground for Global Jihadis," *Terrorism and Political Violence* 20, no. 4 (2008/09/18 2008): 552, https://doi.org/10.1080/09546550802257242.

39 See Nelly Lahoud's analysis of AQI's development in Al-Ubaydi et al., *The Group That Calls Itself a State: Understanding the Evolution and Challenges of the Islamic State*, 11–12. As Lahoud notes, al-Baghdadi made his famous first speech in Mosul's Nouri mosque, which was built by Nour al-Din.

40 Sarah D. Shields, "Mosul Questions: Economy, Identity and Annexation," in *The Creation of Iraq, 1914–1921*, ed. R. S. Simon, E. H. Tejirian, and G. Sick (Columbia University Press, 2004), 50.

41 Dina Rizk Khoury, "Political Relations Between City and State in the Middle East, 1700–1850," in *The Urban Social History of the Middle East, 1750–1950*, ed. Peter Sluglett (New York: Syracuse University Press, 2008), 78.

42 Sarah D. Shields, *Mosul before Iraq: Like Bees Making Five-Sided Cells* (State University of New York Press, 2000), 189. https://books.google.no/books?id=3CO8Z1QWyCQC.

43 Sarah D. Shields, Shields, "Mosul Questions: Economy, Identity and Annexation," 55–7.

44 Andrea Plebani, "Ninawa Province: Al-Qa'ida's Remaining Stronghold," *CTC Sentinel* 3, no. 1 (2010): 21, https://ctc.usma.edu/ninawa-province-al-qaidas-remaining-stronghold/.

45 *Iraq's Provincial Elections: The Stakes*, International Crisis Group (January 27, 2009), https://d2071andvip0wj.cloudfront.net/82-iraq-s-provincial-elections-the-stakes.pdf.

46 Knights, "Al-Qa'ida in Iraq: Lessons from the Mosul Security Operation."

47 Joseph Sassoon, *Saddam Hussein's Ba'th party: inside an authoritarian regime* (New York: Cambridge University Press, 2012), 79.

48 Samuel Helfont, "Saddam and the Islamists: The Ba'thist Regime's Instrumentalization of Religion in Foreign Affairs," *The Middle East Journal* 68, no. 3 (2014): 353, https://doi.org/10.3751/68.3.11.

49 Interview conducted 01.11.2019 in Erbil.

50 Aymenn Jawad Al-Tamimi, "Looking at Violence in Iraq," 2012, http://www.aymennjawad.org/12158/looking-at-violence-in-iraq.

51 Interview conducted 30.10.2019 in Erbil.

52 "Making Themselves at Home. Al Qaeda Ups Mafia-Style Extortion in Mosul," *Niqash*, November 7, 2013, http://www.niqash.org/en/articles/politics/3321/.

53 Plebani, "Ninawa Province: Al-Qa'ida's Remaining Stronghold," 21.

54 "In northern Iraqi city, al-Qaeda gathers strength," *Associated Press*, June 20, 2013.

55 Numbers are from Knights, "Al-Qa`ida in Iraq: Lessons from the Mosul Security Operation."

56 The proliferation of weapons in general, even under Saddam, became clear after 2003. After the fall of the regime, the US administration did no real effort to clear out the massive arsenals around the country. See for instance Charles Tripp, *The Power and the People: Paths of Resistance in the Middle East* (Cambridge: Cambridge University Press, 2013), 45.

57 Benraad, "Iraq's Enduring al-Qaeda Challenge."

58 Reports of the number of fighters involved in the operation vary from a few hundred to around 1,000.

59 The Prophet Muhammad issued a so-called *wathiqat al-madina* to govern the city of Medina in 622. Almost identical city documents were issued in other cities occupied by ISIS.

60 For an in-depth analysis of ISIS's citizenship regime, see Mathilde Becker Aarseth. "Citizenship under the Islamic State," in *Routledge Handbook of Citizenship in the Middle East*, ed. Roel Meijer, James Sater, and Zahra Babar (London: Routledge, 2021).

61 See Aymenn Jawad al-Tamimi (2015). "Unseen Islamic State Pamphlet on Slavery." www.aymennjawad.org/2015/12/unseen-islamic-state-pamphlet-on-slavery. Tamimi's translation.

62 Ibid.

63 Specimen K and L in AJTA. www.aymennjawad.org/17879/the-archivist-unseen-islamic-state-fatwas-on.

64 See for instance Peter Nicolaus & Serkan Yuce (2017). "Sex-Slavery: One Aspect of the Yezidi Genocide." *Iran and the Caucasus* (21); Eda Erdener (2017). "The Ways of Coping with Post-War Trauma of Yezidi Refugee Women in Turkey." *Women's Studies International Forum* 65.

65 See ultimatum for Christians in Mosul, The Islamic State, July 17, 2014, Specimen S in AJTA, http://www.aymennjawad.org/2015/01/archive-of-islamic-state-administrative-documents. Historically, the *jiziya* was also imposed on Jews, but no Jews resided in the Iraqi areas taken over by ISIS.

66 Interview with doctor K in a Mosul hospital, conducted in Erbil 29.10.19.

67 I borrow this distinction from Weigand, "Investigating the Role of Legitimacy in the Political Order of Conflict-torn Spaces (working paper)."

68 Arjona, Kasfir, and Mampilly, *Rebel Governance in Civil War*, 3.

69 Maria J. Stephan, "Civil Resistance vs. ISIS," *Journal of Resistance Studies* 1, no. 2 (2015); Revkin, *Does the Islamic State Have a "Social Contract"? Evidence from Iraq and Syria*, 27; Julia Taleb, "From Assad to ISIS, a tale of Syrian resistance," *Waging Non-Violence*, 2014, https://wagingnonviolence.org/feature/assad-isis-tale-resistance/.

70 Thomas Hegghammer, "Jihadi-Salafis or Revolutionaries? On Religion and Politics in the Study of Militant Islamism," in *Global Salafism: Islam's New Religious Movement*, ed. Roel Meijer (London: Hurst & Company, 2009), 256.

71 Joana Westphal, "Violence in the name of god? A framing processes approach to the Islamic State in Iraq and Syria," *Social Movement Studies* 17, no. 1 (2017): 30, https://doi.org/10.1080/14742837.2017.1381594, http://dx.doi.org/10.1080/14742837.2017.1381594.

72 The founder of the Muslim Brotherhood in Egypt Hassan al-Banna said that Muslims should unite "under one leader," undivided by national borders. Bunzel, *From Paper State to Caliphate: The Ideology of the Islamic State*.

73 Lia, "Understanding Jihadi Proto-States."

74 Audio message by Abu Muhammad al-Adnani, June 2014, "hādhā waʿd allah" ("This Is God's Promise"), https://azelin.files.wordpress.com/2014/06/shaykh-abc5ab-mue1b8a5ammad-al-e28098adnc481nc4ab-al-shc481mc4ab-22this-is-the-promise-of-god22.mp3

75 McCants, *The ISIS Apocalypse: The History, Strategy, and Doomsday Vision of the Islamic State*, 146.

76 Audio message by Abu Muhammad al-Adnani, June 2014, "hādhā waʿd allah" ("This Is God's Promise"), https://azelin.files.wordpress.com/2014/06/shaykh-abc5ab-mue1b8a5ammad-al-e28098adnc481nc4ab-al-shc481mc4ab-22this-is-the-promise-of-god22.mp3

77 Patrick B. Johnston et al., *Foundations of the Islamic State—Management, Money and Terror in Iraq, 2005–2010*, Rand Corporation (Santa Monica, California, 2016), 101–2.

78 Tønnessen, "The Group that wanted to be a State: The 'Rebel Governance' of the Islamic State," 60.

79 Jacob N. Shapiro, "A Predictable Failure: The Political Economy of the Decline of the Islamic State," *CTC Sentinel* 9, no. 9 (2016): 28, https://ctc.usma.edu/posts/a-predictable-failure-the-political-economy-of-the-decline-of-the-islamic-state., Hansen-Lewis and Shapiro, "Understanding the Daesh Economy."

80 Al-Tamimi, "The Evolution in Islamic State Administration: The Documentary Evidence," 118.

81 Andrew F. March and Mara Revkin, "Caliphate of Law," *Foreign Affairs*, April 15, 2015, http://www.foreignaffairs.com/articles/143679/andrew-f-march-and-mara-revkin/caliphate-of-law.

Chapter 3

1 The Islamic State textbook, "Al-siyāsa al-sharʿiyya," 2015/2016, https://azelin.files.wordpress.com/2015/10/the-islamic-state-sharc4abah-politics.pdf, 68.

2 Interviewed 27.04.18 in Mosul.

3 Jesse S. G. Wozniak, "We Are Going to Prove We Are a Civil and Developed Country: The Cultural Performance of Police Legitimacy and Empire in the Iraqi State," *The British Journal of Criminology* 57, no. 4 (2017): 919, https://doi.org/10.1093/bjc/azw046, Mona Mahmood, "Life in Mosul one year on: 'ISIS with all its brutality is more honest than the Shia government,'" *The Guardian*, June 10, 2015, https://www.theguardian.com/world/2015/jun/10/mosul-residents-one-year-on-isis-brutality; Caris and Reynolds, *ISIS Governance in Syria*; Mariam Karouny, "In Raqqa, ISIL governs with fear and efficiency," *The National*, September 4, 2014, https://www.thenational.ae/world/in-raqqa-isil-governs-with-fear-and-efficiency-1.239964; Charles R. Lister, *Profiling the Islamic State*, Brookings Doha Center (Doha, Qatar, 2014), https://www.brookings.edu/wp-content/uploads/2014/12/en_web_lister.pdf.

4 Names and contextual information are removed for the interviewees' own security.

5 Administrative documents are obtained from Aymenn Jawad Al-Tamimi's extensive archive of leaked ISIS documents (from here on shortened to AJTA), my own interviewees, and other trusted online sources. Some of the documents pertaining to policing and education are obtained from George Washington University's project on the ISIS files. Places and dates of origin are reported when these are included in documents. I have also chosen to include several administrative documents from Syrian areas under ISIS control because, according to the group's files, structures and guidelines should be universally enforced in all its provinces. Therefore, many documents are not assigned to a specific *wilāya* or province. This is not to say that the implementation of the group's blueprint for governance was in fact similar in all its provinces, but this was the image it tried to project in its propaganda. Since the provinces in Iraq and Syria were the core of ISIS governance efforts, documents that specifically refer to areas outside of these are not included, although various forms of ISIS police forces have been set up in Libya and to a lesser extent Sinai, Egypt.

6 The interviewees are from sixteen different neighborhoods in eastern and western Mosul and experienced between four months and three years of ISIS rule. Of the main interviewees, nineteen were interviewed in Mosul, and had stayed in Mosul the whole duration of ISIS rule; thirty were interviewed in Iraqi camps for internally displaced people. Interviews for this chapter were conducted in Debaga, Khazer and Hasan Sham IDP camps in territories controlled by the Kurdish Regional Government.

7 For an outline of ISIS legal systems see Mara Revkin, *The legal foundations of the Islamic State*, The Brookings Institutions (2016).

8 O'Driscoll, Dylan. *Past Issues*. Middle East Research Institute, 2016, 16–19, *The Future of Mosul: Before, During, and After the Liberation*.

9 The Islamic State, June 2014, "wathīqat al-madīna, wilāyat nīnawa," https://azelin.files.wordpress.com/2014/06/islamic-state-of-iraq-and-al-shc481m-charter-of-the-city.pdf. ISIS has issued such city documents in Mosul, Tikrit and Hit in Iraq, al-Raqqa in Syria and Sirte in Libya.

10 The Islamic State textbook, "Al-siyāsa al-shar'iyya," 2015/2016, https://azelin.files.wordpress.com/2015/10/the-islamic-state-sharc4abah-politics.pdf, 67

11 The Islamic State, "bayān al-ḥudūd," Aleppo, 2014, https://justpaste.it/hududlistaleppo

12 The Islamic State textbook, "Al-siyāsa al-shar'iyya," 2015/2016, https://azelin.files.wordpress.com/2015/10/the-islamic-state-sharc4abah-politics.pdf, 68

13 The Islamic State, "rasā'il min arḍ al-malāḥim #12," 2013, https://jihadology.net/2013/11/23/al-furqan-media-presents-a-new-video-message-from-the-islamic-state-of-iraq-and-al-sham-messages-from-the-land-of-epic-battles-12/

14 The breadth of powers granted to the *ḥisba* by ISIS, with the right to intervene in private homes, is unusual. The term *ḥisba* is not mentioned in the Quran, but has been used by, among others, the Islamic scholar Abu Al-Hasan Al-Mawardi (974–1058), Abu Hamid Al-Ghazali and Taqi Ad-Din Ahmad Ibn Taymiyya (1263–1328). It has been associated primarily with the personal duty of every Muslim to "promote good and forbid evil," but also "the function of the person who is effectively entrusted in a town with the application of this rule in the supervision of moral behaviour and more particularly of the markets": M. Talbi, "HISBA," in *Encyclopaedia of Islam, Second Edition*, Encyclopaedia of Islam (Brill).

15 The Islamic State video, Ninawa 2015, "Shurtat al-murūr fi wilāyat Nīnawā," https://jihadology.net/2015/08/30/new-video-message-from-the-islamic-state-the-traffic-police-in-wilayat-ninawa/

16 See Anne Speckhard and Ahmet S. Yayla, "The ISIS Emni: The Origins and Inner Workings of ISIS's Intelligence Apparatus," *Perspectives on Terrorism* 11, no. 1 (2017), http://www.terrorismanalysts.com/pt/index.php/pot/article/view/573%J.Perspectives.on.Terrorism.

17 For an interesting analysis of an unofficial document on "Women in the Islamic State," see Charlie Winter, "Women of The Islamic State: Beyond the Rumor Mill," https://jihadology.net/2015/03/31/guest-post-women-of-the-islamic-state-beyond-the-rumor-mill/

18 Specimen O in AJTA, Mosul, July 2015, http://www.aymennjawad.org/17757/the-archivist-26-unseen-islamic-state

19 Reportedly after experiencing "overlapping of the assignments of some of the sectors of *al-ḥisba* in the *wilāyas* (provinces) which has led to bad planning and work," the group clarified the structure of *al-ḥisba* in 2014. Aymenn Jawad Al-Tamimi, "The Internal Structure of the Islamic State's Hisba Apparatus," 2018, http://www.aymennjawad.org/21246/the-internal-structure-of-the-islamic-state-hisba

20 The Islamic State, "al-tawjīhāt wal-taʿmīmāt al-ʿāmma," https://ctc.usma.edu/app/uploads/2018/08/General-Guidance-and-Instructions-Arabic.pdf

21 Zelin, "Picture or It Didn't Happen—A Snapshot of the Islamic State's Official Media Output," 90.

22 See "lāʾiḥat al-ʿuqūbāt al-taʿzīriyya," Mosul 2014, specimen 13S in AJTA, http://www.aymennjawad.org/2016/01/archive-of-islamic-state-administrative-documents-1.

23 The Islamic State video, Fallujah, "taqrīr murʾī ʿan dawr rijāl al-ḥisba fī ṣiānat al-mujtamaʿ al-muslim," "https://azelin.files.wordpress.com/2015/01/the-islamic-state-22men-of-the-hisbah-1-wilc481yat-al-fallc5abjah22.mp4

24 Specimen 19F in AJTA, http://www.aymennjawad.org/2016/01/archive-of-islamic-state-administrative-documents-1; Specimen 2Z in AJTA, Ninawa July 2014, http://www.aymennjawad.org/2015/01/archive-of-islamic-state-administrative-documents; Specimen 3T in AJTA, http://www.aymennjawad.org/2015/01/archive-of-islamic-state-administrative-documents; See "hurmat al-talaffuẓ bi yā Muhammad," February 2016, specimen 18T in AJTA, http://www.aymennjawad.org/2016/01/archive-of-islamic-state-administrative-documents-1

25 The Islamic State video, Fallujah, "taqrīr marʾī ʿan dawr rijāl al-ḥisba fī ṣiyānat al-mujtamaʿ al-muslim," https://azelin.files.wordpress.com/2015/01/the-islamic-state-22men-of-the-hisbah-1-wilc481yat-al-fallc5abjah22.mp4

26 Benraad, "Iraq's Enduring al-Qaeda Challenge."

27 Gary Langer, "Dramatic Advances Sweep Iraq, Boosting Support for Democracy," 2009, https://abcnews.go.com/PollingUnit/story?id=7058272&page=1. This series of surveys, "Iraq: Where Things Stand," was the result of a cooperation between several media networks, and conducted by Oxford Research International, D2 systems of Vienna, and KA Research.

28 Nagorski, "Iraq: Where Things Stand."

29 Revkin, *The Limits of Punishment. Transitional Justice and Violent Extremism* 57.

30 *Middle East 2015. Current and Future Challenges* (Zogby Research Services 2015), https://static1.squarespace.com/static/52750dd3e4b08c252c723404/t/5667940fbfe8731 ec365efa7/1449628687692/Sir+Bani+Yas+2015+Letter+FINAL.pdf.

31 Muʾassasat al-Furqān lil-intāj al-iʿlāmī, "khayr umma," https://jihadology. net/2014/05/28/al-furqan-media-presents-a-new-video-message-from-the-islamic-state-of-iraq-and-al-sham-for-the-good-of-the-ummah/ The Islamic State, "rasāʾil min arḍ al-malāḥim #12," 2013, https://jihadology.net/2013/11/23/al-furqan-media-presents-a-new-video-message-from-the-islamic-state-of-iraq-and-al-sham-messages-from-the-land-of-epic-battles-12/

32 Tom R. Tyler, "Enhancing Police Legitimacy," *The ANNALS of the American Academy of Political and Social Science* 593, no. 1 (2004): 89, https://doi.org/10.1177/0002716203262627.

33 Interview with man from Mosul, conducted in Mosul 27.04.2018.

34 Specimens 33A and 33C in AJTA, http://www.aymennjawad.org/2016/09/archive-of-islamic-state-administrative-documents-2; specimen 24O in AJTA, http://www.aymennjawad.org/2016/09/archive-of-islamic-state-administrative-documents-2

35 Interview with man from Mosul, conducted in Mosul 27.04.2018.

36 Interview with man from Mosul, conducted in Mosul 20.04.2018.

37 See for instance Stephen Carter and Kate Clark, *No Shortcut to Stability. Justice, Politics and Insurgency in Afghanistan* (Chatham House, 2010), https://www.chathamhouse.org/sites/default/files/public/Research/Asia/1210pr_afghanjustice.pdf.

38 See for instance The Islamic State, "rasāʾil min arḍ al-malāḥim #12," 2013, https://jihadology.net/2013/11/23/al-furqan-media-presents-a-new-video-message-from-the-islamic-state-of-iraq-and-al-sham-messages-from-the-land-of-epic-battles-12/

39 The Islamic State, "milaff sijn al-amniyya," Mosul 2014, Specimen 38A-D in AJTA, http://www.aymennjawad.org/2016/09/archive-of-islamic-state-administrative-documents-2

40 Rukmini Callimachi, "The Case of the Purloined Poultry: How ISIS Prosecuted Petty Crime," *The New York Times*, July 1, 2018, https://www.nytimes.com/2018/07/01/world/middleeast/islamic-state-iraq.html. Some have criticized that the documents were taken by Callimachi out of Iraq in the heat of the battle, and there are important and valid objections to removing the documents out of the country. However, through a partnership with George Washington University and others, an important work has been undertaken to digitize, translate and analyze the 15,000 pages of documents that were found. The credibility of the files has been externally verified by multiple sources. The files that can safely be published will gradually be made available to the public in redacted form, in cooperation with Iraqi partners to address ethical questions regarding the files. The originals have been returned to Iraqi authorities.

41 The Islamic State, George Washington University repository, file no. 00_000074AR

42 The Islamic State, George Washington University repository, file no. 02_000263AR

43 The Islamic State, George Washington University repository, file no. 36_001651_25AR

44 The Islamic State, George Washington University repository, file no. 02_000258AR

45 Interview with man in Mosul, conducted in Mosul 21.04.2018.

46 Interview with man in Nour neighborhood, Mosul. Conducted in Mosul 27.04.2018.

47 The Islamic State textbook, "Al-siāsa al-shar'iyya," 2015/2016, https://azelin.files.wordpress.com/2015/10/the-islamic-state-sharc4abah-politics.pdf, 37

48 The Islamic State, Al-Furqan Media, speech released December 26, 2015. https://ia801500.us.archive.org/33/items/ftrbso; The Islamic State, Al-Furqan Media, speech released July 21, 2012. https://jihadology.net/2012/07/23/al-furqan-media-presents-a-new-audio-message-from-the-islamic-state-of-iraqs-shaykh-abu-bakr-al-%E1%B8%A5ussayni-al-qurayshi-al-baghdadi-but-god-will-not-allow-except-that-his-light-should-be/; Aki Peritz, "The Great Iraqi Jail Break," *Foreign Policy*, June 26, 2014, https://foreignpolicy.com/2014/06/26/the-great-iraqi-jail-break/. Anne Speckhard and Ahmet S. Yayla, *Eyewitness Accounts from Recent Defectors from Islamic State: Why They Joined, What They Saw, Why They Quit*, vol. 9, 2015, 106. http://www.terrorismanalysts.com/pt/index.php/pot/article/view/475.

49 Islamic State, "wathīqat al-madīina,wilāyat Ninawa," issued June 2014, https://azelin.files.wordpress.com/2014/06/islamic-state-of-iraq-and-al-shc481m-charter-of-the-city.pdf

50 For an example of a repentance document issued by ISIS in Iraq in July 2016, specimen 32A in AJTA, http://www.aymennjawad.org/2016/09/archive-of-islamic-state-administrative-documents-2; Repentance cards from 2014, specimen 12L in AJTA, http://www.aymennjawad.org/2016/01/archive-of-islamic-state-administrative-documents-1

51 Aymenn Jawad Al-Tamimi, "Repentance: Financial Income for the Islamic State," *Aymenn Jawad Al-Tamimi Blog*, September 28, 2015, http://www.aymennjawad.org/2015/09/repentance-financial-income-for-the-islamic-state

52 See specimen 18H in AJTA, http://www.aymennjawad.org/2016/01/archive-of-islamic-state-administrative-documents-1; The Islamic State, "shurūṭ al-tawba," Ninawa, Specimen 33U in AJTA, http://www.aymennjawad.org/2016/09/archive-of-islamic-state-administrative-documents-2

53 The Islamic State, "milaff sijn al-amniyya," July 2014, specimen 38C in AJTA, http://www.aymennjawad.org/2016/09/archive-of-islamic-state-administrative-documents-2

54 "Islamic State killed 300 former policemen south of Mosul, HRW Says," *Reuters*, November 16, 2016, https://www.reuters.com/article/us-mideast-crisis-iraq-grave-idUSKBN13C0ML; Babb Carla, "UN: Fresh Reports of Extrajudicial Killings by Islamic

State," *VOA News*, October 25, 2016, https://www.voanews.com/a/iraqis-gain-ground-around-mosul-as-islamic-state-fight-intensifies/3564437.html; Caroline Mortimer, "Isis executes 300 Iraqi army troops and civilian activists in Mosul after US-led air strikes on city," *The Independent*, February 8, 2016, https://www.independent.co.uk/news/world/middle-east/isis-executes-300-iraqi-army-troops-and-civilian-activists-in-mosul-after-us-led-air-strikes-on-city-a6861311.html.

55 Reuters, "Islamic State put up to 12,000 people in mass graves, U.N. says" https://www.nbcnews.com/news/world/islamic-state-put-12-000-people-mass-graves-u-n-n933421, November 7, 2018

56 Interview with man in Mosul, 27.04.2018.

57 Suadad Al-Salhy, "How Iraq's 'ghost soldiers' helped ISIL," *Al-Jazeera*, December 10, 2014, https://www.aljazeera.com/news/middleeast/2014/12/how-iraq-ghost-soldiers-helped-isil-2014121072749979252.html.

58 Transparency International, Corruption perceptions index 2017, https://www.transparency.org/news/feature/corruption_perceptions_index_2017

59 The governor of Mosul until June 2014, Atheel Al-Nujaifi, repeated this claim in my interview with him on November 1, 2016 in Erbil. Transparency International has also made this claim, see Katherine Dixon, "Corruption Helped ISIS Take Mosul. Victory Cannot Last While It Persists," *Defense One*, March 10, 2017, https://www.defenseone.com/ideas/2017/03/corruption-helped-isis-take-mosul-victory-cannot-last-while-it-persists/136065/.

60 The Islamic State, June 2015, Dabiq no 10, 33.

61 Aymenn Jawad Al-Tamimi, Twitter, https://twitter.com/ajaltamimi/status/442777401592774656

62 Aymenn Jawad Al-Tamimi, "The Archivist: The Islamic State's Security Apparatus Structure in the Provinces," *Jihadology*, August 2, 2017, https://jihadology.net/2017/08/02/the-archivist-the-islamic-states-security-apparatus-structure-in-the-provinces/.

63 See for example Zaid Al-Ali, *The Struggle for Iraq's Future. How Corruption, Incompetence and Sectarianism Have Undermined Democracy* (New Haven: Yale University Press, 2014), http://www.jstor.org/stable/j.ctt5vksw1.

64 A photo report documenting the lashing of a cigarette smuggler in Salah al-Din: https://web.archive.org/web/20151213044621/http://justpaste.it/pj9y; Video showing burning cigarettes in Al-Raqqa, Syria: Muʾassasat al-Furqān lil-intāj al-iʿalāmī, "khayr umma," https://jihadology.net/2014/05/28/al-furqan-media-presents-a-new-video-message-from-the-islamic-state-of-iraq-and-al-sham-for-the-good-of-the-ummah/

65 Interview with man from Mosul, conducted in Mosul 15.05.18.

66 The Islamic State, *dīwān al-qaḍāʾ wal-shurta al-islamiyya fi al-mosul*. Aymenn Jawad Al-Tamimi, "The Archivist: Unseen Islamic State Regulations for the Mosul

Operations," *Jihadology*, December 31, 2016, https://jihadology.net/2016/12/31/the-archivist-unseen-islamic-state-regulations-for-the-mosul-operations/.

67 Interview with man from Mosul, conducted in Mosul 27.04.2018.

68 Interview with man from Mosul, conducted in Khazer camp, 17.04.2018.

69 Interview with man from Mosul, conducted in Hassan Sham camp, 15.04.2018.

70 Specimen 21B in AJTA, http://www.aymennjawad.org/2016/01/archive-of-islamic-state-administrative-documents-1

71 Similar claims have been made in media reports, see for instance Samya Kullab, "Someone is smuggling desperate civilians out of Mosul. It might be ISIS," *Foreign Policy*, December 7, 2016, https://foreignpolicy.com/2016/12/07/someone-is-smuggling-desperate-civilians-out-of-mosul-it-might-be-isis/.

72 "ISIS Resorts to Selling Drugs in Iraq, Syria for Funding," *Asharq al-Awsat*, April 26, 2017, https://eng-archive.aawsat.com/theaawsat/news-middle-east/isis-resorts-selling-drugs-iraq-syria-funding.

73 Colin P. Clarke, "ISIS is so desperate it's turning to the drug trade," *The Rand Blog*, July 24, 2017, https://www.rand.org/blog/2017/07/isis-is-so-desperate-its-turning-to-the-drug-trade.html.

74 See for example Robert M. Perito, "Police in Armed Conflict," in *The SAGE Handbook of Global Policing*, ed. B. Bradford et al. (London: SAGE Publications, 2016), 444; Rolando Ochoa, "Local Dynamics of a Global Phenomenon: Policing Organized Crime," in *The SAGE Handbook of Global Policing*, ed. B. Bradford et al. (London: SAGE Publications, 2016), 468; Gretchen Peters, "The Afghan Insurgency and Organized Crime," in *The Rule of Law in Afghanistan: Missing in Inaction*, ed. Whit Mason (Cambridge: Cambridge University Press, 2011), 104.

75 Peter T. Underwood, "Pirates, Vikings and Teutonic Knights," in *Pirates, Terrorists, and Warlords: The History, Influence, and Future of Armed Groups Around the World*, ed. J.H. Norwitz (Skyhorse Publishing, 2009), 17.

76 Santiago Ballina, "The crime–terror continuum revisited: a model for the study of hybrid criminal organisations," *Journal of Policing, Intelligence and Counter Terrorism* 6, no. 2 (2011): 130, https://doi.org/10.1080/18335330.2011.605200.

77 Looney, "Reconstruction and Peacebuilding under Extreme Adversity: The Problem of Pervasive Corruption in Iraq," 427.

78 March and Revkin, "Caliphate of Law."

79 The Islamic State, "The Structure of the Khilafa," July 2016, https://videopress.com/v/tv16QF5r

80 See for instance Amre Sarhan, "Source: ISIS throws 5 homosexuals from high building in Mosul," *Iraqi News*, April 21, 2016, https://www.iraqinews.com/iraq-war/source-isis-

throws-5-homosexuals-high-building-mosul/; Mara Revkin, "Law and Lawfare in the Islamic State," *Lawfare Blog*, August 5, 2016.

81 Interview with man from Mosul, conducted in Mosul 27.04.2018.

82 Interview with man from Mosul, conducted in Mosul 27.04.2018

83 See for instance March and Revkin, "Caliphate of Law."

84 Mampilly, "Performing the Nation-State: Rebel Governance and Symbolic Processes," 76.

85 Arjona, "Civilian Cooperation and Non-Cooperation with Non-State Armed Groups: The Centrality of Obedience and Resistance," 765–6.

86 Ideologically committed combatants who care about the group's long-term goals can also be tempted to steal, in what Arjona calls a free-riding problem for rebel groups. Ana Arjona, *Rebelocracy—Social Order in the Colombian Civil War* (Cambridge: Cambridge University Press, 2016), 51.

87 Revkin, *Does the Islamic State Have a "Social Contract"? Evidence from Iraq and Syria*, 19.

88 Interview with man from Mosul, conducted in Mosul 27.04.2018.

89 See for instance Kasfir, "Rebel Governance—Constructing a Field of Inquiry," 39.

90 Arjona, *Rebelocracy—Social Order in the Colombian Civil War*, 48.

91 Weinstein, *Inside Rebellion*, 168.

92 Fransisco Gutiérrez-Sanín, "Organization and Governance: The Evolution of Urban Militias in Medellín, Colombia," in *Rebel Governance in Civil War*, ed. Ana Arjona, Nelson Kasfir, and Zachariah Mampilly (New York: Cambridge University Press, 2015), 248.

93 Douglass C. North and Barry R. Weingast, "Constitutions and Commitment: The Evolution of Institutions Governing Public Choice in Seventeenth-Century England," *The Journal of Economic History* 49, no. 4 (1989): 803, http://www.jstor.org/stable/2122739.

94 Interview with man from Mosul, conducted in Mosul 27.04.2018.

95 Specimen 28R in AJTA, Ninawa, http://www.aymennjawad.org/2016/09/archive-of-islamic-state-administrative-documents-2; Specimen W in AJTA, Anbar July 2015, http://www.aymennjawad.org/17757/the-archivist-26-unseen-islamic-state; Specimen 27W in AJTA, February 2015, Southern Ninawa, http://www.aymennjawad.org/2016/09/archive-of-islamic-state-administrative-documents-2

96 Interview with man from Mosul, conducted on the phone 03.01.2017.

97 Interview with man from Mosul, conducted in Mosul 20.04.2018.

Chapter 4

1. Interviewed in Erbil 03.11.2016.
2. UNAMI and OHCHR, 17 February 2020, "The right to education in Iraq".
3. Interviews with teachers from Mosul University, conducted in Erbil, October 2016.
4. Al-Tamimi, "The Evolution in Islamic State Administration: The Documentary Evidence," 124.
5. Interview with teacher from Mosul University, conducted by phone, 03.12.17.
6. The Islamic State, declaration, September 2014, https://justpaste.it/ninawaschoolsnotice
7. The Islamic State, "taʿmīm ilā kāfat al-muʾassasāt al-tarbawiyya wat-taʿlīmiyya" ("Declaration to all education institutions"), 2014, signed by Dhu al-Qarnayn, http://i.huffpost.com/gen/3765150/thumbs/o-6-570.jpg?6. The Islamic State: "taʿmīm ilā malākāt jāmiʿāt al-mosul wal-maʿāhid min al-tadrisīn wal-idārīīn wal-muwaẓẓafīn" (Declaration to the personnel of Mosul's universities and institutes, its teachers, administrative employees and other employees"), 2014, https://justpaste.it/mosuluninotice. According to my interviewees, the immediate elimination of these courses was carried out as planned.
8. Interview with Muhammad Ali, general director of education in the Ninawa region, conducted in Erbil, 11.04.16.
9. A previous version of this chapter was first published in Mathilde Becker Aarseth "Resistance in the Caliphate's Classrooms: Mosul Civilians Vs Is." *Middle East Policy* 25, no. 1 (2018): 46–63.
10. The interviews lasted between thirty minutes and two hours and were conducted in Baharka and Debaga refugee camps, and in private homes or public offices in Erbil and Duhok in October and November 2016. Six of the interviewees were still in Mosul at the time of the interview, and some interviews were conducted via telephone or social media. The rest were refugees from ISIS-controlled areas at the time of their interviews. Women and men with a range of socioeconomic and professional backgrounds and ages are represented among my informants. Teachers from a range of different school districts in Mosul city and the surrounding areas were interviewed, representing all levels in the Iraqi school system from primary school to university level. The interviews were conducted in Arabic and translated by the author.
11. See for instance Shane Joshua Barter, "The Rebel State in Society: Governance and Accommodation in Aceh, Indonesia," in *Rebel Governance in Civil War*, ed. Nelson Kasfir, Ana Arjona, and Zachariah Mampilly (New York: Cambridge University Press, 2015), 233–4. Timothy Wickham-Crowley, "Del Gobierno de Abajo al Gobierno de

Arriba ... and Back: Transitions to and from Rebel Governance in Latin America, 1956–90," in *Rebel Governance in Civil War*, ed. Nelson Kasfir, Ana Arjona, and Zachariah Mampilly (New York: Cambridge University Press, 2015), 61. William Reno, "Predatory Rebellions and Governance: The National Patriotic Front of Liberia, 1989–92," in *Rebel Governance in Civil War*, ed. Nelson Kasfir, Ana Arjona, and Zachariah Mampilly (New York: Cambridge University Press, 2015). Noman Benotman and Nikita Malik, *The Children of Islamic State* (Quilliam Foundation, 2016), 29.

12 Arjona, *Rebelocracy—Social Order in the Colombian Civil War*, 210.

13 See for example Steven Levitsky and María Victoria Murillo, "Variation in Institutional Strength," *Annual Review of Political Science* 12, no. 1 (2009): 117, https://doi.org/10.1146/annurev.polisci.11.091106.121756, http://www.annualreviews.org/doi/abs/10.1146/annurev.polisci.11.091106.121756.

14 Adnan Abu Zeed, "Decline of Higher Education in Iraq Continues," *Al-Monitor*, 2016, https://www.al-monitor.com/pulse/originals/2016/09/iraq-university-education-academic-accreditation.html; Adnan Abu Zeed, "Iraqi State Education Increasingly Religious," *Al-Monitor*, January 27, 2015, http://www.al-monitor.com/pulse/originals/2015/01/iraq-state-education-religious-curricula.html. A complete overhaul of the curriculum is currently underway in collaboration between the Iraqi government and UNICEF, see http://www.manahj.edu.iq/.

15 This point was also made during the rebuilding efforts starting in late 2017, for example by the blogger Mosul Eye: https://twitter.com/MosulEye/status/933799525180944384.

16 Revkin, *Does the Islamic State Have a "Social Contract"? Evidence from Iraq and Syria*, 25.

17 Linah Alsaafin, "Reclaiming Mosul's vibrant culture after ISIL," *Al-Jazeera*, October 15, 2017, https://www.aljazeera.com/news/2017/10/reclaiming-mosul-vibrant-culture-isil-171015092411699.html.

18 Jane Arraf, "Book Festival That Drew Thousands of People to Downtown Mosul Is Far from Ordinary," *NPR*, November 13, 2018, https://www.npr.org/2018/11/13/667544756/book-festival-that-drew-thousands-of-people-to-downtown-mosul-is-far-from-ordina.

19 Shields, *Mosul before Iraq*.

20 The Islamic State, announcement, 2014, http://www.aymennjawad.org/18600/islamic-state-treatise-on-the-syrian-education. Aymenn Jawad Al-Tamimi's translation from Arabic.

21 The Islamic State, *Dabiq*, no. 8, 2015, 35. The Islamic State, video, 2015, "Al-taʿlīm fī ẓill al-khilāfa" ("Education in the shade of the caliphate"), 2015, https://ia800505.us.archive.org/31/items/ta_rq/ta11.mp4. The Islamic State, "'hākadha turbī al-aṭfāl li-tuṣbiḥ rijāl naṣrak allah yā dawlatul-khilāfa" ("Thus are children raised to become men of God, oh State of the Caliphate"), video, 2015.

22 Ibid.

23 The Islamic State, notice, Mosul, September 2014, specimen A in AJTA, http://www.aymennjawad.org/15946/aspects-of-islamic-state-is-administration-in

24 The Islamic State, 2015, Specimen 5A in AJTA, http://www.aymennjawad.org/2015/01/archive-of-islamic-state-administrative-documents

25 Interview with employee from the education directorate of Mosul, conducted in Baharka camp, 18.10.16.

26 The Islamic State, 2015, Specimens 3C and 5A in AJTA, http://www.aymennjawad.org/2015/01/archive-of-islamic-state-administrative-documents and The Islamic State, video, 2015, "Al-taʿlīm fī ẓill al-khilāfa" ("Education in the shade of the caliphate"), 2015, https://ia800505.us.archive.org/31/items/ta_rq/ta11.mp4

27 The Islamic State, Specimen 3B in AJTA, http://www.aymennjawad.org/2015/01/archive-of-islamic-state-administrative-documents

28 Ibid.

29 The Islamic State, George Washington University's repository, file no. 35_001580AR

30 The Islamic State, video, 2016, https://www.youtube.com/watch?v=vS7zJLjuTcI. In this video, intended to teach children the alphabet, the letters are sung in the form of a *nashīd*, associating each letter with a jihadi or Islamic concept.

31 This introduction is included in most of the new books, for example, ISIS books for science, Qur'an studies and history.

32 The Islamic State, book, "al-qirāʾ, al-ṣaff al-awwal al-ibtiāʾī." ("Reading for first class")

33 The Islamic State, book, "Muqaddamāt al-barmaja bi-istikhdām skratsh li-kāfat ṣufūf al-marḥala al-mutawassiṭa" ("Introduction in the use of the program Scratch for all grades, middle level")

34 The Islamic State, "Al-iʿdād al-badanī, al-mustawa al-awwal" (Physical exercise, first level"). In addition to education, ISIS had programs for forced military training for children. See Max Taylor John G. Horgan, Mia Bloom, Charlie Winter "From Cubs to Lions: A Six Stage Model of Child Socialization into the Islamic State," *Studies in Conflict & Terrorism* (2016); and Malik, *The Children of Islamic State*.

35 Interview with teacher from school in Mosul, conducted in Baharka camp, 18.10.16.

36 The Islamic State, George Washington University repository, file no. 35_001532AR

37 Interview with headmaster from Mosul school, conducted in Baharka camp, 18.10.16.

38 The Islamic State, "Al-tārīkh lil-ṣaff al-khāmis al-ibtidāʾī" ("History for fifth grade")

39 The Islamic State, "Al-adab al-sharaʿiyya lil-ṣaff al-khāmis al-ibtidāʾi" ("Shariʿa manners for fifth grade")

40 The Islamic State, "Al-ʿulūm lil-ṣaff al-awwal al-ibtidāʾi" ("Science for first grade")

41 The Islamic State, "Al-jaghrāfiyya lil-ṣaff al-khāmis al-ibtidā'ī" ("Geography for fifth grade")

42 The Islamic State, George Washington University repository, file no. 30_001484AR

43 These categories are loosely based on Shane Joshua Barter's forms of civilian resistance in war, Barter, "Unarmed Forces: Civilian Strategy in Violent Conflicts," 553–8.

44 James C. Scott, *Weapons of the Weak. Everyday Forms of Peasant Resistance* (New Haven: Yale University Press, 1985), http://www.jstor.org/stable/j.ctt1nq836.

45 Tripp, *The Power and the People: Paths of Resistance in the Middle East*, 10.

46 Interview with Muhammad Ali, the general director of education in the Ninawa region, conducted in Erbil, November 4, 2016. See also example Kinana Qaddour, "Inside ISIS' Dynsunctional Schools," *Foreign Affairs*, October 13, 2017, https://www.foreignaffairs.com/articles/syria/2017-10-13/inside-isis-dysfunctional-schools. Hosam Al-Jablawi, "A Closer Look at the Educational System of ISIS," *Atlantic Council*, April 26, 2016, https://www.atlanticcouncil.org/blogs/syriasource/a-closer-look-at-isis-s-educational-system.

47 Interview with mid-level manager from the education directorate in Mosul, conducted in Baharka camp, 18.10.16.

48 Interview with headmaster of school North of Mosul, conducted in Baharka camp, 18.10.2016.

49 Sallon, Hélène. *L'état Islamique de Mossoul—histoire d'une entreprise totalitaire* (Paris: La Découverte, 2018), 150.

50 Interview with former medical student from Mosul University, conducted by phone, October 19, 2016.

51 Interview with teacher from school in Mosul, conducted in Debaga camp, 11.10.16.

52 Interview with teacher from school in Mosul, conducted in Baharka camp, 18.10.16.

53 Interview with lecturer from Mosul University, conducted on the phone, 06.02.17.

54 Ibid.

55 Mosul Eye, "Education in Mosul under IS rule," 2015, https://mosuleye.files.wordpress.com/2015/12/mosul-eye-education-under-isil.pdf

56 Interviews with teachers, conducted in Erbil, October 2016.

57 Interview with administration employee in the education directorate, conducted in Debaga camp, 11.10.16.

58 Mosul Eye, "Education in Mosul under IS rule," 2015, https://mosuleye.files.wordpress.com/2015/12/mosul-eye-education-under-isil.pdf

59 Interview with mid-level manager from the education directorate in Mosul, conducted in Baharka camp, 18.10.16.

60 Mosul Eye, "Education in Mosul under IS rule," 2015, https://mosuleye.files.wordpress.com/2015/12/mosul-eye-education-under-isil.pdf

61 The Islamic State, George Washington University repository, file no. 35_001577AR

62 Interviews with students from Mosul University, conducted in Erbil, October 2016.

63 Interview with medical student from Mosul University, conducted on social media, 27.06.17.

64 Tripp, *The Power and the People: Paths of Resistance in the Middle East*, 10.

65 Ibid.

66 Interview with headmaster from a school in Mosul, conducted in Debaga camp, 11.10.16.

67 Interview with the assistant manager of a high school in Mosul, conducted in Erbil, 03.11.16.

68 Interview with medical student from Mosul University, conducted on social media, 27.06.17.

69 Ibid.

70 Interview with administrative employee and lecturer from Mosul University, conducted in Erbil, 03.11.16.

71 Interview with administrative assistant manager from a Mosul high school, conducted in Erbil, 03.11.16.

72 Ben Kesling and Margaret Coker, the Wall Street Journal, "Islamic State Hijacks Mosul University Chemistry Lab for Making Bombs," April 1, 2016, https://www.wsj.com/articles/islamic-state-hijacks-mosul-university-chemistry-lab-for-making-bombs-1459503003

73 Barter, "Unarmed Forces: Civilian Strategy in Violent Conflicts," 553.

74 Stephan, "Civil Resistance vs. ISIS," 136.

75 Taleb, "From Assad to ISIS, a tale of Syrian resistance."

76 Revkin, *Does the Islamic State Have a "Social Contract"? Evidence from Iraq and Syria*, 27.

77 Interview with medical student from Mosul University, conducted by phone, 19.10.16.

78 United Nations Assistance Mission for Iraq—Human Rights Office & Office of the United Nations High Commissioner for Human Rights, *Report on the Protection of Civilians in the Armed Conflict in Iraq: December 11, 2014–April 30, 2015*, United Nations (2015), 24, http://www.ohchr.org/Documents/Countries/IQ/UNAMI_ohchr_4th_POCReport-11Dec2014-30April2015.pdf.

79 NRT, "ashwaq al-na'imi ayqunat al-musul," http://www.nrttv.com/ar/Detail.aspx?Jimare=14411.

80 "Hal taʿrifina man aṭlaqa al-raṣāṣ ʿalā raʾs al-shahīda ashwāq al-naʿīmī?," *Al-masala* 2016, http://almasalah.com/ar/NewsDetails.aspx?NewsID=65887.

81 "Man hiyya ashwāq al-naʿīmī. al-muʿallima alatī ʿadamaha dāʿish?" *Rudaw* 2015, http://www.rudaw.net/NewsDetails.aspx?pageid=178700.

82 Interview with teacher from a Mosul primary school, conducted in Duhok, 11.10.16.

83 Ibid.

84 Arjona, "Civilian Cooperation and Non-Cooperation with Non-State Armed Groups: The Centrality of Obedience and Resistance," 766.

85 Interview with administrative employee and lecturer from Mosul University, conducted in Erbil, 03.11.16.

86 The so-called "collective action problem" is described in Mancur Olson, *The Logic of Collective Action: Public Goods and the Theory of Groups, Second Printing with New Preface and Appendix* (Cambridge: Harvard University Press, 1965), https://books.google.no/books?id=jzTeOLtf7_wC.

87 See for example Ana Arjona, "Civilian Resistance to Rebel Governance1," in *Rebel Governance in Civil War*, ed. Ana Arjona, Nelson Kasfir, and Zachariah Mampilly (Cambridge: Cambridge University Press, 2015), 194.

88 Arjona, *Rebelocracy—Social Order in the Colombian Civil War*, 2.

89 Interview with a mid-level manager in the education directorate in Mosul, conducted in Baharka camp, 18.10.16.

90 Barbara F. Walter, "The Extremist's Advantage in Civil Wars," *International Security* 42, no. 2 (2017): 8.

91 See for example Sukanya Podder and Scott Gates, "Social Media, Recruitment, Allegiance and the Islamic State," *Perspectives on Terrorism* 9, no. 4 (2015): 107.

Chapter 5

1 Interviewed 11.10.2016 in Debaga IDP camp

2 Weinstein, *Inside Rebellion*, 52.

3 Reno, "Predatory Rebellions and Governance: The National Patriotic Front of Liberia, 1989–1992," 269.

4 José Ciro Martínez and Brent Eng, "Stifling stateness: The Assad regime's campaign against rebel governance," *Security Dialogue* 49, no. 4 (2018): 4, https://doi.org/10.1177/0967010618768622, http://journals.sagepub.com/doi/abs/10.1177/0967010618768622.

5   When administrative documents from Syria are referred to, this is because they indicate general ambitions for ISIS governance in its territories. Among the informants are general practitioners and specialists in pediatrics, surgery, internal medicine, obstetrics, oncology, hematology and rehabilitation, and all the seven main Mosul hospitals that were under ISIS rule 2014–17 are represented. Informants were interviewed between 2016 and 2018 in Northern Iraq or on the phone and social media. While quotes are attributed to specific individuals, general claims about health governance in Mosul are based on the totality of interviews in combination with other sources. All informants are anonymized for their own security, and direct quotes are separated by the letters A through I in this article.

6   Baghdad's health inspector T. Barrett Heggs wrote in a 1922 report: "All this death, sickness and invalidity means waste. Waste of valuable lives and work to the State, waste of efficiency to the workshops, waste of efforts to the individual and waste or loss of money to all these … Waste is uneconomic; it must be stopped." As cited in Omar Dewachi, *Ungovernable Life: Mandatory Medicine and Statecraft in Iraq* (Stanford: Stanford University Press, 2017), 56.

7   Surveys conducted by Unicef in 1999 estimated that the sanctions had resulted in the death of 500,000 children under-five. Unicef, "Iraq surveys show 'humanitarian emergency'," August 12, 1999, https://www.unicef.org/newsline/99pr29.htm

8   See for example Samira Alaani et al., "Uranium and other contaminants in hair from the parents of children with congenital anomalies in Fallujah, Iraq," *Conflict and Health* 5, no. 1 (2011), https://doi.org/10.1186/1752-1505-5-15. Chris Busby, Malak Hamdan, and Entesar Ariabi, "Cancer, Infant Mortality and Birth Sex-Ratio in Fallujah, Iraq 2005–2009," *International Journal of Environmental Research and Public Health* 7, no. 7 (2010), https://doi.org/10.3390/ijerph7072828, http://www.ncbi.nlm.nih.gov/pmc/articles/PMC2922729/. M. Al-Sabbak et al., "Metal Contamination and the Epidemic of Congenital Birth Defects in Iraqi Cities," *Bulletin of Environmental Contamination and Toxicology* 89, no. 5 (2012), https://doi.org/10.1007/s00128-012-0817-2.

9   Jason H. Calhoun, Clinton K. Murray, and M. M. Manring, "Multidrug-resistant Organisms in Military Wounds from Iraq and Afghanistan," *Clinical Orthopaedics and Related Research* 466, no. 6 (2008), https://doi.org/10.1007/s11999-008-0212-9, http://www.ncbi.nlm.nih.gov/pmc/articles/PMC2384049/. U.S. military doctors have termed Acinetobacter baumannii, one of these superbugs, "Iraqibacter," see Dewachi, *Ungovernable Life: Mandatory Medicine and Statecraft in Iraq*, 179.

10 Valeria Cetorelli and Nazar P. Shabila, "Expansion of health facilities in Iraq a decade after the U.S.-led invasion, 2003–2012," *Conflict and Health* 8 (2014), https://doi.org/10.1186/1752-1505-8-16, http://www.ncbi.nlm.nih.gov/pmc/articles/PMC4163049/.

11 World Health Organization, *Health Profile: Ninawa Governorate* (2015).

12 UN Habitat, *City Profile of Mosul, Iraq. Multi-Sector Assessment of a City under Siege* (2016), https://unhabitat.org/city-profile-of-mosul-iraq-a-city-under-siege/#.

13 Specialized units for treating burns, hepatitis, cancer and forensic medicine were among the novelties. Interview with Dr. Firas Ismail Mustafa, medical doctor and Ninawa representative for WHO, conducted on the phone 28.01.2018.

14 Interview with Dr. Firas Ismail Mustafa, medical doctor and Ninawa representative for WHO, conducted on the phone 28.01.2018.

15 As of December 2017, WHO reported that three Ninawa health facilities were fully damaged and twenty-three partially damaged in the operation. See *Iraq Humanitarian Emergency. Situation Report Issue Number 10, 01–December 31, 2017*, World Health Organization (2017), https://reliefweb.int/sites/reliefweb.int/files/resources/WHO%20Situation%20Report%20for%20Iraq_%201%20to%2031%20December%202017.pdf.

16 See for example Melissa M. Lee, Gregor Walter-Drop, and John Wiesel, "Taking the State (Back) Out? Statehood and the Delivery of Collective Goods," *Governance* 27, no. 4 (2014), https://doi.org/10.1111/gove.12069.

17 Lee, Walter-Drop, and Wiesel, "Taking the State (Back) Out? Statehood and the Delivery of Collective Goods."

18 R. Huang, *The Wartime Origins of Democratization: Civil War, Rebel Governance, and Political Regimes* (Cambridge University Press, 2016), 71–3. https://books.google.no/books?id=lBviDAAAQBAJ.

19 Weinstein, *Inside Rebellion*, 168.

20 Arjona, *Rebelocracy—Social Order in the Colombian Civil War*, 7.

21 See for example Marco Schäferhoff, "External Actors and the Provision of Public Health Services in Somalia," *Governance* 27, no. 4 (2014): 677, https://doi.org/10.1111/gove.12071.

22 Dewachi, *Ungovernable Life: Mandatory Medicine and Statecraft in Iraq*, 3; Sadeer Al-Kindi, "Violence against doctors in Iraq," *The Lancet* 384, no. 9947 (2014), https://doi.org/10.1016/S0140-6736(14)61627-5.

23 Ross I. Donaldson et al., "A Survey of National Physicians Working in an Active Conflict Zone: The Challenges of Emergency Medical Care in Iraq," *Prehospital and Disaster Medicine* 27, no. 2 (2012), https://doi.org/10.1017/S1049023X12000519, https://www.cambridge.org/core/article/survey-of-national-physicians-working-in-an-active-conflict-zone-the-challenges-of-emergency-medical-care-in-iraq/87FE87C78E532F1CE4C8612D17D4BD87.

24 Erika Solomon, Robin Kwong, and Steven Bernard, "Isis Inc: how oil fuels the jihadi terrorists," *Financial Times*, 2016, https://ig.ft.com/sites/2015/isis-oil/.

25 The Islamic State, "The Structure of the Khilafa," video, July 2016, https://videopress.com/v/tv16QF5r

26 The Islamic State, "A call to all Muslims doctors, engineers, scholars and specialists," *Dabiq*, July, 2014.

27 The Islamic State, announcement, Ninawa, 2015, Specimen 5I in Aymenn Jawad Al-Tamimi's online archive of ISIS administrative documents (from here on shortened to AJTA): http://www.aymennjawad.org/2015/01/archive-of-islamic-state-administrative-documents

28 The Islamic State, "Health Services in the Islamic State: Wilāyat al-Raqqah," video, Al-Raqqa, 2015, https://jihadology.net/2015/04/24/new-video-message-from-the-islamic-state-health-services-in-the-islamic-state-wilayat-al-raqqah/

29 The Islamic State, "Vaccination card for children," Aleppo, Specimen 1L in Tamimi's online archive, http://www.aymennjawad.org/2015/01/archive-of-islamic-state-administrative-documents; The Islamic State, "Birth certificate," Aleppo, 2015, Specimen O in AJTA, The Islamic State, "Fatwa 24" and "Fatwa 42," December 2014, http://www.jihadica.com/wp-content/uploads/2015/02/IS-fatwas-35-38-40-53-55-57-59-62-65-71.pdf; The Islamic State, "Travel permit for medical reasons," Al-Raqqa, Specimen 12B in AJTA.

30 The Islamic State, declaration, Ninawa, May 2015, Specimen 5I in Aymenn Jawad Al-Tamimi's online archive of ISIS administrative documents: http://www.aymennjawad.org/2015/01/archive-of-islamic-state-administrative-documents

31 This included any contact between a female nurse and a male doctor in small clinics with few employees. The Islamic State, "Fatwa 24," December 2014, http://www.jihadica.com/wp-content/uploads/2015/02/IS-fatwas-35-38-40-53-55-57-59-62-65-71.pdf

32 See also Erin Cunningham, "Islamic State imposes a reign of fear in Iraqi hospitals," *The Washington Post*, November 25, 2014, https://www.washingtonpost.com/world/middle_east/islamic-state-imposes-a-reign-of-fear-in-iraqi-hospitals/2014/11/25/94476f3e-6382-11e4-ab86-46000e1d0035_story.html?utm_term=.9a3674637e3f.

33 Interview with doctor F in a Mosul hospital, conducted on the phone 05.06.2018.

34 Interview with doctor A in a Mosul hospital, conducted in Mosul 20.04.18.

35 Interview with doctor B in a Mosul hospital, conducted in Mosul 25.04.18.

36 Interviewees who spent time in al-Battoul hospital reported that Yezidi girls held captive as ISIS sex slaves were also taken to al-Battoul for treatment.

37 Interview with doctor C in a Mosul clinic, conducted on the phone, 14.02.18.

38 The Islamic State, "Fatwa 43," December 2014, http://www.jihadica.com/wp-content/uploads/2015/02/IS-fatwas-35-38-40-53-55-57-59-62-65-71.pdf

39 See for example Cunningham, "Islamic State imposes a reign of fear in Iraqi hospitals."

40 Interview with a former patient in a Mosul hospital, conducted on the phone, 03.01.18.

41 The Islamic State, announcement, Mosul, August 2015, https://jihadology.net/2016/12/31/the-archivist-unseen-islamic-state-regulations-for-the-mosul-operations/

42 Interview with doctor D in a Mosul hospital, conducted in Erbil, 19.04.18.

43 Interview with Doctor L in a Mosul hospital, conducted in Mosul, 24.04.2018.

44 Interview with doctor K in a Mosul hospital, conducted in Erbil 29.10.19.

45 See for example Scott Lucas, "Iraq Feature: Women Doctors in Mosul On Strike Over Intimidation by Islamic State," *EA WorldView*, 2014, http://eaworldview.com/2014/08/iraq-feature-women-doctors-mosul-strike-intimidation-islamic-state/; Cunningham, "Islamic State imposes a reign of fear in Iraqi hospitals."

46 See for example David Harris, "Islamic State Executes Women & Doctors in 'Collaborators' Purge," *Clarion Project*, September 7, 2014, https://clarionproject.org/islamic-state-executes-women-doctors-collaborators-purge-9/; Rudaw, "Sources: ISIS executed 10 doctors in Mosul for refusing to treat wounded fighters," *Rudaw*, January 27, 2015, http://www.rudaw.net/english/middleeast/iraq/27012015.

47 For simplicity, I here use the term "ISIS members" for both these groups.

48 Interview with administrative employee in a Mosul hospital, conducted in Mosul 24.04.18.

49 ISIS specifically banned importing medicines from Iran, Specimen 4x in AJTA, http://www.aymennjawad.org/2015/01/archive-of-islamic-state-administrative-documents

50 In Syria, the group distributed its own rudimentary test on basic pharmaceutical knowledge that they demanded pharmacists take. Aymenn Jawad Al-Tamimi, "Could you open a pharmacy in Islamic State territory?" *Aymenn Jawad Al-Tamimi's Blog*, May 7, 2017, http://www.aymennjawad.org/2017/05/could-you-open-a-pharmacy-in-islamic-state. The Islamic State, announcement, Mosul, Specimen C in AJTA, http://www.aymennjawad.org/15952/aspects-of-islamic-state-is-administration-in

51 The Islamic State, announcement, Mosul, Specimen C in AJTA, http://www.aymennjawad.org/15952/aspects-of-islamic-state-is-administration-in

52 Interview with doctor F in a Mosul hospital, conducted on the phone 05.06.2018.

53 Interview with doctor E in a Mosul hospital, conducted in Erbil 19.04.18.

54 A written travel permission was issued on such occasions. For an example of medical travel permissions in Syria see The Islamic State, "Sending someone to the western *wilāyāts* for medical treatment," November 2016, Specimen 40S in Tamimi's online archive, http://www.aymennjawad.org/2017/08/archive-of-islamic-state-administrative-documents-3

55 The Islamic State, "Fatwa 37," December 2014, http://www.jihadica.com/wp-content/uploads/2015/02/IS-fatwas-35-38-40-53-55-57-59-62-65-71.pdf

56 Interview with civilian from Mosul, conducted in Erbil 03.11.16.

57 See also "dāʿish tuḥāṣir mustashfayāt al-mosul ('IS Besieges Mosul Hospitals')," *Al-Araby*, September 26, 2014, https://www.alaraby.co.uk/society/2014/9/26/الموصل-مستشفيات-تحاصر-داعش.

58 Interview with administrative manager under ISIS in a Mosul hospital, conducted in Mosul 24.04.2018.

59 Interview with doctor H in a Mosul hospital, conducted in Mosul 21.04.18.

60 ISIS documents from Syria mete out lashes as punishment for doctors who were accused of causing an ISIS member's death. See The Islamic State, "Complaint about Doctor's Negligence," *Deir Azzour*, April 2017, Specimen 41G in Tamimi's online archive, http://www.aymennjawad.org/2017/08/archive-of-islamic-state-administrative-documents-3

61 See for example "dāʿish yaftaḥ mustashfa bi-aḥdath al-tajhīzāt janūb al-Mosul," ("ISIS opens hospital with modern equipment South of Mosul"), *Al-Siasi*, 2015, http://alsiasi.com/254574-/داعش-يفتتح-مستشفى-بأحدث-التجهيزات-جنوب-الموصل-حدث-بالصور.html

62 Administrative records from Syria indicate an ISIS-run vaccination program for children, see for example The Islamic State, "Vaccination schedule for children," specimen 1M in Tamimi's online archive, http://www.aymennjawad.org/2015/01/archive-of-islamic-state-administrative-documents However, as Tamimi has pointed out, these were a copy of the government run programs. The actual implementation of this program is uncertain.

63 Interview with doctor I in a Mosul hospital, conducted in Mosul 26.04.18.

64 The Islamic State, "al-Nabaʾ," nr 18, s 12.

65 Interview with doctor G in Jumhuri hospital, conducted in Mosul 23.04.18.

65 The Islamic State, announcement, Mosul, October 2016, https://jihadology.net/2016/12/31/the-archivist-unseen-islamic-state-regulations-for-the-mosul-operations/

67 Interview with doctor J in a Mosul hospital, conducted in Mosul 13.04.18.

68 Aymenn Jawad Al-Tamimi, "Aspects of Islamic State (IS) Administration in Ninawa Province: Part I," *Aymenn Jawad Al-Tamimi Blog*, January 17, 2015, http://www.aymennjawad.org/15946/aspects-of-islamic-state-is-administration-in.

69 Reno, "Predatory Rebellions and Governance: The National Patriotic Front of Liberia, 1989–1992," 269.

70 Stathis N. Kalyvas, "'New' and 'Old' Civil Wars: A Valid Distinction?," *World Politics* 54, no. 1 (2001), http://www.jstor.org.ezproxy-test.uio.no/stable/25054175.

Chapter 6

1. Audio message by Abu Muhammad al-Adnani, June 2014, "hādhā waʿd allah" ("This is God's Promise"), https://azelin.files.wordpress.com/2014/06/shaykh-abc5ab-mue1b8a5ammad-al-e28098adnc481nc4ab-al-shc481mc4ab-22this-is-the-promise-of-god22.mp3

2. Interview conducted on the phone 05.06.2018.

3. Mampilly, *Rebel Rulers. Insurgent Governance and Civilian Life during War*, 13.

4. Thomas Joscelyn, "Town of Dabiq falls to Turkish-backed forces," *Long War Journal Blog*, October 17, 2016, https://www.longwarjournal.org/archives/2016/10/town-of-dabiq-falls-to-turkish-backed-forces.php.

5. Ahmed S. Yayla and Colin P. Clarke, "Turkey's Double ISIS Standard," *Foreign Policy*, April 12, 2018, https://foreignpolicy.com/2018/04/12/turkeys-double-isis-standard/

6. Daniel Byman, "Understanding the Islamic State—A Review Essay," *International Security* 40, no. 4 (2016): 136, https://doi.org/10.1162/ISEC_r_00235.

7. Bart Schuurman and Max Taylor, "Reconsidering Radicalization: Fanaticism and the Link between Ideas and Violence," *Perspectives on Terrorism* 12, no. 1 (2018): 15, http://www.terrorismanalysts.com/pt/index.php/pot/article/view/675/1347

8. Charlie. "Apocalypse, Later: A Longitudinal Study of the Islamic State Brand," 103–21.

9. Ibid., 112.

10. Ibid., 108.

11. Nelly Lahoud, "How will the Islamic State endure?" *The Survival Editor's Blog*, October 31, 2017.

12. Brynjar Lia, "The Jihādī Movement and Rebel Governance: A Reassertion of a Patriarchal Order?" *Die Welt des Islams* 57, no. 3–4 (2017): 476–7, https://doi.org/10.1163/15700607-05734p09.

13. Audio message by Abu Muhammad al-Adnani, July 2014, "hādhā waʿd allah" ("This is God's Promise"), https://azelin.files.wordpress.com/2014/06/shaykh-abc5ab-mue1b8a5ammad-al-e28098adnc481nc4ab-al-shc481mc4ab-22this-is-the-promise-of-god22.mp3

14. John Davison, "No plan for Mosul: chaos and neglect slow Iraqi city's recovery," *Reuters*, February 4, 2019, https://www.reuters.com/article/us-iraq-mosul/no-plan-for-mosul-chaos-and-neglect-slow-iraqi-citys-recovery-idUSKCN1PT0JV.

15. Ghaith Abdul-Ahad, "'I just wanted to die': the torture of an Iraqi protester," *The Guardian*, February 18, 2020, https://www.theguardian.com/world/2020/feb/18/i-just-wanted-to-die-the-torture-of-an-iraqi-protester.

Notes on Sources and Methodology

1 See for instance The Islamic State, Mosul, "rumūz al-kulliyyāt wal-maʿāhid" ("Names of university colleges and institutes), specimen 81 and «idārat al-jāmiʿa" (Administration of the university), specimen 8X in Aymenn Jawad Al-Tamimi's online archive of ISIS records (from hereon shortened to AJTA), http://www.aymennjawad.org/2015/01/archive-of-islamic-state-administrative-documents. Note: The information about each documents produced by ISIS varies, e.g. issue date, title, or place of origin. In this book, references include the information given in each document.

2 The Islamic State, Mosul 2016, specimen 26J in AJTA, http://www.aymennjawad.org/2016/09/archive-of-islamic-state-administrative-documents-2

3 The Islamic State, Mosul 2015, specimen 16B in AJTA, http://www.aymennjawad.org/2016/01/archive-of-islamic-state-administrative-documents-1

4 See for instance The Islamic State, South Ninawa, specimens 32Z, 33A and 33B in AJTA, http://www.aymennjawad.org/2016/09/archive-of-islamic-state-administrative-documents-2

5 The Islamic State, Mosul, "qāʾima li-ḥuḍūr ṣalāt al-fajr wal-ʿishā fil-masjid" ("List of attendance of morning and night prayer in the mosque"), specimen 21R in AJTA, http://www.aymennjawad.org/2016/09/archive-of-islamic-state-administrative-documents-2

6 Representatives from Doctors without Borders, Norwegian Refugee Council, and Global Response Management.

7 J.A. Maxwell, *Qualitative Research Design: An Interactive Approach* (Thousand Oaks, California: SAGE Publications, 2005), 111. https://books.google.no/books?id=OJFrFmpGSnUC.

8 H.S. Becker, *Sociological work: method and substance* (London: Aldine Pub. Co., 1970), 51–62. https://books.google.no/books?id=7rxkAAAAIAAJ.

9 Maxwell, *Qualitative Research Design: An Interactive Approach*, 106.

10 Anssi Peräkylä, "Analyzing Talk and Text," in *The Sage Handbook of Qualitative Research, Third Edition*, ed. Norman K. Denzin and Yvonna S. Lincoln (Thousand Oaks/ London/ New Delhi: SAGE Publications, 2005), 869.

11 K. Charmaz and A. Bryant, "Grounded Theory and Credibility," in *Qualitative Research*, ed. David Silverman (London: SAGE Publications, 2011), 299.

12 The Islamic State, announcement, Mosul 2015, specimen 12R in AJTA, http://www.aymennjawad.org/2016/01/archive-of-islamic-state-administrative-documents-1

13 Maxwell, *Qualitative Research Design: An Interactive Approach*, 94.

14 Ibid., 112.

15 This distinction is taken from Stephane J. Baele et al., "The Ethics of Security Research: An Ethics Framework for Contemporary Security Studies," *International Studies Perspectives* 19, no. 2 (2018): 108, https://doi.org/10.1093/isp/ekx003.

16 Baele et al., "The Ethics of Security Research: An Ethics Framework for Contemporary Security Studies," 120.

17 Ibid., 121.

Bibliography

Abdul-Ahad, Ghaith. "'I Just Wanted to Die': The Torture of an Iraqi Protester." *The Guardian*, February 18, 2020. https://www.theguardian.com/world/2020/feb/18/i-just-wanted-to-die-the-torture-of-an-iraqi-protester.

Abdulrazaq, Tallha and Gareth Stansfield. "The Enemy Within: Isis and the Conquest of Mosul." *The Middle East Journal* 70, no. 4 (2016): 525–42.

Abu Zeed, Adnan. "Decline of Higher Education in Iraq Continues." *Al-Monitor*, 2016. https://www.al-monitor.com/pulse/originals/2016/09/iraq-university-education-academic-accreditation.html.

Al-Ali, Zaid. *The Struggle for Iraq's Future. How Corruption, Incompetence and Sectarianism Have Undermined Democracy*. New Haven: Yale University Press, 2014. http://www.jstor.org/stable/j.ctt5vksw1.

Al-Jablawi, Hosam. "A Closer Look at the Educational System of Isis." *Atlantic Council*, April 26, 2016. https://www.atlanticcouncil.org/blogs/syriasource/a-closer-look-at-isis-s-educational-system.

Al-Kindi, Sadeer. "Violence against Doctors in Iraq." *The Lancet* 384, no. 9947 (2014): 954–5. https://doi.org/10.1016/S0140-6736(14)61627-5.

Al-Sabbak, M., S. Sadik Ali, O. Savabi, G. Savabi, S. Dastgiri, and M. Savabieasfahani. "Metal Contamination and the Epidemic of Congenital Birth Defects in Iraqi Cities." *Bulletin of Environmental Contamination and Toxicology* 89, no. 5 (2012): 937–44. https://doi.org/10.1007/s00128-012-0817-2.

Al-Salhy, Suadad. "How Iraq's 'Ghost Soldiers' Helped Isil." *Al-Jazeera*, December 10, 2014. https://www.aljazeera.com/news/middleeast/2014/12/how-iraq-ghost-soldiers-helped-isil-2014121072749979252.html.

Al-Tamimi, Aymenn Jawad. "The Archivist: The Islamic State's Security Apparatus Structure in the Provinces." *Jihadology*, August 2, 2017. https://jihadology.net/2017/08/02/the-archivist-the-islamic-states-security-apparatus-structure-in-the-provinces/.

Al-Tamimi, Aymenn Jawad. "The Archivist: Unseen Islamic State Regulations for the Mosul Operations." *Jihadology*, December 31, 2016. https://jihadology.net/2016/12/31/the-archivist-unseen-islamic-state-regulations-for-the-mosul-operations/.

Al-Tamimi, Aymenn Jawad. "Aspects of Islamic State (Is) Administration in Ninawa Province: Part I." *Aymenn Jawad Al-Tamimi Blog*, January 17, 2015. http://www.aymennjawad.org/15946/aspects-of-islamic-state-is-administration-in.

Al-Tamimi, Aymenn Jawad. "Could You Open a Pharmacy in Islamic State Territory?" *Aymenn Jawad Al-Tamimi's Blog*, May 7, 2017. http://www.aymennjawad.org/2017/05/could-you-open-a-pharmacy-in-islamic-state.

Al-Tamimi, Aymenn Jawad. "The Evolution in Islamic State Administration: The Documentary Evidence." *Perspectives on Terrorism* 9, no. 4 (2015): 117–29. http://www.terrorismanalysts.com/pt/index.php/pot/article/view/447.

Al-Tamimi, Aymenn Jawad. "The Internal Structure of the Islamic State's Hisba Apparatus," 2018. http://www.aymennjawad.org/21246/the-internal-structure-of-the-islamic-state-hisba.

Al-Tamimi, Aymenn Jawad. "Looking at Violence in Iraq," 2012. http://www.aymennjawad.org/12158/looking-at-violence-in-iraq.

Al-Tamimi, Aymenn Jawad. "Repentance: Financial Income for the Islamic State." *Aymenn Jawad Al-Tamimi Blog*, September 28, 2015. http://www.aymennjawad.org/2015/09/repentance-financial-income-for-the-islamic-state

Al-Ubaydi, Muhammad, Nelly Lahoud, Daniel Milton, and Bryan Price. *The Group That Calls Itself a State: Understanding the Evolution and Challenges of the Islamic State*. Combatting Terrorism Center (Westpoint, 2014). https://ctc.usma.edu/the-group-that-calls-itself-a-state-understanding-the-evolution-and-challenges-of-the-islamic-state/.

Alaaldin, Ranj. "Iraq's Next War." *Foreign Affairs*, 2018. https://www.foreignaffairs.com/articles/middle-east/2018-09-13/iraqs-next-war?cid=int-fls&pgtype=hpg.

Alaani, Samira, Muhammed Tafash, Christopher Busby, Malak Hamdan, and Eleonore Blaurock-Busch. "Uranium and Other Contaminants in Hair from the Parents of Children with Congenital Anomalies in Fallujah, Iraq." *Conflict and Health* 5, no. 1 (2011): 15. https://doi.org/10.1186/1752-1505-5-15.

Alsaafin, Linah. "Reclaiming Mosul's Vibrant Culture after Isil." *Al-Jazeera*, October 15, 2017. https://www.aljazeera.com/news/2017/10/reclaiming-mosul-vibrant-culture-isil-171015092411699.html.

Amarasingam, Amarnath. "Talking to Foreign Fighters: Insights into the Motivations for Hijrah to Syria and Iraq Au—Dawson, Lorne L." *Studies in Conflict & Terrorism* 40, no. 3 (2017): 191–210. https://doi.org/10.1080/1057610X.2016.1274216.

"Another Iraq Candidate Killed Ahead of Provincial Polls." *The Daily Star Lebanon*, June 14, 2013. http://www.dailystar.com.lb/News/Middle-East/2013/Jun-14/220395-gunmen-kill-election-candidate-in-iraq.ashx#axzz2X550kr6J.

Arjona, Ana. "Civilian Cooperation and Non-Cooperation with Non-State Armed Groups: The Centrality of Obedience and Resistance." *Small Wars & Insurgencies* 28, no. 4–5 (2017): 755–8. https://doi.org/10.1080/09592318.2017.1322328.

Arjona, Ana. "Civilian Resistance to Rebel Governance." In *Rebel Governance in Civil War*, edited by Ana Arjona, Nelson Kasfir, and Zachariah Mampilly, 158–79. Cambridge: Cambridge University Press, 2015.

Arjona, Ana. *Rebelocracy: Social Order in the Colombian Civil War*. Cambridge: Cambridge University Press, 2016.

Arjona, Ana, Nelson Kasfir, and Zachariah Mampilly, eds. *Rebel Governance in Civil War*. New York: Cambridge University Press, 2015.

Arraf, Jane. "Book Festival That Drew Thousands of People to Downtown Mosul Is Far from Ordinary." *NPR*, November 13, 2018. https://www.npr.org/2018/11/13/667544756/book-festival-that-drew-thousands-of-people-to-downtown-mosul-is-far-from-ordina.

Asher-Schapiro, Avi. "The Us-Led Coalition Bombed the University of Mosul for Being an Islamic State Headquarters," 2016. https://news.vice.com/article/the-us-led-coalition-bombed-the-university-of-mosul-for-being-an-islamic-state-headquarters.

Atwan, Abdel Bari. *Islamic State: The Digital Caliphate*. University of California Press, 2015. https://books.google.no/books?id=yHolDQAAQBAJ.

Baele, Stephane J., David Lewis, Anke Hoeffler, Olivier C. Sterck, and Thibaut Slingeneyer. "The Ethics of Security Research: An Ethics Framework for Contemporary Security Studies." *International Studies Perspectives* 19, no. 2 (2018): 105–27. https://doi.org/10.1093/isp/ekx003.

Bakker, Edwin, and Mark Singleton. "Foreign Fighters in the Syria and Iraq Conflict: Statistics and Characteristics of a Rapidly Growing Phenomenon." In *Foreign Fighters under International Law and Beyond*, edited by Andrea de Guttry, Francesca Capone, and Christophe Paulussen, 9–25. The Hague: T.M.C. Asser Press, 2016.

Balcells, Laia. *Rivalry and Revenge: The Politics of Violence during Civil War*. Cambridge: Cambridge University Press, 2017.

Ballina, Santiago. "The Crime–Terror Continuum Revisited: A Model for the Study of Hybrid Criminal Organisations." *Journal of Policing, Intelligence and Counter Terrorism* 6, no. 2 (2011): 121–36. https://doi.org/10.1080/18335330.2011.605200.

Barrett, Richard. *The Islamic State*. The Soufan Group, 2014. http://www.soufangroup.com/the-islamic-state/.

Barter, Shane Joshua. "The Rebel State in Society: Governance and Accommodation in Aceh, Indonesia." In *Rebel Governance in Civil War*, edited by Nelson Kasfir, Ana Arjona, and Zachariah Mampilly. New York: Cambridge University Press, 2015.

Barter, Shane Joshua. "Unarmed Forces: Civilian Strategy in Violent Conflicts." *Peace & Change* 37, no. 4 (2012): 544–71. https://doi.org/10.1111/j.1468-0130.2012.00770.x.

Becker, H.S. *Sociological Work: Method and Substance*. London: Aldine Pub. Co, 1970. https://books.google.no/books?id=7rxkAAAAIAAJ.

Benmelech, Efraim, and Esteban F. Klor. "What Explains the Flow of Foreign Fighters to Isis?." *Terrorism and Political Violence*, no. October (2018): 1–24. https://doi.org/10.1080/09546553.2018.1482214.

Benraad, Myriam. "Iraq's Enduring Al-Qaeda Challenge." *The Washington Institute*, 2009, November 18. https://www.washingtoninstitute.org/policy-analysis/view/iraqs-enduring-al-qaeda-challenge.

Bertelsen, Preben, and Michael Stohl. "Who Goes, Why, and with What Effects: The Problem of Foreign Fighters from Europe Au—Lindekilde, Lasse." *Small Wars & Insurgencies* 27, no. 5 (2016): 858–77. https://doi.org/10.1080/09592318.2016.1208285.

Biddle, Stephen, Jeffrey A. Friedman, and Jacob N. Shapiro. "Testing the Surge: Why Did Violence Decline in Iraq in 2007?." *International Security* 37, no. 1 (2012): 7–40. https://doi.org/10.1162/ISEC_a_00087.

"Bil-Arqām … Hadhihi Al-Asʿār Alatī Dafaʿaha Dāʿish Limuqātilihi Muqābil Kull Sabiyya ('in Numbers … These Are the Prices Payed by Is Fighters for One Sabiyya')." *Akhbar Alan*, March 22, 2018. https://www.akhbaralaan.net/news/exclusive/2018/3/22/%D8%A8%D8%A7%D9%84%D8%A3%D8%B1%D9%82%D8%A7%D9%85%D9%87%D8%B0%D9%87-%D8%A7%D9%8

4%D8%A3%D8%B3%D8%B9%D8%A7%D8%B1-%D8%A7%D9%84%D8-
%AA%D9%8A-%D8%AF%D9%81%D8%B9%D9%87%D8%A7-
%D8%AF%D8%A7%D8%B9%D8%B4-%D9%84%D9%85%D9%82%D8%A7%D8%A
A%D9%84%D9%8A%D9%87-%D9%85%D9%82%D8%A7%D8%A8%D9%84-%D9%-
83%D9%84-%D8%B3%D8%A8%D9%8A%D8%A9.

Brisard, J.C., and D. Martinez. *Zarqawi: The New Face of Al-Qaeda*. Polity, 2005. https://books.google.no/books?id=F6SNDMjJW4YC.

Bunzel, Cole. *From Paper State to Caliphate: The Ideology of the Islamic State*. The Brookings Institution, 2015. https://www.brookings.edu/research/from-paper-state-to-caliphate-the-ideology-of-the-islamic-state/.

Busby, Chris, Malak Hamdan, and Entesar Ariabi. "Cancer, Infant Mortality and Birth Sex-Ratio in Fallujah, Iraq 2005–2009." *International Journal of Environmental Research and Public Health* 7, no. 7 (2010): 2828–37. https://doi.org/10.3390/ijerph7072828. http://www.ncbi.nlm.nih.gov/pmc/articles/PMC2922729/.

Byman, Daniel. "Understanding the Islamic State—A Review Essay." *International Security* 40, no. 4 (2016): 127–65. https://doi.org/10.1162/ISEC_r_00235.

Calhoun, Jason H., Clinton K. Murray, and M. M. Manring. "Multidrug-Resistant Organisms in Military Wounds from Iraq and Afghanistan." *Clinical Orthopaedics and Related Research* 466, no. 6 (2008): 1356–62. https://doi.org/10.1007/s11999-008-0212-9.

Callimachi, Rukmini. "The Case of the Purloined Poultry: How Isis Prosecuted Petty Crime." *The New York Times*, July 1, 2018. https://www.nytimes.com/2018/07/01/world/middleeast/islamic-state-iraq.html.

Callimachi, Rukmini. "The Isis Files." *The New York Times*, April 4, 2018. https://www.nytimes.com/interactive/2018/04/04/world/middleeast/isis-documents-mosul-iraq.html?action=click&module=RelatedCoverage&pgtype=Article&region=Footer.

Caris, Charles C., and Samuel Reynolds. *Isis Governance in Syria*. Institute for the Study of War, 2014. http://www.understandingwar.org/sites/default/files/ISIS_Governance.pdf.

Carla, Babb. "Un: Fresh Reports of Extrajudicial Killings by Islamic State." *VOA News*, October 25, 2016. https://www.voanews.com/a/iraqis-gain-ground-around-mosul-as-islamic-state-fight-intensifies/3564437.html.

Carter, Stephen, and Kate Clark. *No Shortcut to Stability. Justice, Politics and Insurgency in Afghanistan*. Chatham House, 2010. https://www.chathamhouse.org/sites/default/files/public/Research/Asia/1210pr_afghanjustice.pdf.

Cetorelli, Valeria, and Nazar P. Shabila. "Expansion of Health Facilities in Iraq a Decade after the U.S.-Led Invasion, 2003–2012." *Conflict and Health* 8 (2014). https://doi.org/10.1186/1752-1505-8-16.

Chambers, Peter. "Abu Musab Al Zarqawi: The Making and Unmaking of an American Monster (in Baghdad)." *Alternatives: Global, Local, Political* 37, no. 1 (2012).

Charmaz, K., and A. Bryant. "Grounded Theory and Credibility." In *Qualitative Research*, edited by David Silverman, 291–309. London: SAGE Publications, 2011.

Clarke, Colin P. "Isis Is So Desperate It's Turning to the Drug Trade." *The Rand Blog*, July 24, 2017. https://www.rand.org/blog/2017/07/isis-is-so-desperate-its-turning-to-the-drug-trade.html.

Clunan, Anne L. Clunan and Harold A. Trinkunas, eds. *Ungoverned Spaces*. Stanford, CA: Stanford Security Studies, 2010.

Cockburn, Patrick. *The Rise of Islamic State: Isis and the New Sunni Revolution*. London: Verso, 2015.

Colas, Brandon. "What Does Dabiq Do? Isis Hermeneutics and Organizational Fractures within Dabiq Magazine." *Studies in Conflict & Terrorism* 40, no. 3 (2017): 173–90. https://doi.org/10.1080/1057610X.2016.1184062.

Cunningham, Erin. "Islamic State Imposes a Reign of Fear in Iraqi Hospitals." *The Washington Post*, November 25, 2014. https://www.washingtonpost.com/world/middle_east/islamic-state-imposes-a-reign-of-fear-in-iraqi-hospitals/2014/11/25/94476f3e-6382-11e4-ab86-46000e1d0035_story.html?utm_term=.9a3674637e3f.

"Dāʿish Tuḥāṣir Mustashfayāt Al-Mosul ('Is Besieges Mosul Hospitals')." *Al-Araby*, September 26, 2014. https://www.alaraby.co.uk/society/2014/9/26/داعش-تحاصر-مستشفيات-الموصل.

Davison, John. "No Plan for Mosul: Chaos and Neglect Slow Iraqi City's Recovery." *Reuters*, February 4, 2019. https://www.reuters.com/article/us-iraq-mosul/no-plan-for-mosul-chaos-and-neglect-slow-iraqi-citys-recovery-idUSKCN1PT0JV.

Dewachi, Omar. *Ungovernable Life: Mandatory Medicine and Statecraft in Iraq*. Stanford: Stanford University Press, 2017.

Dixon, Katherine. "Corruption Helped Isis Take Mosul. Victory Cannot Last While It Persists." *Defense One*, March 10, 2017. https://www.defenseone.com/ideas/2017/03/corruption-helped-isis-take-mosul-victory-cannot-last-while-it-persists/136065/.

Donaldson, Ross I., Patrick Shanovich, Pranav Shetty, Emma Clark, Sharaf Aziz, Melinda Morton, Tariq Hasoon, and Gerald Evans. "A Survey of National Physicians Working in an Active Conflict Zone: The Challenges of Emergency Medical Care in Iraq." *Prehospital and Disaster Medicine* 27, no. 2 (2012): 153–61. https://doi.org/10.1017/S1049023X12000519. https://www.cambridge.org/core/article/survey-of-national-physicians-working-in-an-active-conflict-zone-the-challenges-of-emergency-medical-care-in-iraq/87FE87C78E532F1CE4C8612D17D4BD87.

Downes, Alexander B. *Targeting Civilians in War*. Ithaca, NY: Cornell University Press, 2008.

Dyer, Owen. "Hospitals and Medical Staff Are Targeted in Syria, as Un Report Blames Regime Forces." 10.1136/bmj.j1189. *BMJ* 356, 2017. http://www.bmj.com/content/356/bmj.j1189.abstract.

Gerges, Fawaz A. *Isis: A History*. Princeton, New Jersey: Princeton University Press, 2017.

Gerring, John. "Mere Description." *British Journal of Political Science* 42, no. 4 (2012): 721–46. https://doi.org/10.1017/S0007123412000130. https://www.cambridge.org/core/article/mere-description/833643C6242D3A45D48BAAC3EF0C33D0.

Giustozzi, Antonio. "The Taliban's 'Military Courts.'" *Small Wars & Insurgencies* 25, no. 2 (2014): 284–96. https://doi.org/10.1080/09592318.2014.903638.

Gutiérrez-Sanín, Fransisco. "Organization and Governance: The Evolution of Urban Militias in Medellín, Colombia." In *Rebel Governance in Civil War*, edited by Ana Arjona, Nelson Kasfir, and Zachariah Mampilly. New York: Cambridge University Press, 2015.

Habitat, UN. *City Profile of Mosul, Iraq. Multi-Sector Assessment of a City under Siege*, 2016. https://unhabitat.org/city-profile-of-mosul-iraq-a-city-under-siege/#.

Hafez, Mohammed M. "Suicide Terrorism in Iraq: A Preliminary Assessment of the Quantitative Data and Documentary Evidence." *Studies in Conflict & Terrorism* 29, no. 6 (2006): 591–619. https://doi.org/10.1080/10576100600790878.

"Hal Taʿrifina Man Aṭlaqa Al-Raṣāṣ ʿalā Raʾs Al-Shahīda Ashwāq Al-Naʿīmī?" *Al-masala*, 2016. http://almasalah.com/ar/NewsDetails.aspx?NewsID=65887.

Hamming, Tore Refslund. "The Al Qaeda–Islamic State Rivalry: Competition Yes, but No Competitive Escalation." *Terrorism and Political Violence* (2017): 1–18. https://doi.org/10.1080/09546553.2017.1342634.

Hansen-Lewis, Jamie, and Jacob N. Shapiro. "Understanding the Daesh Economy." *Perspectives on Terrorism* 9, no. 4 (2015): 142–55.

Harris, David. "Islamic State Executes Women & Doctors in 'Collaborators' Purge." *Clarion Project*, September 7, 2014. https://clarionproject.org/islamic-state-executes-women-doctors-collaborators-purge-9/.

Hassan, Hassan. "The Sectarianism of the Islamic State: Ideological Roots and Political Context," June 13, 2016. https://carnegieendowment.org/2016/06/13/sectarianism-of-islamic-state-ideological-roots-and-political-context-pub-63746.

Hegghammer, Thomas. "Jihadi-Salafis or Revolutionaries? On Religion and Politics in the Study of Militant Islamism." In *Global Salafism: Islam's New Religious Movement*, edited by Roel Meijer. London: Hurst & Company, 2009.

Helfont, Samuel. "Saddam and the Islamists: The Ba'Thist Regime's Instrumentalization of Religion in Foreign Affairs." *The Middle East Journal* 68, no. 3 (2014): 352–66. https://doi.org/10.3751/68.3.11.

Huang, R. *The Wartime Origins of Democratization: Civil War, Rebel Governance, and Political Regimes*. Cambridge University Press, 2016. https://books.google.no/books?id=lBviDAAAQBAJ.

"In Northern Iraqi City, Al-Qaeda Gathers Strength." *Associated Press*, June 20, 2013.

Iraq's Provincial Elections: The Stakes. International Crisis Group, January 27, 2009. https://d2071andvip0wj.cloudfront.net/82-iraq-s-provincial-elections-the-stakes.pdf.

Iraq Humanitarian Emergency. Situation Report Issue Number 10, 01-31 December 2017. World Health Organization, 2017. https://reliefweb.int/sites/reliefweb.int/files/resources/WHO%20Situation%20Report%20for%20Iraq_%201%20to%2031%20December%202017.pdf.

Iraq: Isis Executed Hundreds of Prison Inmates. Human Rights Watch, October 30, 2014. https://www.hrw.org/news/2014/10/30/iraq-isis-executed-hundreds-prison-inmates.

"Isis Resorts to Selling Drugs in Iraq, Syria for Funding." *Asharq al-Awsat*, April 26, 2017. https://eng-archive.aawsat.com/theaawsat/news-middle-east/isis-resorts-selling-drugs-iraq-syria-funding.

"Islamic State Killed 300 Former Policemen South of Mosul, Hrw Says." *Reuters*, November 16, 2016. https://www.reuters.com/article/us-mideast-crisis-iraq-grave-idUSKBN13C0ML.

John G. Horgan, Max Taylor, Mia Bloom, Charlie Winter "From Cubs to Lions: A Six Stage Model of Child Socialization into the Islamic State". *Studies in Conflict & Terrorism* (2016).

Johnston, Patrick B., Jacob N. Shapiro, Howard J. Shatz, Benjamin Bahney, Danielle F. Jung, Patrick K. Ryan, and Jonathan Wallace. *Foundations of the Islamic State—*

Management, Money and Terror in Iraq, 2005–2010. Rand Corporation Santa Monica, California, 2016.

Joscelyn, Thomas. "Town of Dabiq Falls to Turkish-Backed Forces." *Long War Journal Blog*, October 17, 2016. https://www.longwarjournal.org/archives/2016/10/town-of-dabiq-falls-to-turkish-backed-forces.php.

Kalyvas, Stathis N. "'New' and 'Old' Civil Wars: A Valid Distinction?." *World Politics* 54, no. 1 (2001): 99–118. http://www.jstor.org.ezproxy-test.uio.no/stable/25054175.

Kalyvas, Stathis N., Ian Shapiro, and Tarek Masoud, eds. *Order, Conflict, and Violence*. Cambridge: Cambridge University Press, 2008.

Karam, Zeina. *Life and Death in Isis: How the Islamic State Builds Its Caliphate*. Associated Press Books, 2015.

Karouny, Mariam. "In Raqqa, Isil Governs with Fear and Efficiency." *The National*, September 4, 2014. https://www.thenational.ae/world/in-raqqa-isil-governs-with-fear-and-efficiency-1.239964.

Kasfir, Nelson. "Rebel Governance—Constructing a Field of Inquiry." In *Rebel Governance in Civil War*, edited by Ana Arjona, Nelson Kasfir, and Zachariah Mampilly. Cambridge: Cambridge University Press, 2015.

Keister, Jennifer. "States within States: How Rebels Rule." PhD, University of California, 2011.

Khoury, Dina Rizk. "Political Relations between City and State in the Middle East, 1700–1850." In *The Urban Social History of the Middle East, 1750–1950*, edited by Peter Sluglett. New York: Syracuse University Press, 2008.

Knights, Michael. "Al-Qa`Ida in Iraq: Lessons from the Mosul Security Operation." *CTC Sentinel* 1, no. 7 (2008). https://ctc.usma.edu/al-qaida-in-iraq-lessons-from-the-mosul-security-operation/.

Kullab, Samya. "Someone Is Smuggling Desperate Civilians Out of Mosul. It Might Be Isis." *Foreign Policy*, December 7, 2016. https://foreignpolicy.com/2016/12/07/someone-is-smuggling-desperate-civilians-out-of-mosul-it-might-be-isis/.

Lacina, Bethany, and Nils Petter Gleditsch. "Monitoring Trends in Global Combat: A New Dataset of Battle Deaths." *European Journal of Population/Revue Européenne de Démographie* 21, no. 2/3 (2005): 145–66. http://www.jstor.org/stable/20164300.

Lahoud, Nelly. "How Will the Islamic State Endure?" *The Survival Editor's Blog*, October 31, 2017.

Lahoud, Nelly. *The Jihadis' Path to Self-Destruction*. London: Hurts & Company, 2010.

Langer, Gary. "Dramatic Advances Sweep Iraq, Boosting Support for Democracy," 2009. https://abcnews.go.com/PollingUnit/story?id=7058272&page=1.

Le Billon, Philippe. "Corruption, Reconstruction and Oil Governance in Iraq." *Third World Quarterly* 26, no. 4–5 (2005): 685–703. https://doi.org/10.1080/01436590500127966.

Lee, Melissa M., Gregor Walter-Drop, and John Wiesel. "Taking the State (Back) Out? Statehood and the Delivery of Collective Goods." *Governance* 27, no. 4 (2014): 635–54. https://doi.org/10.1111/gove.12069.

Levitsky, Steven, and María Victoria Murillo. "Variation in Institutional Strength." *Annual Review of Political Science* 12, no. 1 (2009): 115–33. https://doi.org/10.1146/annurev.polisci.11.091106.121756.

Lia, Brynjar. "The Jihādī Movement and Rebel Governance: A Reassertion of a Patriarchal Order?." *Die Welt des Islams* 57, no. 3–4 (2017): 458–79. https://doi.org/10.1163/15700607-05734p09.

Lia, Brynjar. "Understanding Jihadi Proto-States." *Perspectives on Terrorism* 9, no. 4 (2015). http://www.terrorismanalysts.com/pt/index.php/pot/article/view/441.

Lister, Charles R. *Profiling the Islamic State*. Brookings Doha Center. Doha, Qatar, 2014. https://www.brookings.edu/wp-content/uploads/2014/12/en_web_lister.pdf.

Looney, Robert E. "Reconstruction and Peacebuilding under Extreme Adversity: The Problem of Pervasive Corruption in Iraq." *International Peacekeeping* 15, no. 3 (2008): 424–40. https://doi.org/10.1080/13533310802059032.

Lucas, Scott. "Iraq Feature: Women Doctors in Mosul on Strike over Intimidation by Islamic State." *EA WorldView*, 2014. http://eaworldview.com/2014/08/iraq-feature-women-doctors-mosul-strike-intimidation-islamic-state/.

MacDiarmid, Campbell "Mosul University after Isil: Damaged but Defiant." *Al-Jazeera*, January 26, 2017. http://www.aljazeera.com/indepth/features/2017/01/mosul-university-isil-damaged-defiant-170120090207277.html.

Mahmood, Mona. "Life in Mosul One Year On: 'Isis with All Its Brutality Is More Honest Than the Shia Government.'" *The Guardian*, June 10, 2015. https://www.theguardian.com/world/2015/jun/10/mosul-residents-one-year-on-isis-brutality.

"Making Themselves at Home. Al Qaeda Ups Mafia-Style Extortion in Mosul." *Niqash*, November 7, 2013. http://www.niqash.org/en/articles/politics/3321/.

Malik, Noman and Benotman Nikita. *The Children of Islamic State* (Quilliam Foundation: 2016).

Mampilly, Zachariah. "Performing the Nation-State: Rebel Governance and Symbolic Processes." In *Rebel Governance in Civil War*, edited by Ana Arjona, Nelson Kasfir, and Zachariah Mampilly. Cambridge: Cambridge University Press, 2015.

Mampilly, Zachariah Cherian. *Rebel Rulers. Insurgent Governance and Civilian Life during War*. 1st ed. Cornell University Press, 2011. http://www.jstor.org/stable/10.7591/j.ctt7zfvj.

"Man Hiyya Ashwāq Al-Naʿīmī. Al-Muʿallima Alatī ʿadamaha Dāʿish?." *Rudaw*, 2015. http://www.rudaw.net/NewsDetails.aspx?pageid=178700.

March, Andrew F., and Mara Revkin. "Caliphate of Law." *Foreign Affairs*, April 15, 2015. http://www.foreignaffairs.com/articles/143679/andrew-f-march-and-mara-revkin/caliphate-of-law.

Marr, Phebe and Ibrahim Al-Marashi. *The Modern History of Iraq*. 4th ed. Boulder: Westview Press, 2017.

Martínez, José Ciro and Brent Eng. "Stifling Stateness: The Assad Regime's Campaign against Rebel Governance." *Security Dialogue* 49, no. 4 (2018): 0967010618768622. https://doi.org/10.1177/0967010618768622.

"Maṣdar Yuʾakkid Hurūb 600 Najīl Min Sijn Abū Ghrayb Baynahum Akhṭar Al-Irhābīīn ('Source Confirms the Escape of 600 Prisoners from Abu Ghraib Prison, among Them Dangerous Terrorists')." *Almada Press*, July 22, 2013. http://www.almadapress.com/ar/news/15489/ابو-سجن-من-نزيل-600-هروب-يؤكد-مصدر.

Maxwell, J. A. *Qualitative Research Design: An Interactive Approach*. Thousand Oaks, CA: SAGE Publications, 2005. https://books.google.no/books?id=OJFrFmpGSnUC.

McCants, William. *The Isis Apocalypse: The History, Strategy, and Doomsday Vision of the Islamic State*. New York: St Martin's Press, 2015.

Meijer, Roel. "'Defending Our Honor': Authenticity and the Framing of Resistance in the Iraqi Sunni Town of Falluja." *Etnofoor* 17, no. 1/2 (2004): 23–43. http://www.jstor.org/stable/25758067.

Middle East 2015. Current and Future Challenges. (Zogby Research Services 2015). https://static1.squarespace.com/static/52750dd3e4b08c252c723404/t/5667940fbfe8731ec365efa7/1449628687692/Sir+Bani+Yas+2015+Letter+FINAL.pdf.

Mortimer, Caroline. "Isis Executes 300 Iraqi Army Troops and Civilian Activists in Mosul after Us-Led Air Strikes on City." *The Independent*, February 8, 2016. https://www.independent.co.uk/news/world/middle-east/isis-executes-300-iraqi-army-troops-and-civilian-activists-in-mosul-after-us-led-air-strikes-on-city-a6861311.html.

Mosul: Isil's Economic Engine. RAND Corporation, September 13, 2017. https://www.rand.org/nsrd/projects/when-isil-comes-to-town/case-studies/mosul.html#population.

Nagorski, Tom. "Iraq: Where Things Stand," 2007. https://abcnews.go.com/International/story?id=2962206&page=1.

Napoleoni, Loretta. *The Islamist Phoenix: The Islamic State and the Redrawing of the Middle East.* New York: Seven Stories Press, 2014.

North, Douglass C. and Barry R. Weingast. "Constitutions and Commitment: The Evolution of Institutions Governing Public Choice in Seventeenth-Century England." *The Journal of Economic History* 49, no. 4 (1989): 803–32. http://www.jstor.org/stable/2122739.

Ochoa, Rolando. "Local Dynamics of a Global Phenomenon: Policing Organized Crime." In *The Sage Handbook of Global Policing*, edited by B. Bradford, B. Jauregui, I. Loader, and J. Steinberg. London: SAGE Publications, 2016.

Office, Unesco Iraq. *Unesco National Education Support Strategy 2010–2014.* Unesco Iraq Office, 2011.

Olson, Mancur. *The Logic of Collective Action: Public Goods and the Theory of Groups, Second Printing with New Preface and Appendix.* Cambridge: Harvard University Press, 1965. https://books.google.no/books?id=jzTeOLtf7_wC.

Organization, World Health. *Health Profile: Ninawa Governorate.* (2015).

Perito, Robert M. "Police in Armed Conflict." In *The Sage Handbook of Global Policing*, edited by B. Bradford, B. Jauregui, I. Loader, and J. Steinberg. London: SAGE Publications, 2016.

Peritz, Aki. "The Great Iraqi Jail Break." *Foreign Policy*, June 26, 2014. https://foreignpolicy.com/2014/06/26/the-great-iraqi-jail-break/.

Peräkylä, Anssi. "Analyzing Talk and Text." In *The Sage Handbook of Qualitative Research, Third Edition*, edited by Norman K. Denzin and Yvonna S. Lincoln. Thousand Oaks/London/New Delhi: SAGE Publications, 2005.

Peters, Gretchen. "The Afghan Insurgency and Organized Crime." In *The Rule of Law in Afghanistan: Missing in Inaction*, edited by Whit Mason. Cambridge: Cambridge University Press, 2011.

Plebani, Andrea. "Ninawa Province: Al-Qa'ida's Remaining Stronghold." *CTC Sentinel* 3, no. 1 (2010). https://ctc.usma.edu/ninawa-province-al-qaidas-remaining-stronghold/.

Podder, Sukanya, and Scott Gates. "Social Media, Recruitment, Allegiance and the Islamic State." *Perspectives on Terrorism* 9, no. 4 (2015): 107–16.

Qaddour, Kinana. "Inside Isis' Dynsunctional Schools." *Foreign Affairs*, October 13, 2017. https://www.foreignaffairs.com/articles/syria/2017-10-13/inside-isis-dysfunctional-schools.

Rabasa, Angel, Steven Boraz, Peter chalk, Kim Cragin, Theodore W. Karasik, Jennifer D.P. Moroney, Kevin A. O'Brien, and John E. Peters. *Ungoverned Territories. Understanding and Reducing Terrorism Risks*. Santa Monica, CA: RAND Corporation, 2007.

Reno, William. "Predatory Rebellions and Governance: The National Patriotic Front of Liberia, 1989–1992." In *Rebel Governance in Civil War*, edited by Ana Arjona, Nelson Kasfir, and Zachariah Mampilly. New York: Cambridge University Press, 2015.

Revkin, Mara. *Does the Islamic State Have a "Social Contract"? Evidence from Iraq and Syria*. Yale University and University of Gothenburg The Program on Governance and Local Development, 2016.

Revkin, Mara. "Law and Lawfare in the Islamic State." *Lawfare Blog*, August 5, 2016.

Revkin, Mara. *The Legal Foundations of the Islamic State* The Brookings Institutions (2016).

Revkin, Mara. *The Limits of Punishment. Transitional Justice and Violent Extremism* Institute for Integrated Transitions, United Nations University (2018).

Richards, Anthony. "Conceptualizing Terrorism." *Studies in Conflict & Terrorism* 37, no. 3 (2014): 213–36. https://doi.org/10.1080/1057610X.2014.872023.

Rights, United Nations Assistance Mission for Iraq—Human Rights Office & Office of the United Nations High Commissioner for Human. *Report on the Protection of Civilians in the Armed Conflict in Iraq: 11 December 2014–30 April 2015*. United Nations (2015). http://www.ohchr.org/Documents/Countries/IQ/UNAMI_ohchr_4th_POCReport-11Dec2014-30April2015.pdf.

Rudaw. "Sources: Isis Executed 10 Doctors in Mosul for Refusing to Treat Wounded Fighters " *Rudaw*, January 27, 2015. http://www.rudaw.net/english/middleeast/iraq/27012015.

"Rule of Fear: Isis Abuses in Detention in Northern Syria." *Amnesty International*, 2013. https://www.amnesty.org/download/Documents/16000/mde240632013en.pdf.

Sarhan, Amre. "Source: Isis Throws 5 Homosexuals from High Building in Mosul." *Iraqi News*, April 21, 2016. https://www.iraqinews.com/iraq-war/source-isis-throws-5-homosexuals-high-building-mosul/.

Sassoon, Joseph. *Saddam Hussein's Ba'th Party: Inside an Authoritarian Regime*. New York: Cambridge University Press, 2012.

Schuurman, Bart. "Research on Terrorism, 2007–2016: A Review of Data, Methods, and Authorship." *Terrorism and Political Violence* (2018): 1–16. https://doi.org/10.1080/09546553.2018.1439023.

Schuurman, Bart and Max Taylor. "Reconsidering Radicalization: Fanaticism and the Link between Ideas and Violence." *Perspectives on Terrorism* 12, no. 1 (2018). http://www.terrorismanalysts.com/pt/index.php/pot/article/view/675/1347.

Schäferhoff, Marco. "External Actors and the Provision of Public Health Services in Somalia." *Governance* 27, no. 4 (2014): 675–95. https://doi.org/10.1111/gove.12071.

Schweitzer, Yoram, Omer Einav (eds.). *The Islamic State: How Viable Is It?* Institute for National Security Studies, Tel Aviv University (2016). http://www.inss.org.il/publication/the-islamic-state-how-viable-is-it/.

Scott, James C. *Weapons of the Weak. Everyday Forms of Peasant Resistance*. New Haven: Yale University Press, 1985. http://www.jstor.org/stable/j.ctt1nq836.

Shapiro, Jacob N. "A Predictable Failure: The Political Economy of the Decline of the Islamic State." *CTC Sentinel* 9, no. 9 (2016): 28–32. https://ctc.usma.edu/posts/a-predictable-failure-the-political-economy-of-the-decline-of-the-islamic-state.

Shields, Sarah D. "Mosul Questions: Economy, Identity and Annexation." In *The Creation of Iraq, 1914-1921*, edited by R. S. Simon, E. H. Tejirian, and G. Sick Columbia University Press, 2004.

Shields, Sarah D. *Mosul before Iraq*. New York: State University of New York Press, 2000.

Silverman, David. *Interpreting Qualitative Data*. 2011.

Smith, Benjamin K., Andrea Figueroa-Caballero, Samantha Chan, Robert Kovacs, Erinn Middo, Lauren Nelson, Richard Palacios, Supriya Yelimeli, and Michael Stohl. "Framing Daesh: Failures and Consequences." *Perspectives on Terrorism* 10, no. 4 (2016): 40–50. http://www.jstor.org/stable/26297617.

Solomon, Erika, Robin Kwong, and Steven Bernard. "Isis Inc: How Oil Fuels the Jihadi Terrorists." *Financial Times*, 2016. https://ig.ft.com/sites/2015/isis-oil/.

Speckhard, Anne and Ahmet S. Yayla. *Eyewitness Accounts from Recent Defectors from Islamic State: Why They Joined, What They Saw, Why They Quit*. Vol. 9, 2015. http://www.terrorismanalysts.com/pt/index.php/pot/article/view/475.

Speckhard, Anne and Ahmet S. Yayla. "The Isis Emni: The Origins and Inner Workings of Isis's Intelligence Apparatus." *Perspectives on Terrorism* 11, no. 1 (2017). http://www.terrorismanalysts.com/pt/index.php/pot/article/view/573%J.Perspectives.on.Terrorism

Speckhard, Anne and Ahmet S. Yayla. *Isis Defectors: Inside Stories of the Terrorist Caliphate*. McLean, Virginia: Advances Press, 2016.

State, Islamic. "A Call to All Muslims Doctors, Engineers, Scholars and Specialists." *Dabiq*, July 2014, 11.

Steinberg, Guido. "Jihadi-Salafism and the Shi'is. Remarks About the Intellectual Roots of Anti-Shi'ism." In *Global Salafism: Islam's New Religious Movement*, edited by Roel Meijer Columbia University Press, 2009.

Stephan, Maria J. "Civil Resistance Vs. Isis." *Journal of Resistance Studies* 1, no. 2 (2015): 127–50.

Stern, Jessica and J.M. Berger. *Isis. The State of Terror*. London: William Collins, 2015.

Talbi, M. "Hisba." In *Encyclopaedia of Islam, Second Edition*. Encyclopaedia of Islam, III:485b: Brill.

Taleb, Julia. "From Assad to Isis, a Tale of Syrian Resistance." *Waging Non-Violence*. (2014). https://wagingnonviolence.org/feature/assad-isis-tale-resistance/.

Tønnessen, Truls Hallberg. "Al-Qaida in Iraq: The Rise, the Fall and the Comeback." PhD, PhD thesis, University of Oslo, 2015.

Tønnessen, Truls Hallberg "The Group That Wanted to Be a State: The 'Rebel Governance' of the Islamic State." In *Islamists and the Politics of the Arab Uprisings. Governance, Pluralisation and Contention*, edited by Hendrik Kraetzschmar and Paola Rivetti. Edinburgh: Edinburgh University Press, 2018.

Tønnessen, Truls Hallberg. "Heirs of Zarqawi or Saddam? The Relationship between Al-Qaida in Iraq and the Islamic State." *Perspectives on Terrorism* 9, no. 4 (2015). http://www.terrorismanalysts.com/pt/index.php/pot/article/view/443/874.

Tønnessen, Truls Hallberg. "Motstand Og Politikk I Irak." *Babylon* 8, no. 1 (2010): 20–31.

Tønnessen, Truls Hallberg. *The Origins of the Islamic State*. Forthcoming.
Tønnessen, Truls Hallberg. "Training on a Battlefield: Iraq as a Training Ground for Global Jihadis." *Terrorism and Political Violence* 20, no. 4 (2008): 543–62. https://doi.org/10.1080/09546550802257242.
Tripp, Charles. *The Power and the People: Paths of Resistance in the Middle East*. Cambridge: Cambridge University Press, 2013. 10.1017/CBO9781139028721.
Tyler, Tom R. "Enhancing Police Legitimacy." *The ANNALS of the American Academy of Political and Social Science* 593, no. 1 (2004/05/01 2004): 84–99. https://doi.org/10.1177/0002716203262627.
Underwood, Peter T. "Pirates, Vikings and Teutonic Knights." In *Pirates, Terrorists, and Warlords: The History, Influence, and Future of Armed Groups around the World*, edited by J.H. Norwitz Skyhorse Publishing, 2009.
Unmaking Iraq: A Constitutional Process Gone Awry. International Crisis Group, September 26, 2005. https://www.crisisgroup.org/middle-east-north-africa/gulf-and-arabian-peninsula/iraq/unmaking-iraq-constitutional-process-gone-awry.
Wagemakers, Joas. "Invoking Zarqawi: Abu Muhammad Al-Maqdisi's Jihad Deficit." *CTC Sentinel* 2, no. 6 (2009).
Walt, Stephen M. "Isis as Revolutionary State." *Foreign Affairs*, November/December 2015. https://www.foreignaffairs.com/articles/middle-east/isis-revolutionary-state.
Walter, Barbara F. "The Extremist's Advantage in Civil Wars." *International Security* 42, no. 2 (2017): 7–39.
Warrick, Joby. *Black Flags: The Rise of Isis*. New York: Anchor Books, 2015.
Weigand, Florian. "Investigating the Role of Legitimacy in the Political Order of Conflict-Torn Spaces (Working Paper)." (2015).
Weinstein, Jeremy M. *Inside Rebellion*. New York: Cambridge University Press, 2007.
Weiss, Michael and Hassan Hassan. *Isis. Inside the Army of Terror*. New York: Regan Arts, 2015.
Westphal, Joana. "Violence in the Name of God? A Framing Processes Approach to the Islamic State in Iraq and Syria." *Social Movement Studies* 17, no. 1 (2017): 19–34. https://doi.org/10.1080/14742837.2017.1381594.
Whiteside, Craig. "A Pedigree of Terror: The Myth of the Ba'athist Influence in the Islamic State Movement." *Perspectives on Terrorism* 11, no. 3 (2017): 2–18.
Who Report on the Global Tobacco Epidemic, 2017. Country Profile, Iraq. World Health Organization (2017).
Wickham-Crowley, Timothy. "Del Gobierno De Abajo Al Gobierno De Arriba ... and Back: Transitions to and from Rebel Governance in Latin America, 1956–1990." In *Rebel Governance in Civil War*, edited by Ana Arjona, Nelson Kasfir, and Zachariah Mampilly. New York: Cambridge University Press, 2015.
Winter, Charlie. "Apocalypse, Later: A Longitudinal Study of the Islamic State Brand." *Critical Studies in Media Communication* 35, no. 1 (2018): 103–21. https://doi.org/10.1080/15295036.2017.1393094.
Wolff, Michael Jerome. "Building Criminal Authority: A Comparative Analysis of Drug Gangs in Rio De Janeiro and Recife." *Latin American Politics and Society* 57, no. 2 (2015): 21–40. https://doi.org/10.1111/j.1548-2456.2015.00266.x.

Wood, Elisabeth J. *Insurgent Collective Action and Civil War in El Salvador*. New York: Cambridge University Press, 2003.

Wozniak, Jesse S. G. "We Are Going to Prove We Are a Civil and Developed Country: The Cultural Performance of Police Legitimacy and Empire in the Iraqi State." *The British Journal of Criminology* 57, no. 4 (2017): 906–23. https://doi.org/10.1093/bjc/azw046.

Yayla, Ahmed S., and Colin P. Clarke. "Turkey's Double Isis Standard." *Foreign Policy*, April 12, 2018. https://foreignpolicy.com/2018/04/12/turkeys-double-isis-standard/.

Zelin, Aaron Y. "Picture or It Didn't Happen—a Snapshot of the Islamic State's Official Media Output." *Perspectives on Terrorism* 9, no. 4 (2015): 85–97. http://www.jstor.org/stable/26297417.

Zelin, Aaron Y. *The War between Isis and Al-Qaeda for Supremacy of the Global Jihadist Movement*. The Washington Institute for Near East Policy, 2014. http://www.washingtoninstitute.org/uploads/Documents/pubs/ResearchNote_20_Zelin.pdf

Index

al-Abadi, Haider 36, 122
accountability 48, 57, 58, 62–5, 69, 81
al-Adl, Sayf 21, 29
al-Adnani, Abu Muhammad 29, 41–2
al-adab al-shara'iyya 81
al-jaghrafiyya (geography) 81
al-Qaida 1, 17–21, 31–3, 40, 51, 58
al-Qa'ida in Iraq (AQI) 17, 18, 20, 23, 26, 32–4
al-'ulum (science) 81
Arjona, Ana 39, 64, 65, 74, 91, 94, 100
al-Assad, Bashar 17
awwama (civilian) 108–12

al-Baghdadi, Abu Bakr 4, 5, 27, 29, 48, 55, 89, 116–17, 125, 126
al-Baghdadi, Abu Umar 22
Barzani, Masoud 15, 16
bin Laden, Osama 20, 21
Breaking the Walls campaign 26

caliphate 5, 7, 9, 21, 29, 40–2, 45–8, 68–9, 76, 80, 81, 92, 93, 94, 101, 102, 111, 125, 130, 138
   civilians 62–3
   corruption 57–8
   justice 63–5
   predictability 65–8
   safety and security 50–7
cigarettes 53, 59–62
civilians 7, 9–14, 21, 39, 47, 49, 51, 55, 57, 59, 62–9, 73, 81, 91–3, 96–9, 102, 105, 107–14, 116–19, 121–4, 126–39
classrooms resistance 71–3

defiance 89–91
engagement 86–9
everyday resistance 81–5
institutions 91–3
ISIS plan 76–81
Mosul education 74–6
clothing rules 103–8
corruption 8, 17, 26, 31, 33, 36, 48, 57–8, 69, 127
crime 49, 51–6, 62, 69, 107, 129, 130

dawa'ish 59, 63
dawla 41, 58
da'ish 52, 54, 55, 60, 63, 64, 67, 83–5, 91, 112, 113, 115
defiance 89–91
diwan al-hisba 50, 67
diwan al-sihha 110, 112, 116
diwan al-ta'lim 76–7, 85
diwans 39
drugs 110

education 71–3, 93. *see also* classrooms resistance
   Mosul 74–6
ethics 139–41
everyday resistance 81–5

Faith Campaign 31
fatwa 105, 111, 124
Free Syrian Army (FSA) 17

gender segregation rules 103–8
Gutiérrez-Sanín, Fransisco 66

hijra 40
al-hisba 49–51, 61, 63, 67, 87, 89, 90, 103, 105, 112, 113, 131, 152 n.14, 153 n.19
Huang, R. 100
hudud 48, 49

ikhwa (brother) 108–12
Iraq healthcare 98–101
ISI 18, 22, 25–7, 31–5

Jabhat al-Nusra (JN) 27
jihad/jihadi/jihadism/jihadi-Salafi 3, 4, 12, 15, 16, 18, 20–2, 33, 34, 39–43, 73, 76, 96, 123, 125–9, 140, 142 n.4
jiziya 34, 38, 149 n.65
justice 13, 17, 21, 32, 37, 47–9, 51, 53, 55, 57, 63–6, 123

kafir 40
khilafa 41, 42, 58
khimar 45
Kurdish region (KRG) 132–4
Kurds 30, 33, 36, 132

Lahoud, Nelly 12
legitimacy 12, 13, 39, 47, 48, 51, 66, 68–9, 75, 99, 124
Lia, Brynjar 41

McCants, William 42
al-Maliki, Nouri 23–7, 30, 35, 36, 50
Mampilly, Zachariah 10, 64, 124
al-Maqdisi, Abu Muhammad 20, 21, 40, 72
March, Andrew F. 43
media 17, 46–7, 49, 59, 68, 73, 125, 129, 131
Mosul before Iraq (Shields) 75
Mosul education 74–6
Mosul's health system 95–8, 118–19
    gender segregation and clothing rules 103–8
    ikhwa/awwama 108–12
    in Iraq 98–101

    management 112–18
    Muslims and 101–3
mushrikun 37, 40
Muslims
    and Mosul's health system 101–3
    population 33
    Shia 13, 20, 27, 29, 40, 140
    Sunni 22, 24, 63, 103, 125, 132

Ninawa province 4, 29–30, 73, 97, 125
al-Nujaifi, Abdallah 15–16
al-Nujaifi, Athil 15, 16, 33

police forces 13, 45–59, 62–9, 124
predictability 13, 46–7, 65–9
punishment 39, 46, 47, 49, 52, 55, 59, 64, 84, 107, 109

al-Qarnayn, Dhu 72, 76, 78, 85, 87
Quran 31, 34, 72, 78, 80

rawafid (rejectionists) 40
rebels 4, 8–14, 27, 39, 41, 43, 47–8, 64–6, 73, 74, 91, 94, 96–8, 100, 101, 118, 119, 123–9
Reno, W. 96, 118
Revkin, Mara 43, 65, 75, 144 n.19

Saddam Hussein 19, 21, 24, 28, 30, 31, 35, 57, 58, 74, 145 n.3
Salafis 1, 18–20, 30–1, 34–5, 40
Sallon, Hélene 83
security 134–5
shari'a 5, 13, 47, 50, 68, 76, 81, 103
Shields, Sarah D. 75
smoking 59–60, 67–8
smuggling 23, 54, 58, 60–2
social contract 13, 37, 38, 48, 65–7, 99
social media 16, 47, 90, 131, 136
Soldiers' Harvest campaign 35
Sunni Arabs 12, 19, 23–30, 35

takfir 12, 35, 40
Al-Tamimi, Aymenn Jawad 43, 118, 131
tawaghit (tyrants) 40

al-tawba 55, 56
tawhid 40
taxation 68
Tel Abyad 58
Tel Kaif 53–4
Tonnessen, Truls Hallberg 17, 20
Tripp, Charles 82, 86

validity 137
violence 6, 7, 9, 11, 13, 17, 18, 23–7, 32, 33, 48, 51, 66, 81, 101, 140, 142 n.4

Walter, Barbara F. 93
Weinstein, J. M. 96
Westphal, Joana 40
Winter, Charlie 125
World Health Organization (WHO) 99

Yezidis 28, 36–8, 40, 106, 140

al-Zarqawi, Abu Musab 19–23, 29, 42, 72
al-Zawahiri, Ayman 20–2, 27
Zelin, Aaron 49